ggle · Wander · Amble · Ambulat
nter · Sidle · Slink · Shuffle ol
ke · Shudder · Shiver · Plod · Trudg
t · Stagger · Sashay · Gallop · Gambo
Bound · Buck · Bounce · Pounce · Bol
Whirl · Swirl · Spring · Jump · Jostl
e · Dance · Rock · Roll · Rove · Roan
aver · Dodder · Teeter · Totter · Quive
ad · Agitate · Peregrinate · Nod · Mov
le · Wiggle · Wander · Amble · Ambulat
nter · Sidle · Slink · Shuffle · Shambl
Shudder · Shiver · Plod · Trudge · Lurcl
· Sashay · Gallop · Gambol · Galumpl
uck · Bounce · Pounce · Bob · Minc
irl · Spring · Jump · Jostle · Jiggle · Joggl
ll · Rove · Roam · Ramble · Turn · Vee
tter · Quiver · Quaver · Tiptoe · Traips
Nod · Cavort · Hop · Hike · Walk · Wen
· Ambulate · Perambulate · Step · Strid
mble · Swing · Sway · Swerve · Shimm

HOW TO MAKE

ANIMATED

TOYS

DAVID WAKEFIELD

Published by Popular Science Books
New York, New York

Distributed to the trade by Rodale Press, Inc.
Emmaus, Pennsylvania

Copyright © 1986 by David Wakefield

Published by

Popular Science Books
Times Mirror Magazines, Inc.
380 Madison Avenue
New York, NY 10017

Distributed to the trade by
Rodale Press, Inc.
33 East Minor Street
Emmaus, PA 18049

Special thanks to the PK Building Center and Newton's Book Store of Englewood, Ohio

Book design by Linda Watts
Produced by Bookworks, Inc.

Library of Congress Card Number: 86-042771
ISBN: 0-943822-68-8

Manufactured in the United States of America

To my father,
who put the laughter in my blood.

Great Expectations

In the rolling Ohio hills, west of the Appalachian mountains and east of Liar's Corner, there is a treehouse. This is unremarkable in itself. There are many trees in Ohio, and many children. If you mix trees and children and let the mixture stand for a few weeks, you'll get treehouses.

However, this particular treehouse is not what we've all come to expect in treehouses. It looks like a small Victorian mansion that was plucked from an historical neighborhood in Boston or Philadelphia by a whimsical tornado, and dropped onto the unsuspecting Ohio wilderness. The two-story structure roosts in two ancient oaks, who bear the burden proudly. This wonderful vision was my *second* introduction to David Wakefield.

My first introduction was a wooden turtle. This turtle was pulled across the floor of a friend's home by a child named Sebastian. I've seen many wooden pull-toys before, and I think I know what to expect from pull-toys. But I had never seen one as clever as this. As Sebastian pulled, the turtle's head and tail disappeared inside the shell, then reappeared a few moments later. Sebastian was captivated by the motion, and so was I. As soon as I could coax the toy away from the child, I began to explore the insides. Aha! Wheels with offset axles hooked to the head and tail pieces...

"That's one of David Wakefield's toys," said Sebastian's mother. "He also makes these." She opened Sebastian's toy chest and showed me a hippo whose mouth opened and closed, a lobster with claws that snapped and clattered, and others. They were all skillful combinations of wheels, axles, cams, and levers that would move together in some wonderful, unexpected way when you moved the toys. On the floor or in the chest, the toys looked quite ordinary. But when you played with them, they came alive!

As a fair-to-middlin' woodworker, I admire well-designed, well-crafted projects. I said that I'd like to meet the toymaker and shake his hand. So that afternoon we drove over to David's place. He wasn't at home, so we admired his treehouse.

When I eventually did meet David Wakefield, I got another brush with the unexpected. Most of us harbor the notion that all the best toys are crafted by small, bearded, grandfatherly creatures. David was clean-shaven, youthful, as tall as a tree, with a shock of wild red hair. Nonetheless, he was an experienced, knowledgeable woodworker.

As we talked, I learned that David was a native of Australia, born into show business. His father was a comedian and his mother an actress. He traveled around the world with his folks, but came to rest in the forest just outside of Millfield, Ohio. He liked working with his hands, so he began making things out of wood. He made musical instruments, custom furniture, and finally settled on toys. His 'animated' toys—David called them "animatables"—were by far his most popular designs, so he began to produce them exclusively. Making and selling these toys for nine years eventually gave rise to a full-blown woodworking business, *Howling Wolf Woodworks*. David asked if Popular Science would consider publishing a book on toymaking. I thought that they might.

That's how this book came to be: a wooden turtle, a treehouse, two woodworkers swapping shop stories. All the rest just fell into place. Getting David's book published was a simple matter. One day, I just took a box of his animated toys into an editorial meeting and let everyone play with them. We all agreed then and there to publish the book. (However, it was many months before David got his toys back.)

When he finished the manuscript, David came to New York to deliver it. I went with him, and took him around to meet the folks at *Popular Science Books*. Afterwards, one of the editors mentioned to me, "He's not at all what I expected."

No, I have to agree, he's not. He packs quite a few wonderful surprises. It's the same with his treehouse. And his toys.

Nick Engler
April, 1986

Contents

Prehistoric MONSTERS

Pure MOTION

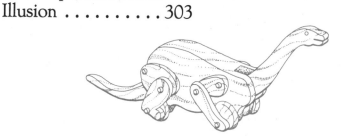

ESSENTIAL Information

- Techniques and Production Procedures
- Materials and Tools
- Designing Animated Animals

Techniques and Production Procedures

To the untrained eye, toymaking appears to be quite simple. Just cut out a shape, slap on some wheels, and there you are. In actuality, though, making a quality toy demands a fair amount of knowledge, skill, and patience. I don't say this to discourage you, but to encourage you to read this chapter. It will help you to avoid most of the mistakes that I've made (and learned from) during my years as a toymaker. In toymaking, as in most things, there is a hard way and an easy way. The potential is there for either frustration or satisfaction. I'd like to help you achieve the latter.

Some of you are already skilled woodworkers. Remember, though, that toymaking is a specific area of woodworking, and as such it has its own particular problems and solutions. So whether you are a novice woodworker or a skilled cabinetmaker, whether you want to make a few toys for friends and relatives or you are planning to go into production and become a professional toymaker, the information here will prove invaluable.

Enlarging Patterns

Let's start at the beginning. Every project starts with a design, and toymaking is no different. But toy designs generally incorporate a lot of *patterns*—shapes that can't be described by simple measurements. A furniture project may have one or two patterns for a turned leg or a decorative molding, but you'll notice the toys in this book generally have five or more!

To help you deal with all these patterns, the good folks at Popular Science decided to publish them either full size or at 57% scale. There's a reason for this, and I'll explain it as I go along.

Enlarging with photocopier. The full-size patterns don't need to be enlarged, of course, so let's set them aside for the moment. The reason the other patterns in this book are 57% scale is that, first of all, they were too big to publish full-size. Secondly, they are published at this specific scale so that you could enlarge them on a photocopier.

Many photocopiers have enlargement and reduction capabilities. If you call around to 'quick-print' shops, you can probably find one that enlarges from letter to legal size. The standard percentage for this enlargement, according to the copier manufacturers that I called, is 121%. If you enlarge the 57% patterns *three* times, letter-to-legal size, you get a photocopied pattern that's very close to full-size. (*See Figures 1 and 2.*) Here's the math:

$$.57 \times 1.21 \times 1.21 \times 1.21 = 1.01 \text{ (approximately)}$$

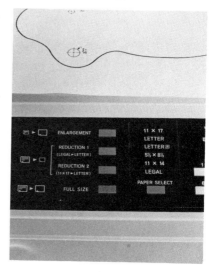

Figure 1. Look for a photocopier that can enlarge from letter size to legal size. On most copiers, this enlargement will be approximately 121%.

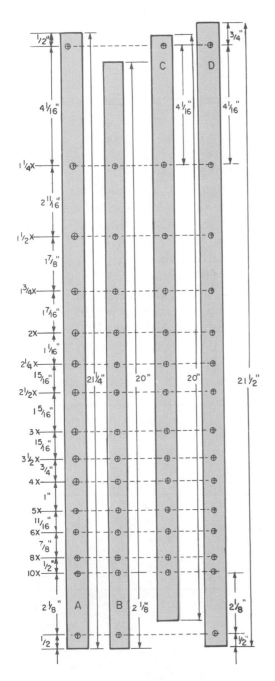

PANTOGRAPH LAYOUT

Figure 2. Using the letter-to-legal size enlargement, photocopy the original drawing *three* times to get it up to full size.

Figure 3. Following these plans, you can make your own pantograph. *Pantograph plans courtesy Nick Engler. From the Popular Science Woodworking Projects 1985 Yearbook.*

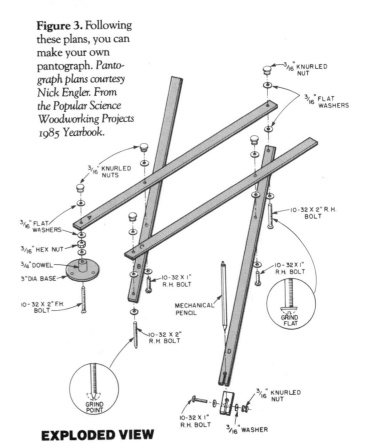

EXPLODED VIEW

Of course, some copiers use different percentages. In calling around, I found percentages from 120% to 129%. But the majority used 121%. One or two percentage points shouldn't make that much difference in the patterns, provided you remember to adjust the position of the wheels, cams, and other moving parts so that they work together properly. If you don't get good results from a standard letter-to-legal-size enlargement, try to find a copier with 'variable reduction and enlargement' capability. Have the operator punch in 121% and copy each pattern over three times.

Enlarging with a pantograph. A pantograph is a simple drawing device that will make accurate enlargements. They're available at most drafting and art supply stores. Or, you can make your own following the plans in Figure 3.

To use this to enlarge a pattern in this book, first make a photocopy of the pattern and tape the copy flat on a drawing board. (If you don't have a drawing board, you can use a sheet of plywood.) Adjust the two movable pivots to enlarge 1¾ x (175%). Once again, here's the math:

$$.57 \times 1.75 = 1.00 \text{ (approximately)}$$

Tack or screw the fulcrum to the board, to the left and slightly below the pattern. Tape a large sheet of paper to the board, to the right and slightly above the pattern. Carefully trace the pattern with the stylus. The pencil will make an enlarged pattern on the paper. *(See Figure 4.)* If there are gaps in the lines of the enlarged drawing, adjust the height of the pencil so the lead rests firmly on the paper.

Enlarging with a projector. Make a photocopy of the pattern and mount it flat on a board. Take a picture of this with a 35mm camera on *slide film*. When you take the picture, make sure the camera lens is perpendicular to the pattern, not skewed off to the top, bottom, or side. *(See Figure 5.)* Let me repeat: Take the picture *straight on*. If you take it at an angle, the pattern will be distorted on the film.

Have the slides developed. Tape some paper onto a wall, and project the slide of the pattern onto the paper. Once again, you must project this slide straight on. Like the camera, the projector lens must be perpendicular to the wall to avoid distortion. Move the projector forward and back until the pattern is the proper size on the paper. Trace the projected pattern with a pencil onto the paper.

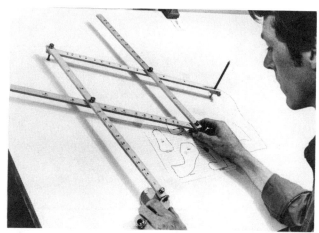

Figure 4. Set the pantograph enlargement to 1¾ X (175%). As you trace the 57% scale patterns with the stylus, the pencil will draw them full-size.

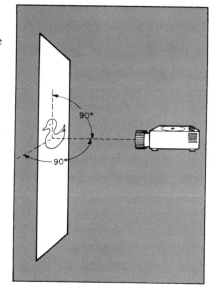

Figure 5. If you use camera and slide projector to enlarge the patterns, you must be careful to position the lenses so that they are perfectly perpendicular first to the pattern, and then to the paper. If the lenses are skewed, the pattern will be distorted.

You can do the same thing with an opaque projector, if you have access to one. The advantage here is that you don't have to develop any film. Just tape the photocopy of the pattern to the projector, and project the image on a wall. For the last time, project the pattern straight on, not off to the side.

Enlarging with a grid. If you don't want to resort to any of these 'high-tech' methods, you can always fall back on the old 'squares' method. Make a grid of ½″ squares on a piece of paper. Number the horizontal and vertical lines on the grid you've just drawn *and* the grid behind the pattern in the book. Carefully examine the pattern and note where the pattern line touches each grid line. Make a pencil dot at the corresponding points on the ½″ grid that you drew. Repeat for every point where the grid and pattern touches. Then simply connect the dots, using french curves. *(See Figure 6.)*

Be extremely careful when locating holes and drawing shapes that must somehow move, such as the head of the Hippo or the claws of the Lobster. Measure twice to make sure that you've reproduced these shapes as accurately as possible before you transfer the enlarged pattern to the wood.

Transferring Patterns

Once you have full-size patterns, there are several ways to transfer them onto wood. The first is to tape the patterns to the wood with a piece of carbon paper between them. Carefully trace the pattern with a stylus. A ballpoint pen that's run out of ink makes an excellent stylus. Or you can sand a ¼″ dowel to a rounded point. *(See Figure 7.)* Using either instrument, the carbon paper will transfer the pattern to the wood.

The second method is to cut the pattern out, and tape it to the wood using see-through tape. Tape the entire perimeter of the pattern so that it stays perfectly flat. Then saw it out and discard the paper.

If you plan on making several copies of the toy, you may want to make a stencil. If that's the case, tape the pattern to a piece of ⅛″ hardboard and cut it out. Cut wide of the line, and break the fuzz off the edges of the cut hardboard with 120# sandpaper. Drill all the hole locations in the stencil with a ¼″ bit. (A ¼″ hole is just the right size for you to make a neat, round mark with a pencil.) You can use this stencil to trace the pattern and locate the holes over and over again.

Figure 6. If you rely on the old 'squares' method to enlarge the patterns, use a french curve to connect the dots. This will help ensure that all your curves are 'fair'.

Figure 7. A ¼″ dowel with the tip sanded to a slightly rounded point makes a good stylus for transferring patterns.

It's also a good idea to transfer any pertinent information onto the stencil with a pen or marker—hole sizes, depth of dado slots, position of dowel drive holes, and so on.

Using the Bandsaw

Once you've transferred the patterns for the toys to the wood, the next step is to cut the patterns out. Chances are, the tool that you'll use for this job will be a bandsaw.

Choosing blades. When cutting on the bandsaw, I usually use a ¼" blade with a 'pitch' of 4 or 6. The pitch refers to the number of teeth per inch. A six-pitch blade (six teeth per inch) is good for general use. A four-pitch blade is more suitable for production. I also use a ⅛" blade with a pitch of ten for cutting tight curves. If the blades that are available have a higher pitch, that's fine. You'll just have to cut a little slower with a high-pitch blade.

Always buy skip-tooth blades. These blades clear the sawdust from the cut more efficiently, and they enable you to cut hardwood more quickly without clogging the blade. You can purchase ¼" skip-tooth blades from the Woodcraft Supply Corporation, 313 Montvale Avenue, Woburn, MA 01888. The Do-All Company, 1547 Lockbourne Avenue, Columbus, OH 43210, will make up ⅛" and ¼" bandsaw blades of any length and pitch that you require. (Do-All is a large company with shops in most major cities. Consult your Yellow Pages or write the head office in Columbus to find the shop nearest you.)

The use of the bandsaw is pretty straightforward, but there are a few simple tips that you can take advantage of to speed up your work. First of all, always make sure that the table is *precisely* perpendicular to the blade before you begin cutting. (Unless, of course, you're making angle cuts.) This will save you time and aggravation when you start edge sanding. It will also ensure that the mechanisms of the toys will work properly.

Follow good safety practices when using this tool. It may look fairly benign, but it can turn on you if you aren't careful. Don't wear jewelry or loose clothing—these can catch in the blade. Use eye protection, and always adjust the upper blade guides so that they are never more than ¼" above the work. This limits your exposure to the blade. Finally, keep your fingers out of danger. Many bandsaws have a small, round insert in the worktable, around the blade. These inserts are usually 1"-2" in diameter. Treat this insert as if it marked the boundary of a "danger zone", and never let your fingers stray closer to the blade than the edge of the insert. If your bandsaw doesn't have an insert, paint a red circle on your bandsaw to remind yourself of the danger. Remember, small parts can be cut just as quickly with a coping saw—you don't have to use the bandsaw for *everything*.

Cutting dowels. When cutting dowels on the bandsaw, clamp a scrap block to the rip fence just in front of the blade. To cut a specific length, adjust the position of the rip fence, measuring from the scrap block to the blade. Place the end of the dowel stock against the scrap block and roll it forward into the blade. Repeat to make as many dowels of the same length as you need. (This setup will also work for other small parts. However, when working with flat stock, simply slide the wood forward.)

You can also cut three to five dowels at once, without them binding as they pass through the blade. If you're cutting lots and lots of dowels, put a tray or box under the outfeed side of the table to catch the dowels as you cut them. (See Figure 8.)

Ripping and resawing. You can also use a scrap block clamped to the fence to help gauge the length of a rip cut. In this case, mount the block to fence the same distance beyond the cutting edge as the length of the cut. This block will serve as a stop. (See Figure 9.)

Make the cut by feeding the stock forward slowly. Don't feed too fast, or the blade will tend to 'cup' in the wood and you won't get a straight cut. Repeat as needed—each rip cut will be exactly the same.

You may want to rip stock to get it down to a specific thickness. This is called resawing. The procedure for resawing is similar to the one I just outlined; but omit the stop block. If the stock that you need to rip is taller than the rip fence—such as the decks of the River Queen—you'll need to make a taller fence. This is nothing more than two boards, each as long as the table, joined together at right angles and clamped to the bandsaw table. (*See Figure 10.*)

When resawing wide boards, it's advisable to use a wider blade—⅜" or ½". Smaller blades want to follow the wood grain, and the cut may not be perfectly straight. However, you can use a ¼" blade successfully for resawing *if* the blade is sharp, the guides are adjusted correctly, and you set the blade tension just a little more taut than normal. Pass the board through as slowly as necessary to keep the blade cutting in a straight line. If you see the blade start to wander, slow down.

Hold the board firmly against the fence in front of the blade as you push it. Don't apply any pressure against the blade or beyond it; this will bind the blade. Another problem that could cause binding is internal stresses in the board that are released as you resaw. These may cause the resawn portions of a board to press together, squeezing the blade. A small wedge between the resawn portions will counteract this. (*See Figure 11.*)

Figure 8. The scrap clamped to the fence will help you to cut several dowels to the same length. The scrap is clamped in front of the blade so the pieces don't bind as they pass the blade. (Note the tray to catch the dowels as they come off the table.)

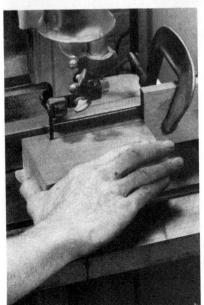

Figure 9. A scrap clamped to the fence beyond the blade will help you to make accurate dead-end lengthwise cuts.

Figure 10. Clamp the rip fence to the bandsaw table, making sure it is parallel to the blade.

Towards the end of the pass, a push stick will come in handy. *(See Figure 12.)* I've included two simple designs for push sticks that you can make in Figure 13. Keep one or the other handy at all times.

If you have trouble keeping the blade straight when you rip or resaw on the bandsaw, there are several possible causes. (1) The blade may be dull; (2) the guides may be out of adjustment; (3) you're not holding the board firmly against the fence; (4) you're trying to cut too quickly, or (5) the fence isn't parallel to the blade.

Cutting pegs to length. There will be many times when you'll need to cut a number of store-bought pegs to a specific length. To do this, first feed a scrap piece of ⅛" thick hardboard into the bandsaw blade, leaving as much material to the right of the blade as the length of the peg you want to cut. Butt the underside of the head of the peg against the edge of the hardboard. Hold it firmly and slowly pass it by the blade. *(See Figure 14.)* Repeat as needed, and hand sand the sawn tips to knock off any feathers or burrs.

Cutting curves. If you need to cut an outside curve that's too tight for the blade you're using, make several short cuts. Cut off a little bit of stock each time,

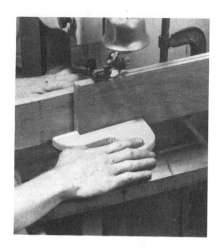

Figure 12. You'll want to use a push stick at the end of the pass.

Figure 13. Push sticks are quite helpful and easy to make. Simply cut them out on the bandsaw and rout the edges of the handles to make them more comfortable to use.

3/4" STOCK

7"

4 5/8"

REMOVE 3/4" X 3/4" FOR ONE

REMOVE 3/4" X 6" FOR OTHER

(FOR TWO PUSH STICKS)

Figure 11. Sometimes there are internal stresses in a board that are released as the board is resawn. This can cause the resawn pieces to press together, binding the blade. A small wedge (kerf keeper) pressed into the kerf, beyond the blade, will counteract this tendency.

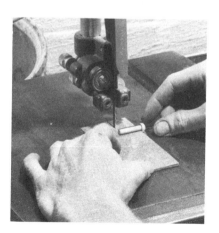

Figure 14. To cut a peg to length, butt the head against the edge of a scrap of hardboard. Hold it firmly as you pass it by the blade.

Figure 15. Sometimes you can cut tight curves with a ¼″ blade by making more than one cut.

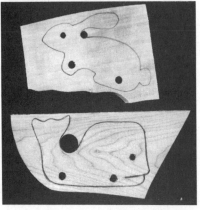

Figure 16. Drilling holes in tight inside corners will make bandsawing easier.

Figure 17. This jig is essential for accurately drilling peg holes and offset axle holes in wheels.

coming closer and closer to the cutline with each pass. Or, you can drill several holes along the curve before you cut, just to the outside of the cutline. These will help you turn sharp corners.

If you need to cut a tight inside curve, sometimes you can do it in two passes. Cut in from one side, back the blade out, then cut in from the other side. (*See Figure 15.*) If you make 'dead end' cuts like this, you may have to turn off the bandsaw in order to back the blade out without pulling it off the bandsaw wheels.

You can also drill holes where there are tight curves so that you don't have to worry about sawing them. (*See Figure 16.*) Just make sure that the holes are the same radius as the curves.

Whether cutting tight outside curves or tight inside curves, you can use your bandsaw to 'nibble' away stock from cuts that you couldn't make any other way. In this operation, you carefully advance the board up to the blade and press it *very* lightly against the teeth, using the blade as an ultra-thin power rasp. Nibbling usually leaves an extremely rough surface, but you can clean these up with sandpaper, a drum sander, or a rat-tail file.

Making do. If you don't have a bandsaw, a coping saw will do the job with a little muscle and a lot of patience. The trick to using a coping saw is that you have to trace the pattern on *both* sides of the wood. To get the patterns properly positioned, first trace the pattern on one side of the wood, marking the holes. Drill these holes; turn the piece over; and use the holes to position the pattern on the other side of the workpiece. Clamp the stock in a vise and saw out the shape, keeping to the pattern on both sides of the wood.

Using the Drill Press

When using the drill press in making toys, you will find it useful to make several jigs or fixtures to help hold or position the work as you drill. The purpose of all of these jigs is to somehow support or position the work.

This is done not only for the sake of accuracy, but also for safety. The drill press may not look dangerous; however, *any* power tool can turn on you if used improperly. When drilling small parts, the workpieces must be supported or held down so that the bit doesn't catch and fling them across the room—or at you. Many of the same rules that I mentioned on the bandsaw also apply here: Don't wear jewelry or loose clothing, use eye protection, and keep your hands clear of the bit.

Preventing tear-out. The first of these jigs is as simple as they get: just a board. When drilling all the way through a workpiece, put a board underneath it to keep the back of the hole from splintering out. Any scrap (except particle board) will do. If you're going to drill several holes all the same size, clamp the board down so that it doesn't slip around. If you allow it to slip, the drill will gradually make an enlarged hole in the board. When you drill through the workpiece, there won't be enough stock backing up the bit to prevent the tear-out.

Drilling offset axle holes. Another essential jig is a board for drilling offset axle holes and peg holes accurately in the wheels. Use a board about six inches longer than the width of your drill press table. Drill two ⅝″ holes, 1/16″ deep, about 3″ apart at the center of the board. When you're drilling the inside of a wheel, the protruding axle hub on the outside of the wheel can be set in one of these shallow holes. This will allow the wheel to sit flat on the board.

Drill a ⅜″ hole, ½″ deep in the center of one of the ⅝″ holes. Drill a ¼″ hole in the center of the other. These holes will support dowels that will serve as locating posts for the wheels. Cut a ⅜″ and a ¼″ dowel long enough so that they will protrude a little bit more than the thickness of the wheel when they are seated in their respective holes. Sand the diameter of each dowel and round the protruding ends so the wheels slip on and off easily, but with no slop. Clamp the board to the table of the drill press so that the drill bit will make a

hole precisely the same distance from the center hole each time you put a new wheel in the jig. (*See Figure 17.*)

Some wheels need to have their axle hole plugged with a dowel, then a new axle hole drilled just a few fractions of an inch off from the original hole. To drill several 'plugged' wheels all precisely the same, tack two 3″ lengths of wood, approximately ½″ thick, to the jig board so that they form a 'V'. Locate this V under the drill bit so that when you cradle a wheel in the V, the bit will make a hole in the wheel that is slightly off center.

Sanding tight curves. You can use your drill press to sand tight inside curves by making a simple drum sander out of a dowel. Just cut a slot in the end of the dowel with your bandsaw, and insert a small strip of sandpaper. Clamp the other end of the dowel in the chuck. When you turn on the drill press, the sandpaper will wind up on the dowel forming a 'drum', slightly larger than the diameter of the dowel. (*See Figure 18.*) You may wish to make several of these sanders, using different diameter dowels.

Woodcraft Supply Corporation offers a set of small drum sanders that will mount on your drill press, as well as replacement drums. Their address is in the appendix.

Figure 18. If you don't have drum sanders, you can make passable ones yourself. Cut slots in the end of several sizes of dowels. Slip sandpaper into the slots and twist it around the dowels so that the direction of the dowel's spin will tend to keep the paper wrapped in position.

There are other fixtures that you'll need to make for the drill press, but they are used for one or two specific toys. I'll explain them as they're needed.

Making do. If you don't have a drill press, I suggest you purchase a jig for your hand drill that converts it into a benchtop drill press. There are several of these available on the market today, for most makes of hand drills. These jigs are fine for most of the operations described in this book. However, they don't provide the weight or the stability to use a fly cutter safely. Nor do they have the 'throw' needed to drill long holes, such as the holes through the bodies of the Tyrannosaurus or the Toucan.

If you don't wish to purchase a drill press or a jig for your hand drill, you can still make most of the toys in this book, provided you take your time and work carefully. However, it's much harder to be accurate and your toys may require a good deal of handwork to get them to work properly.

Using the Sander/Grinder

This is sometimes called a one-inch belt sander, or 'edge sander'. Before using this tool, always check that the table is perpendicular to the belt. This will make a big difference in the results, especially if you're sanding thicker stock.

When working on this tool, try to sand the edge of the pieces to a smooth, fluid line. Don't stop moving the piece while it's pressed against the belt—this will create flat spots. Make long sweeping passes, pressing the piece lightly against the belt.

Every power tool has its dangers, and this is no different. The danger in using a sander/grinder is that your fingers may catch between the belt and the work-table. To lessen this danger, adjust the tool so that the space between the table and the belt is ⅛″ or less. Once again, take off your jewelry and don't wear loose clothing. Wear eye protection and a dust mask, and keep your fingers at least 1″ away from the belt at all times.

Sanding inside curves. Some sander/grinders have a removable backing plate (or platen) behind the belt to support it. Remove this platen to sand inside curves. On my sander/grinder, the platen can't be removed. So I modified the tool so that the belt tracks off center, leaving half the belt unsupported. With this arrangement the belt can follow concave curves. *(See Figure 19.)* I use the unsupported part of the belt for inside curves and the supported part for straightaways and outside curves.

Cleaning the belts. If you haven't tried an abrasive belt cleaner yet, now is the time. They are made of neoprene rubber that grabs the sawdust particles and thoroughly cleans the belt. They will increase belt life by as much as five times and will keep belts from burning your work. Clean your sanding belts after every two-three minutes of use. Press the cleaner firmly against the belt for three or four seconds, until the belt is restored to its original color. *(See Figure 20.)* By the

Figure 19. If the platen, or backing plate, on your sander/grinder is not removable you can bend the arm to the top pulley and get the belt to track off-center. This will leave part of the width of the belt unsupported and enable you to follow inside curves.

way, these belt cleaners are manufactured by the Abrasive Service Company, Inc., 398 Broad Street, Forestville, CT 06010. If you write them, they'll tell you the supplier nearest you.

Collecting the sawdust. You'll want to set up some sort of dust collection system if you don't already have one. If your sander/grinder doesn't have a fitting for a vacuum cleaner hose, you can make one easily. Take a section of vacuum cleaner tube and cut a slot diagonally down it so that it will fit around the belt as it passes under the table. Fashion a clamp that will hold this tube in place while you work, and hook the tube up to a good shop vac. *(See Figure 21.)* By the way, the dust from sander/grinders is very fine. Clean out and replace your vacuum filters frequently to prevent problems.

Making do. This is a hard tool to do without. There are many sander/grinders on the market at a wide range of prices. If you're serious about making toys, you should invest in one. If you want to keep your investment to a minimum, write to Divindacom Products, Inc., P.O. Box 12, Jackson, WI 53037 and ask for information on their sanders.

If you want to do without a sander/grinder, you'll have to do a lot of hand rasping and hand sanding.

Smooth out rough edges with a four-in-hand rasp and a rat-tail file. Follow this up with 80# sandpaper, then 120#.

Using the Stationary Belt Sander

This is another indispensable power tool for toy-makers. If you don't already have a stationary belt sander, you don't need to spend a fortune to get one. Divindacom, the company I mentioned just a few paragraphs back, manufactures an inexpensive 6" stationary belt sander. When you're deciding on what belt sander to purchase, stay away from those that have complex housings that interfere with belt changes. You'll be changing grits quite often, and fooling with the housing can get tiresome.

When using a belt sander, I always wear eye protection, a dust mask, and hearing protection. The eye protection is a must when using any power tool, of

Figure 21. You can convert your vacuum cleaner into a dust remover by slotting the tube so that it encases the belt. Then you can fashion a jig to hold it in place on your sander/grinder.

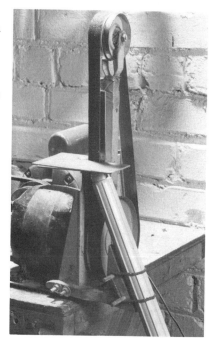

Figure 20. Belt cleaners will extend the life of your belts by as much as five times. Press it against the belt, with the sander running, and it will remove most of the built-up dust particles and restore the belt to near its original color.

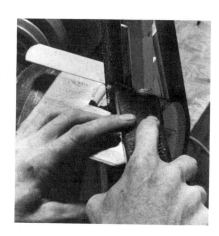

course. But the sander kicks up quite a bit of sawdust, and it's a noisy tool. You can rig up a simple dust collection system easily enough. *(See Figure 22.)* But you'll never capture all the dust, nor will you be able to make the tool any quieter.

There is also a 'pinch point' on most belt sanders, where the belt goes under the housing or the backstop. Keep your fingers clear of this point, and adjust the distance between the belt and the backstop to less than ⅛" to keep the danger to a minimum. Never work without a backstop. This piece of hardware is there for your safety, like the blade guard on a table saw.

Sanding techniques. Usually, you'll want to start sanding with 80#. This belt will leave a flat surface on the wood and remove any millmarks and saw marks. It will also remove dents left by C-clamps after gluing up a piece.

When you first touch your work to the sander, hold it firmly but pay attention to the way the work hits the belt. You want the piece to lie flat on the belt, with as much surface contact as possible. As you sand, check your work often to see that you are sanding the whole surface equally. If some part of the surface isn't being sanded equally, press harder over that area. But always keep the entire surface on the belt. If you try to sand just the unsanded areas, the surface will become uneven and give you trouble the rest of the way through assembly.

The more often you check your work while you're sanding, the closer you'll come to a flat, even surface. I can't stress the importance of this too much. If you sand a piece so that it's thicker on one side than on the other, not only will it look bad, but it may affect the moving parts.

Always sand with the grain running in the same direction as the belt. Sometimes you may have to lay out pieces so that the grain runs diagonally, so beware of simply holding pieces the 'long way' on the belt sander. Check the grain direction on each piece before you sand.

Move the piece back and forth over the full width of the belt as you sand. This will spread out the wear on the belt and use it up evenly. It will also slow down the tendency of the belt to become clogged with dust particles. Lastly, it will speed up the sanding process, always exposing the piece to the cleanest, sharpest grit.

While I'm talking about clogging, let me harken back to the sander/grinder section and remind you about abrasive belt cleaners. These cleaners work for

Figure 22. You can make a jig to hold a vacuum cleaner head up to your belt sander. Notice the flap of cardboard extending above the vacuum head to catch the dust as it flies up.

Figure 23. Abrasive belt cleaners also work well on belt sanders. They will, in fact, clean any abrasive tool you use—disc sanders, pad sanders, even rasps and files.

any abrasive tool—sander/grinders, belt sander, disc sanders, etc. (*See Figure 23.*)

Finish sanding on the belt sander with 120#. Use this belt to remove all scratch marks from the 80#. The 120# belt will not remove material quickly, like the 80#. It will simply polish the surface. So make sure that you don't move from the 80# to the 120# too soon.

Rounding over. Many of the toys in this book require that you round over the edges of some of the parts. If this part is a dowel, hold it at a 45° angle to the belt and slowly rotate the dowel while pressing it down against the abrasive. (*See Figure 24.*) The process is similar for square or rectangular parts, but they require a little more care when you rotate them. Remember, always keep the piece moving as you sand.

Making do. If you don't have a stationary belt sander, several companies make jigs that will hold your portable belt sander stationary. You can also clamp a portable belt sander upside down in a wood vise while you use it. However, be sure that it is clamped securely.

You can also make do with hand sanding. Purchase or make a sanding block with a soft backing of felt or rubber, and wrap sandpaper around it. The backing helps the paper hit as much of the surface as possible.

Figure 24. To round off the ends of dowels, hold them at a 45° angle to the stationary belt sander, across the direction of the belt travel. Twist them gingerly as you touch them down lightly.

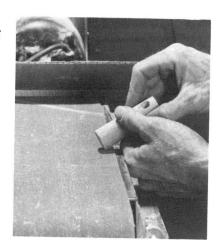

Clamp the sanding block in a vise, and rub the piece back and forth over it. If you are trying to build up your finger and arm muscles, this will do it!

Using the Router

While all power tools require special caution when you use them, this goes double for the router. I consider the router the most dangerous tool that I use in toy-making. Wear eye *and* ear protection when you use a router, and keep your fingers as far as possible from the spinning bit.

Use your common sense when deciding what pieces to shape on the router and what pieces should be done by hand. There are many small parts to toys, and some of these are too small to shape safely on a machine. Sometimes, you can mount a small part on the end of a dowel or in a clamp so that it can be safely shaped. But if you can't get a good, solid grip, shape the piece by hand. I use this rule of thumb: If, during any portion of the routing operation, I have to bring my finger closer than 3" to the bit, then I do the operation by hand. I've found that the edges of small pieces can sometimes be shaped quicker with a four-in-hand rasp or sandpaper than they can with a router.

One more warning: If you are not absolutely confident of your ability to complete a routing operation safely, DON'T DO IT! Doubts can be a powerful force for good when you're woodworking, if you pay attention to them.

Router bits. I use a quarter-round bit exclusively for shaping the edges of toys. This is primarily an aesthetic judgement. Of course, all hard corners on toys should be 'broken' to make the toy safer for children, but this can be done with a variety of bits. Some toymakers prefer a chamfering bit. I like the quarter-round bit.

I recommend purchasing carbide-tipped bits for two reasons. First, carbide-tipped bits will stay sharp much longer than steel bits. This saves you sharpening costs, and helps prevent the bit from burning the wood. Second, the carbide-tipped bits are available with a roller bearing guide that travels slowly along the edge of a piece while the bit is spinning much faster. This, too, prevents burns on the edges of the toy parts. The bearing surface of the steel router bit will inevitably burn a dark line along the edge of the toy no matter how carefully you work.

Using a router table. For toymaking, you want to set your router up as a shaper, with the bit facing upwards. To do this, you'll need to make or purchase a routing table about 18″ square. If you make your own, use a hard, smooth material (such as Formica®) on the work surface. Wax the surface often, to help the work glide across it.

To attach your router to the table, first remove the work surface from the router. It usually comes off with a few screws. Then use these screws to attach the router to the table with the bit poking up through a hole in the center of the table. If you've built your own table, you'll need to rout out the area under the table about the same diameter as the router's work surface, to make the table in this area the same thickness as the router's work surface. Mark and drill holes for the screws, then attach the router.

Shaping techniques. Keep in mind that when you use the router as a shaper, the bit spins clockwise as you look down at it. Pieces must be passed from left to right past the 'front' of the bit (the side closest to you). This will feed the work *against* the direction of rotation. If you pass the work by the bit in the opposite direction, the bit will want to push the work along. It may even grab the work and fling it out of your hands.

Never start routing on an outside curve or corner. The bit will either chip the wood or fling the workpiece out of your hands. Start on a straightaway or a gentle curve whenever possible. Avoid end grain when starting a cut. End grain is much harder to rout, and it can catch the bit. So always start your pass on long grain.

As you make your pass, maintain a constant feed rate. Never stop moving the workpiece when it's pressed against the router bit. If the bit spins in just one place on the wood, for even a fraction of a second, it will burn your work. This is especially important to remember on sharp curves where there is a tendency to slow down as you change feed directions. It's better to make many short overlapping passes at a constant speed, than to slow down at turning points and burn the wood.

Feeding the work at a constant rate is a skill, and it will take some practice. If you haven't done much work on a router, you can reduce the risk of ruining your workpiece by making the cut in two passes. Set the bit at half the proper height, so that it removes just half of the stock. Make a pass, then raise the bit to the proper setting and make another to complete the cut.

A word of warning. I don't recommend that you use a shaper for shaping these toy parts. Most shapers have ½″ shanks, and the cutters are quite large—too large to do delicate work safely. Routers, on the other hand, take bits with ¼″ shanks. The cutters are smaller, and they will accommodate smaller workpieces safely.

Making do. Although the router will make short work of your shaping chores, it is also quite easy to do without one. Simply use a four-in-hand rasp or a rat-tail file to break the edges, then smooth them out with hand sanding.

Several mail order tool supply companies, such as the Woodcraft Supply Corporation, sell quarter-round and chamfering spokeshaves that can be used to break the corners on some of the larger toy parts. These tools won't reach tight corners, and they are awkward to use on small parts. Nonetheless, they will save you some work over just using a rasp and file.

Using the Table Saw and Jointer

Both of these tools are essential to woodworking in general. You need them to make smaller, true boards out of larger, uneven boards. Other than cutting a dado slot here and there, there are hardly any specific applications to toymaking that I need to explain. But I do want to review some safety rules with you.

Because toymaking involves so many small parts, sooner or later you'll be tempted to saw or joint a small board. DON'T DO IT! Use a bandsaw or hand saw to cut the piece, and a sander or sandpaper to true it up. If you must cut small pieces on the table saw, use feather board and push sticks to hold the piece as you feed it into the blade. Never cut anything so small that it might be pinched between the blade and the table insert.

When using the jointer, there is just no way to joint small pieces safely, even if you use push blocks. I use this rule of thumb: If the workpiece is less than 12″ long, less than 1″ wide, or less than ¼″ thick, I true it up on the sander or by hand. Remember that if you should slip when attempting to join a small part, the rotation of the cutter head will drag your hand down into the machine. That's not a pleasant thought.

Of course, it goes without saying that you should never remove the saw guard or cutter guard to make it easier to work. There are only three operations on the table saw where it's necessary to remove the guard: cutting a dado, a groove, or a rabbet. If you have to remove a tool guard to perform any other toymaking operation, you should be using another tool.

Keep your own guard up at all times. Power tools are dangerous; there's no getting around that. It behooves you to develop good safety habits when using them. Don't ever think that safety practices hamper or restrict your woodworking. You'll quickly find that they actually improve the speed and accuracy of your work. They also make you more confident, and reduce the stress of working around power tools. All this works together to make your toymaking more enjoyable.

Using a Dust Collection System

Whirling bits and cutters are clear and present dangers in woodworking that you can see and hear. There is another danger that is not quite so readily apparent: sawdust. Not only is dust a nuisance, it can irritate your skin, your eyes, or the linings of your nose and lungs. Several studies have shown that long-term exposure can cause medical problems. Finally, sawdust may work its way into the bearings and bushings of your machinery, dry up the lubrication, and ruin your power tools. For these reasons, if you're going to do any serious toymaking, sawdust collection is essential.

I've been using a small shop vacuum for years, along with some simple jigs that I've made to collect dust from my sanders. So much fine dust, however, puts a strain on shop vacs. The dust clogs the filters, causes the vacuum motor to race, and the vacuum wears out in no time.

So instead of relying solely on a shop vac, I've also invested in a small dust collection system. There are many of these on the market, and their prices range from a few hundred dollars on up to thousands. Mine was made by Holub Industries. (See the appendix for their address.) They make several modest systems for small shops that will mount to 30-gallon and 50-gallon drums.

These systems are much more powerful than a vacuum cleaner and will remove almost all the dust that comes off your sanders. With a little ingenuity, you can also hook the system to your bandsaw, jointer, table saw, radial arm saw, even your router table. All you need is some PVC pipe, some flexible tubing, and a few 'shut-offs' to restrict the vacuum lines to those tools that aren't running.

Gluing and Clamping

There are five different gluing operations in toymaking. I'll cover these one at a time.

Gluing boards edge to edge. Choose the two boards that you want to glue together, and joint the edges. Be sure that the fence on the jointer is perfectly square to the table so that the edges of the boards will be perfectly perpendicular to the faces. Lay out as many bar clamps as you need to keep the entire length of the joint under pressure. Open the clamps up a little wider than the combined width of the board that you will be gluing up. Lay waxed paper on the clamps to keep glue from dripping onto them and onto the work surface.

Stand the boards up on edge, with the edges to be glued facing up. Apply glue evenly to both edges. I use my fingers to spread the glue, but you may prefer a small brush. Try not to let the glue drip down the faces of the board as you spread it. With practice, you'll figure out just how much glue to apply and how to spread it without making a mess.

As soon as you spread the glue, lay the board down in the clamps. Bring the boards together and start to tighten the clamps. Hold the joint between your fingers as you tighten the clamps to make sure that both surfaces end up flush. (See Figure 25.) As you clamp the boards, a little glue should squeeze out of the seam, along the entire length. If it doesn't, you've done one of four things wrong: (1) You haven't applied enough glue. (2) You haven't tightened the clamps sufficiently. (3) You haven't used enough clamps. (4) The edges aren't jointed properly.

The first three problems are easily corrected. If your problem is the jointed edges, scrape the glue off and rejoint them. If you're having trouble jointing the edges, check the alignment of your jointer tables and knives. Remember, when you're jointing, once you start the pass you should apply pressure only to the outfeed table. Putting pressure on the infeed table will simply duplicate the edge that you already have. If there is a bow in the board, always joint the concave side.

There are two ways to keep the board flat as you clamp them. The first is to use bar clamps above *and* below the workpieces. (See Figure 26.) This will work for most of the projects in this book. Toy parts are relatively small, and you'll rarely need more than three bar clamps—one above the stock and two below—to glue up wide boards. Opposing the bar clamps in this way counteracts the tendency for the joint to 'lift' in the center.

If you're gluing up very wide or very thin stock, you'll need to do a bit more to keep the boards flat. Wrap a piece of waxed paper around the ends of the boards. Put a rigid piece of stock at least 1″ wide above and below both ends of the boards and clamp them with C-clamps. (See Figure 27.)

The best time to remove excess glue squeeze-out is twenty to thirty minutes after you've clamped the boards. The glue should be the consistency of cottage cheese—just starting to set up. At this point it can be scraped off easily with a chisel without smearing. If you wipe it off earlier, you will press some of the glue into the wood grain. This will make it harder to sand and finish later on. If you wait too long to remove the glue, the glue beads will become brittle and stuck to the wood. There will be a tendency for the glue to pull off tiny chips of wood as you scrape it off.

I usually leave the boards edge clamped for forty-five minutes to an hour. It's best to let the glue set up overnight before you start working with a piece.

Gluing flat surfaces together. The surfaces that are to be glued together should be perfectly flat. Any deep planer millmarks or saw marks should be removed before gluing. 80# sandpaper is sufficient to flatten surfaces that won't be seen after gluing.

Once again, experience will teach you how much glue to use. For areas like the top edge of the Hippo's mouth, the squeeze-out doesn't matter. You will either be sanding or sawing that area again, and this will remove the excess glue.

In some areas, however, the squeeze-out is difficult to remove. For example, it would be hard to get the glue off the rear legs of the Hound. For places like this, you should put a thin layer of glue on the piece that is to be attached and work it away from the edges toward the center of the piece. This will minimize squeeze-out.

As you bring the pieces together, be careful to position them properly so that you won't have to move them and expose smeared glue. Before you clamp the pieces, press them together firmly. This will create a suction that will help keep the pieces from shifting when you clamp them.

If the area to be clamped is not going to be sanded again and will be seen, use something to prevent the faces of the clamps from marring the wood. You can use thin scraps of wood (called 'cauls'), rubber pads, or you can glue thick pieces of leather to the clamp's faces to avoid the bother of positioning the cauls or pads every time you glue up something.

When you first apply the clamps, rock them back and forth slightly as you snug them up, until the surfaces engage completely. This will help to prevent the workpieces from shifting under the building clamp pressure. It also helps to have the C-clamps set to the proper opening before you apply the glue. Otherwise, the pieces may fall apart while you're fiddling with the C-clamps.

To remove any squeeze-out or smears, wait twenty to thirty minutes after clamping up the parts and work carefully with a chisel or scraper. Generally, I leave the workpieces in the clamps for at least half an hour, then let them sit for two or three hours before I work with them.

Gluing dowels in place. When you are gluing a dowel all the way through a piece, cut the dowel just a little bit longer so that it will protrude slightly from both sides. This way you can saw it off and sand it flush to the surface.

To glue the dowel in place, first put down waxed paper under your work. Using a wooden matchstick, a toothpick, or a long, thin glue applicator, smear the glue

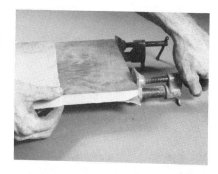

Figure 25. Line the edges up with your fingers as you tighten the clamps.

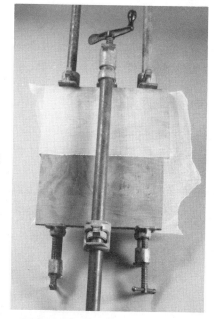

Figure 26. Using clamps on *both* sides of the boards will counteract the tendency of the joint to lift up in the center.

Figure 27. Clamping 1″ boards above and below either end of the glue-up will keep all the boards flat. Note the waxed paper wrapped around the ends of the glue-up to prevent the 1″ boards from being glued to the assembly.

evenly on the inside of the hole. Here again, experience will tell you how much glue to apply. Lay the part flat on the waxed paper and drive the dowel in place, making sure that it protrudes from both sides. A sixteen-ounce or twenty-ounce hammer will provide the concentrated mass you need to drive the dowel easily, without smashing the end of the dowel or splitting it. Wipe off the glue that's been driven out by the dowel, then let the glue cure. Afterwards, cut and sand the dowels flush. Don't sand the dowel too quickly, or you'll burn the tough end grain of the dowel. This will give your toy a 'black eye' or a 'mole'.

If the hole to be doweled is near the edge of the piece, it's best to drill and plug the hole *before* you cut out the shape of the part. That way, you avoid splitting out a thin area with the pressure of a snug dowel.

When you're gluing dowels in a blind hole (such as the dowels that attach the Bulldozer's blade to its wheels), be careful not to put too much glue in the dowel hole. This will prevent the dowel from seating properly, and it may make for a weak joint. Use less glue in the hole, and cut several long grooves running down the side of the dowel. These grooves can be cut with a V-gouge chisel, scratched into the dowel with an awl, or pressed in by crimping the dowel with a pair of pliers. The grooves will allow the excess glue to escape from the hole as you drive the dowel in.

Gluing pegs. Gluing pegs in a toy is similar to gluing dowels in a blind hole, with one important difference. When you peg a part of a toy to another part, you must leave a tiny clearance between the peg head and the toy. If you leave no clearance, the parts will bind. With practice, you'll be able to leave the proper clearance by instinct. But if you're just beginning to make toys, you'll want to make a clearance gauge. This jig guarantees perfect results every time. (*See Figure 28.*)

Remember that pegs need to be different lengths for different situations. The length is measured from the bottom of the peg head to the end of the peg. This dimension is determined by the depth of your peg hole, plus the thickness of the part that the peg goes through, plus the clearance, *minus* 1/64"-1/32" to leave room for glue at the bottom of the hole.

Gluing wheels to axles. When you cut the axles for your toys, double-check the lengths on the bills of materials. The length of an axle is determined by the thickness of the wheels, plus the thickness of the part

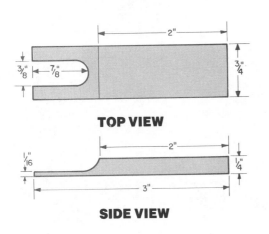

TOP VIEW

SIDE VIEW

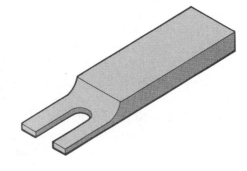

Figure 28. This simple gauge will ensure that pegs are driven in to the proper depth when you are joining pivoting parts.

that the axle goes through, plus the clearances needed between the wheels and the part, *plus* another 1/16"-1/8" so that the axles will protrude slightly from the wheel hubs when you glue them in place. The axle lengths will change slightly depending on how much you sand the toy parts before you assemble the wheels to the axles.

The glue joint between the axle and the wheel has to be as strong as you can make it. To increase the strength, cut several grooves in the ends of the axles where the wheels will fit over them. The grooves will allow more glue to stay in the joint when you press the wheels onto the axles.

Some toymakers recommend rubbing the middle of the axle with paraffin. This will decrease the friction where the axle goes through the toy. This is not necessary if you build your toys from hard, close-grained woods (such as cherry) as I do. But if you use softer, more fibrous woods, treating the axles with paraffin will help the wheels spin freely and decrease the wear of the axle in the hole. Be careful not to get paraffin on the ends of the dowels where the wheels are glued.

To glue the wheels to the axles, first put a piece of waxed paper down on the workbench. Put all the wheels on the paper with the insides facing up. Use a matchstick or a long, thin applicator to smear glue evenly inside the holes. Don't apply glue to more wheels than you can glue up in five minutes, or the glue inside the wheels will start to set up and the joints will be weakened.

Drive an axle into a wheel until you feel it hit the workbench. Turn the wheel/axle assembly over and carefully remove any glue that has been driven out of the hole. Give the axle a twist as you press your finger in toward an imaginary point directly above the center of the axle. Your finger will spiral in, lifting the glue off the wheel without smearing it outward from the hub. *(See Figure 29.)*

Now slip the dowel through the axle hole and set the glued-up wheel on the workbench with the axle

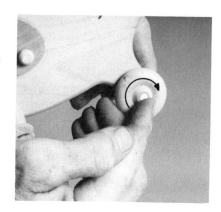

Figure 29. Use a circular motion inward and upward to remove the excess glue without smearing it on the face of the wheel.

pointing straight up. Drive the second wheel onto the axle until the axle protrudes slightly from the hub. Remove the excess glue in the same way you did with the first wheel. Wipe the glue off your hammer head and your finger—I keep a piece of carpet scrap on my workbench just for this purpose. Let the glue cure and sand the axle flush with the hubs of the wheels.

Gluing assemblies that pivot on pegs. Assemblies that pivot on pegs, such as the Hippo's head, require a simple jig to line up the pivot holes as the pieces are glued together. This will ensure that all parts move smoothly when assembled.

To make the jig, square up a block of scrap wood to 1¾" x 4" x 6". Stand the block on its end on the drill press table and drill a ¼" hole in the end, as shown in Figure 30. Cut a ¼" dowel 4" long and round off both ends. Hand sand 3" of its length until it will easily slip in and out of a 9/32" pivot hole. Glue the unsanded end of the dowel in the hole in the block. Lastly, cut away the back part of the block as shown in the drawing. This will allow you to clamp the block to your workbench.

To use the block, first fasten it to the bench. (Some of the assemblies may require a scrap block under the jig to raise it the proper height.) Slip the parts that are to be joined onto the dowel—usually these will be two sides that are joined by a spacer block. Apply glue to the inside surfaces of the sides and position the spacer between them. Carefully bring the whole assembly together with one of the sides pressed against the jig. (*See Figure 31.*) Press the parts together firmly so they won't shift when you apply the clamps. Clamp the accessible end of the assembly. Then slip the assembly off the jig and apply one or two more clamps, taking care that the parts don't shift. (*See Figure 32.*)

Hand Sanding

By the time you get to hand sanding a toy, it usually has all its edges and surfaces smoothed already. You only need to do a little touch-up work on the routed edges and the sharp corners. For this reason, I use a scrap of carpet to cushion the toys as I do the final sanding. This way, you can apply as much pressure as you want without fear that you will mar the surfaces that are already smooth.

Because most of the toy's surfaces are already sanded with 120# at this stage, be careful to only sand those surfaces that *need* sanding. You can scratch a smooth surface easily when you're hand sanding with 80#. These scratches will show up prominently when you finish the toy.

To speed up the chore of sanding routed edges, I hold the paper between my thumb and palm, and use all four fingers to apply pressure. This way, you'll get the most cutting action from each stroke. You'll also use more of the paper surface.

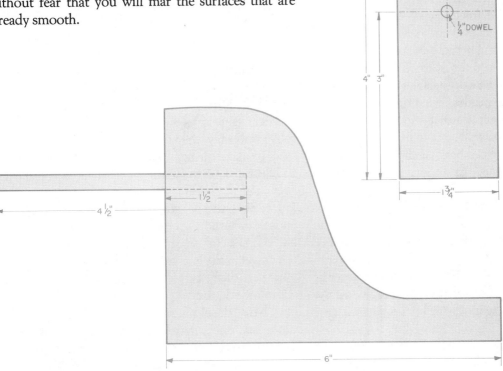

Figure 30. This jig will help you to accurately glue up pivoting assemblies such as the Hippo's head.

Finishing

The best finish for toys is a synthetic oil finish. It's quick to apply, it wears well, and it can be easily repaired if the toy is scratched. The oil finish that I prefer is Watco Danish Oil—there's more information on Danish oil in the "Materials and Tools" chapter.

Finishing one toy at a time. If you're making one toy at a time, the simplest way to finish it is to apply oil with a brush. The instructions on most oil finishes tell you to sand it into the wood, but this is difficult with a toy because there are so many tiny surfaces. A brush will reach into all the cracks and crevices with a minimum of effort. Let the oil soak in for half an hour or so, then rub off any excess before it gets gummy and hard to remove. Apply a second coat and repeat. Let the finish set up overnight, then apply a final coat. Once again, rub off the excess before it sets up. If you wish, wax the toy with a good carnauba wax.

Finishing many toys at once. If you're making many toys at once, dipping the toys in oil is the way to go. But don't use the five-gallon container that the finish comes in to do the dipping. If you break the seal on the lid, the finish will start to evaporate and will get too thick to soak in properly. Instead, just open the screw-on cap and pour as much finish as you need to cover the toys in a plastic bucket.

I made a simple trough to drain the toys after dipping, so that the excess oil runs back into the bucket. (*See Figure 33.*) Dip the first toy, put it on the trough next to the bucket, dip the second, push the first on a little further up the trough to make room for the second, and repeat. This way, most of the excess oil will run back to the bucket by the time a toy leaves the trough. When a toy reaches the top of the trough, put it on a clean surface and let the remaining oil soak in.

As you set the toy down to let the oil soak in, separate any surfaces that want to stick together with toothpicks. If the moving parts touch each other, this will prevent the oil from soaking in properly. It will also

leave a lot of residue on the surface. It's also a good idea to flip the toy over. If it drained in the trough resting on its wheels, let it soak with the wheels up.

After half an hour, wipe off the excess oil with a rag. You don't have to really rub the toy down. Just wipe off the wet areas. However the type of rag you use *is* important. Cotton rags, like old T-shirts, make the best rags. They are absorbent and lint-free. Synthetic materials don't work well at all. If you wait too long and

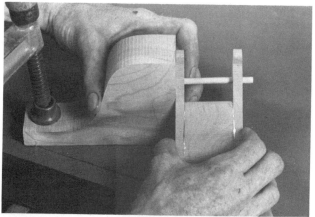

Figure 31. Using the jig to line up the two sides of the assembly, press the three pieces firmly together. Make sure the side next to the jig is flat against it and that the whole assembly can slide freely along the ¼″ dowel.

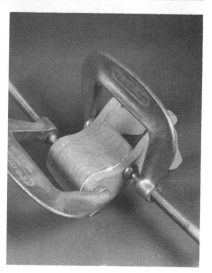

Figure 32. Be careful not to let the parts shift as you apply the clamps. Take the assembly off the jig to apply the second and possibly the third clamp.

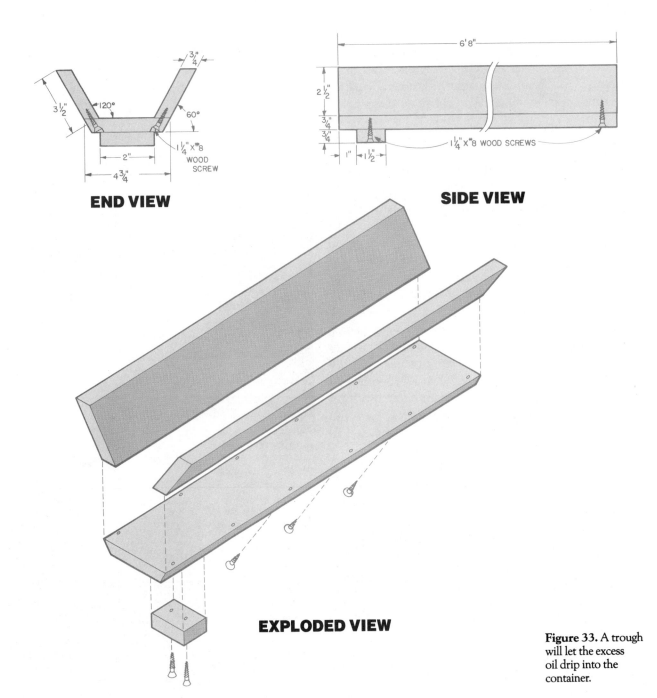

END VIEW

SIDE VIEW

EXPLODED VIEW

Figure 33. A trough will let the excess oil drip into the container.

the toys get gummy, you can use a rag dampened with oil to dissolve the excess. Pay special attention to surfaces where parts might have been touching—between the wheels and body, behind pegged pieces, and so on. Put the oil back in its container and let the toys dry overnight.

The next day, repeat the process. But this time, after you wipe off the toys the first time, let them sit for another half an hour and really give them a good rubdown.

Some woods may require a third coat, it may supersaturate the toy and the excess may bleed out. If this happens, rub the toy down with mineral spirits.

Painting. In general, I think these toys look best with a clear finish to show off the natural color and grain of the wood. Some toys, however, look much better when painted. For example, the Hummingbird and the Toucan need a bit of color. (But don't paint any of the parts that rub together!) When you paint a toy, it's sometimes necessary to assemble the parts *after* you've applied the paint and it's had time to dry. Keep this in mind if you plan to paint your toys.

Attaching Pull Cords and Handles

Before attaching an acrylic or nylon cord to a toy, melt the ends with a match or lighter. This prevents the cord from unraveling, and helps you to insert the cord in its hole. Hold the cord close enough to the flame that it will begin to shrivel up, but not so close that it catches on fire. (If it does catch on fire, simply blow it out.) Let the end cool for a minute or two; then, while the melted material is still warm and pliable, give the end a twist with your finger. *(See Figure 34.)* This will bring the end to a slight taper.

If you have to thread the cord through a long hole, twist the cord as you feed it into the hole. This twist stiffens and tightens the cord, making it easier to feed through the hole. If this doesn't work, use a nail or awl.

Catch the point of the awl behind on the melted tip, and push it through.

When you've threaded the cord through the hole, tie a square knot in one end so that it won't pull out. To hide the knot, drill a 'countersink' for it before you drill the hole for the cord. This countersink is nothing more than a slightly larger hole ⅜"-½" deep. For example, if you're using ¼" cord, drill a ½" blind hole for a countersink, then drill a ¼" hole through the middle of the ½" hole, all the way through the part. Thread the cord through the ¼" hole, and press the knot into the ½" countersink.

Fasten a wooden bead to the other end of the cord in the same fashion to make a handle. These wooden beads are commercially available.

Figure 34. Melt the end of the cord with a match or lighter and give the end a twist when it is still soft, but not hot enough to burn your fingers.

Materials and Tools

When I first started making toys several years ago, I got my wood from a kiln drying operation. I bought the rest of my supplies at a local hardware store. In both cases, I paid extremely high prices for materials and tools that were mediocre at best.

In a dogged search for simplicity, economy, and quality, I've located better suppliers. I find my wood closer to home. After I stopped buying kiln-dried lumber, I tried a local solar kiln with cheaper prices. After that, I began air-drying wood from local saw mills. Today, I call upon a friend with a portable bandsaw mill who cuts trees from my own land.

On the other hand, my search for better materials and tools has led me further and further afield. Currently, I use suppliers from Maine to California.

After many years of looking, I've gathered quite a resource list for the toymaker—where to get the best supplies at reasonable prices, tools and materials that can help your work go faster. In this chapter, I'll share those resources with you. Hopefully, this will save you some time and money.

Of course, I can't guarantee that all the resources listed here are the highest quality or the least expensive —they're just the best and the most economical that I've found after many years. However, new businesses are always springing up; woodworking companies are always developing new products. If you know of a better tool for a job, or a place where you can buy better supplies, by all means use them. But if you need a place to start looking, use this resource guide.

I'm also mindful that not all of these resources will be useful to all readers. For those of you who only plan to make one or two toys, there's no sense in cutting down a tree and drying your own lumber. For short runs, it's more economical to buy a few boards from a lumberyard. (Better yet, you can probably use the scraps left over from other woodworking projects.) Some 'purists' among you will want to make the *entire* toy—including the wheels and pegs—without buying anything but the wood and the glue. But for those readers who would rather save the time it takes to make these parts, I've found some reliable wheel and peg suppliers. In short, use what you want from this chapter as you need it.

What Wood Shall I Use?

I recommend that in most cases, you use a good grade of hardwood. I'm not a hardwood chauvinist by any means. Softwood is excellent for framing, trim, cabinetry, furniture, and any number of other uses. Although it is readily available and relatively inexpensive, it is inappropriate for toymaking for several reasons. First of all, it splinters easily. This makes it hazardous for children. Secondly, it isn't strong enough. If you're going to spend long hours making a toy, you don't want it to break the first time a child drops it on the floor. Thirdly, softwoods are so resinous that they will clog sandpaper sheets and belts in no time. And finally, a finished hardwood toy looks so much better than one made from softwood. You can sand a piece of pine, fir, or spruce all the way down to 400# sandpaper and it still won't come near to the beautiful lustre and grain patterns of hardwood.

Enough said about softwood. Now, what types of hardwood are appropriate? Several factors are involved.

Does it matter whether I use a heavy or a light wood? When you're designing or building a toy with moving parts, weight is an important consideration. *(See Figure 1.)* In the case of the Lobster, you wouldn't want to make the claws out of oak or hard maple because they would be too heavy to lift easily. But you could make the body out of a heavy wood. This would give the toy stability and the momentum to help lift the claws. If you were making the Frog, you wouldn't want to use osage orange for the body because it would be too heavy for the eccentric wheel to lift easily. That same wood, however, would be fine for the legs. These parts are so small (compared to the mass of the body) that they wouldn't inhibit the toy's movement.

Weight is something that needs to be reconsidered with each toy—and each *part* of each toy. The rule of thumb is that light wood is best for those parts that are to be lifted. For the rolling or stationary mass of the toy, you can use a heavier wood. Keep in mind, though, that the heavier the wood, the heavier and more awkward the toy will be for a child to play with.

How strong must the wood be? Ironically, the rolling mass of the toy, which can be made from a heavier wood, needn't be as strong as other parts. For example, the shell of the Turtle could be made from strong, heavy woods such as oak or hickory. But it could also be made from mahogany or poplar, which are lighter and not quite as strong. What you make these parts from really depends on your own tastes and the availability of the woods.

The thinner parts, however, must be made from strong woods, especially where there are holes near the edges of pieces. Two examples of this are the Frog's feet and the Hippo's head.

Further thoughts on wood selection: There is something else you should consider as you choose your wood. You may have tropical woods in your shop. Many of these will make beautiful toys, but here's a word of caution: Many dark tropical woods, such as rosewood, coco-bolo, and purpleheart, have *toxic resins*. Avoid these woods if you are making a toy for an infant who may chew on it. And if you're making a lot of toys, exposure to the fine sawdust from these toxic woods could cause respiratory problems, skin rashes, and eye irritations. Wear goggles, a face mask, and protective shop clothing while you work.

So what wood do I think is best for toys? Cherry. It's relatively light, quite strong, sands easily, and looks beautiful when finished. I also use walnut and poplar sometimes. They're not quite as strong as cherry, but they're strong enough for all but the thinnest parts. They also look good when you mix them with cherry in a toy.

Comparative Weight and Strength of Hardwoods

Very Light	Poplar, Aspen, Basswood
Light	Cherry, Walnut, Butternut, Mahogany, Hickory
Heavy	Maple, Birch, Beech, Oak, Ash
Soft	Basswood
Medium	Butternut, Mahogany
Hard	Cherry, Walnut, Maple, Birch, Beech, Oak, Ash, Hickory

Figure 1. A quick look at this chart shows that cherry and walnut are the only common hardwoods that are both light and strong. This makes them the best choice for toymaking. Of the two, I prefer cherry.

Where can I get the wood I need?

As I mentioned before, some of you may simply use the scraps you have around your shop. Others may buy what the local lumberyard carries. Or maybe you're planning to become a professional toymaker and you're looking for a reliable source of reasonably priced hardwoods. Where you get your lumber will depend on any number of factors—what woods are available where you live, how much you want to build, how much you want to pay, and so on.

One thing that makes toymaking appealing to many beginning woodworkers is that they can start right in on their first toy without a huge cash outlay for materials. Most of the toys in this book can be made with what you have in your scrap bin. You may not have any 8/4 (2″ thick) hardwood laying around, but you probably have some small pieces of ¾ or 4/4 wood that you can laminate to make a board of the proper thickness. There is plenty of room here for imagination. Glue up different woods to make striped stock. (A *striped* Hippo? Why not!) Give strength to weak woods by sandwiching them between stronger pieces. You can also change the design of the toy to accommodate the wood in your scrap bin. For example, the Frog can be made out of 6/4 stock. Simply adjust the length of the axles.

You may be just starting out in woodworking and not have any hardwood scraps available. How about that mahogany desk with the broken legs? Or the pallets thrown out behind the factory? Have you noticed that the crates behind the local motorcycle shop are made from unusual Asian woods? All of these things can be recycled to make some beautiful toys.

Another good source of inexpensive hardwood is old barns. I once took down an old corn crib and found the corner posts were walnut, all the diagonal braces and rafters were cherry, and the rest of the structure was white oak. When looking at an old building, keep an eye out for excessive checking, rot, and whether or not the nails have rusted off below the surface. Demolition is hard work, and you want to be sure that you are going to get some usable lumber for your efforts.

A note of caution: If you use old wood, be extremely carefully to remove all nails, screws, and staples. One nail can take a big chip out of jointer knives, dull a bandsaw blade, or completely ruin a carbide-tooth saw blade. Also, some woods, like white oak, become extremely tough after many years. They will take a toll on your blades, cutters, and knives. I think, though, that the beauty of old, air-dried wood more than compensates for the added trouble of dealing with it.

Surprisingly, the most likely place to get cheap wood is a wood shop! There may be a furniture or cabinet shop near you that throws away scraps that would be excellent for toys. If you use your head, there's no end to the places where you can find hardwoods for little or nothing.

You may be saying, "This is all fine and good, but I don't have the time to browse through dumps or search out discarded woods." Well, most lumberyards have at least a modest selection of hardwoods. These are usually priced quite high because of the limited demand, but remember that a few board feet will go a long way for a toymaker. You can also buy hardwoods through several mail-order companies. Once again, the prices are high—especially when you add in the freight.

Buying Wood in Quantity

Some of you are going to make a lot of toys and will need large quantities of reasonably priced wood. If so, there are two avenues open to you. The first is to search out a hardwood supplier. If you live in an area where there are hardwood forests, there will probably be a kiln or a hardwood distributor nearby where you can order lumber. In both cases, you will have to buy somewhere in the neighborhood of 500 board feet to get the best prices.

A *note on kiln-dried woods:* Beware of case-hardening and surface checks. (*See Figure 2.*) Sometimes a kiln operation will dry the wood too quickly and it will develop cracks in the surface. (This is most common in oak.) Or the wood will develop an internal 'honeycombed' checking (called case-hardening) that can't be seen until you saw the board. If you find either of these, the operation is in a big hurry and you would be better off to stay away from them.

Another note on planing: Some kiln operators and most hardwood distributors will plane your lumber to the desired thickness for a small additional fee. If you want the mill to do your planing, select only straight-grained woods. If you buy figured woods, such as curly maple, you will be better off to resaw and sand the wood to the proper thickness. There's too much 'tear-out' and chipping when you plane figured woods.

The other way to get hardwood economically is to go directly to the sawmill. In many states, if you write to the Department of Natural Resources, they will send you a book with all the registered sawmills in the state, listed by county. This book will also tell you the number of board feet that each sawmill cuts per year (which will give you a good idea of the size of the operation), and the services available: planing, resawing, kiln-drying, and so on.

If you live in a rural wooded area, as I do, there will probably be three small unlisted sawmills for every large one listed. Look around. Check the phone book. Sometimes these mills will be sawing mostly railroad ties and have stacks of 4/4 board left over. They may sell these cheap to get rid of them. Also, railroad tie and pallet sawmills will know enough to set aside walnut and cherry logs, but won't have the established market to sell the lumber at top prices. You may be able to get some real bargains.

Many sawmills will grade their desirable hardwoods and have low grade hardwoods that furniture companies don't want. Even though you want to use high-quality wood in your toys, you can buy #3 grade lumber and simply cut around the knots. If you find a piece of wood with solid knots, you can incorporate these into the toy to give it character. The pieces of wood used in toys are generally so small that the instability caused by knots (which makes the wood unsuitable for furniture) is not a problem with toys.

Kiln-drying—Pros and cons: You may have found a sawmill that will supply you with green lumber, and you're considering having it kiln-dried. Or, you may simply be looking for a supplier of kiln-dried hardwood. In either case, you'll want to know a few things about kiln-drying.

The main advantage of kiln-drying is that it's fast. Air-drying wood takes at least a year. In a kiln, however, green wood can be dried in as little as two weeks. Although most kilns will dry only their own wood, you may find one that will dry your lumber. This could enable you to get started working in a matter of weeks.

The other advantage to kiln-drying is that it takes the moisture content a bit lower than air-drying because it drives out the 'bound water'—water held

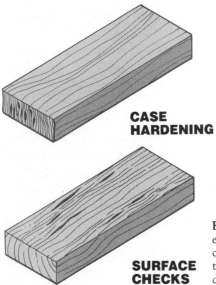

CASE HARDENING

SURFACE CHECKS

Figure 2. Case hardening and surface checks are a sign that the wood has been dried too quickly.

inside the cell walls. This process, however, makes wood 'thirsty'. Kiln-dried lumber will have a tendency to take on moisture in your shop unless the ends of the boards are painted and you store your lumber in a very dry area, such as a loft or attic. Be careful that the storage area isn't *too* hot, though, or the ends of the boards may check. There is still some moisture present in kiln-dried lumber (about 7%) that excessive heat can drive out too quickly. However, if you have to choose between a hot storage area or a wet one, take the heat. Changes in humidity are far more destructive to wood than changes in temperature. And if you want to control the humidity, a dehumidifier will keep the air dry in your shop.

There are three distinct disadvantages to kiln-drying. First, kiln-dried lumber tends to be more brittle. Some woodworkers use air-dried wood exclusively because it has a lively resilience that is lost in kiln-drying. Secondly, drying wood too quickly can cause surface checking and/or case hardening, as previously mentioned. And finally, the color may be changed slightly. This is especially true of walnut. When walnut is kiln-dried, it's usually steamed. The steam disperses the tannins responsible for the dark colors evenly throughout the rest of the wood. The dark and light areas (heartwood and sapwood) blend together. This process makes more of the wood into high-grade lumber, since sapwood is worth less than heartwood, but it washes out the depth and intensity of the color. A piece of air-dried walnut often has a rich purple cast to it which is lost in the steaming process.

Air-drying—Pros and cons: The main advantage to air-drying lumber is that you can do it yourself for free. Once you've built a drying rack, your only cost is for transportation from the sawmill. And you'll find that the price of green lumber at the sawmill is substantially lower than dried lumber from the kiln or the distributor. In some cases, it may be several dollars per board foot lower. This will vary quite a bit, depending on the type of wood and the area of the country, but the savings will be attractive in any case.

There are three disadvantages to air-drying lumber. The first is that it requires space. Five hundred board feet of lumber will make a stack 4' wide by 8' long by 2½' tall. The second disadvantage is that it takes time. Generally speaking, it takes a year to dry a 4/4 (1" thick) board, 2 and a quarter years for a 8/4 board, and four to five years for a 12/4 board.

The third disadvantage is that air-drying doesn't remove as much moisture from the wood as kiln-drying, and the wood is less stable. I haven't found this to be a problem for toymaking, though. The pieces used in toys are usually so small that any movement through shrinking or swelling is negligible. There is also little chance of checking or cracking. Because the pieces are small, internal stresses are released before they build to the point of cracking. I've also found that a Danish oil finish slows down the passage of water enough to prevent rapid changes in moisture content which might otherwise cause checking.

How to air-dry your own lumber: The most important factor in air drying is the air circulation. Although the basement may seem to be the perfect place to dry your wood, the opposite is probably true. Usually, the air in a basement is stagnant and humid. There is little circulation to remove the humidity. More often than not, green lumber stored in a basement will mildew and rot, rather than dry.

An attic, on the other hand, is usually too hot, and will dry the wood too quickly. As I said before, this results in surface checking. The wood on the outside of the board dries faster than the inside. As it dries, it shrinks and cracks develop.

The best place to dry wood, believe it or not, is outside. Look for a spot that gets a breeze and isn't exposed to a lot of direct sunlight. This will allow the wood to dry at a slow, even rate. You can build a simple drying rack, as shown in Figure 3. Make sure this rack is

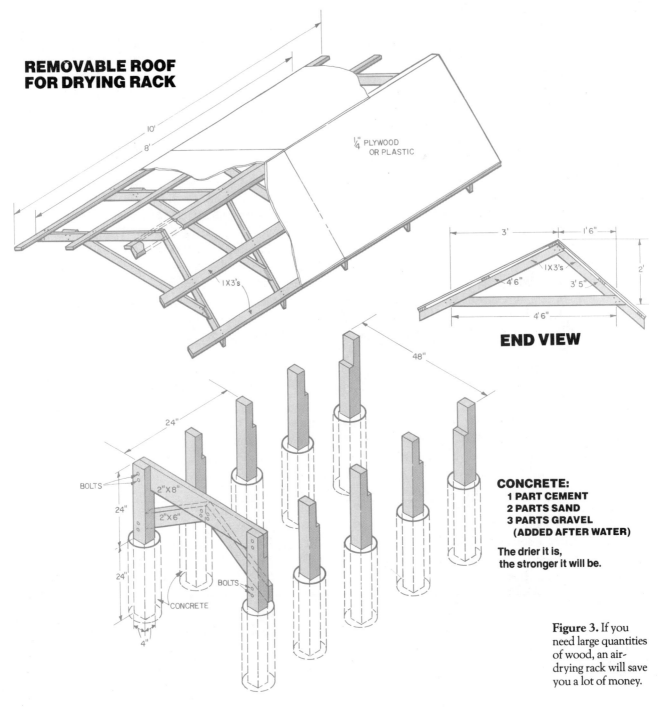

REMOVABLE ROOF FOR DRYING RACK

10'

8'

1/4" PLYWOOD OR PLASTIC

1 X 3's

END VIEW

3'   1' 6"

1 X 3's

4' 6"   3' 5"

2'

4' 6"

48"

24"

BOLTS

2" X 8"

24"

2" X 6"

BOLTS

24"

CONCRETE

4"

CONCRETE:
1 PART CEMENT
2 PARTS SAND
3 PARTS GRAVEL
(ADDED AFTER WATER)

The drier it is,
the stronger it will be.

Figure 3. If you
need large quantities
of wood, an air-
drying rack will save
you a lot of money.

well off the ground and perfectly flat. Do not put the cross supports more than two feet apart or the boards will sag as they dry.

Once you've built the drying rack, you're ready to stack the lumber. To allow proper air circulation between each board, you'll need to put 'stickers' (small sticks) in between the rows to ensure proper air circulation. I use commercial furring strips for stickers, but any dry wood will do. The stickers should be as long as the width of the drying rack, at least ¾" thick, and no more than 1½" wide. The narrower the stickers are, the less likely they are to trap moisture and encourage fungus or rot.

The structures within a tree—the xylem and the phloem—pass water up and down the trunk. Because of this, water leaves a board more quickly through the ends of the boards than it does through the faces and edges. This can result in the ends of the boards checking. (*See Figure 4.*) To prevent this, paint the ends of the boards as soon after they are cut as possible. This will seal the end grains and let the water leave the wood slowly and evenly. If the boards are all the same length, you can paint the ends after you've stacked them. If not, you'll have to paint them before you stack them.

A note on sealing end grains: The Chapman Chemical Company, P.O. Box 9158, Memphis, TN 38109, manufactures a wax emulsion called Sealtite #60 to seal the ends of boards as they dry. It will work with both air-drying and kiln-drying processes, and comes in a variety of colors and container sizes.

As you stack the lumber, arrange each layer so that it's as wide as the layer beneath it. That way, each layer will be properly supported, and the weight of the boards from above *and* below will help to keep all the boards from cupping. Leave space in between the edges of each board to allow for air circulation. Pressing them too close together will keep boards on the inside of the stack from drying properly. (*See Figures 5 and 6.*)

Figure 4. When drying your own wood, the ends of the boards should be painted or the ends may check.

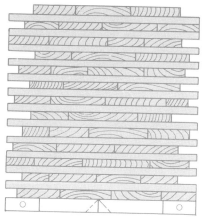

Figure 5. It's important to leave space between the boards as you stack them. This allows for air circulation. It's also important that you spread out each layer so that it's just as wide as the layer above it and below it. This properly supports the stack and helps to control cupping.

Figure 6. This wood has been improperly stacked. The edges of the boards touch, and the layers are of an uneven width.

Be careful to place the stickers directly over each other, in line with the supports. (*See Figures 7 and 8.*) Don't stack the wood more than 4'- 5' thick. When you've finished, build a simple roof and lay it on top of the stack. This roof should have plenty of overhang, to keep the rain from dripping on the stack. If you can't build your rack in the shade, paint the roof with aluminum paint. This will reflect the sunlight and prevent the stack from getting too hot.

For toymaking, you can be fairly comfortable using 4/4 wood after it's dried for a year. For 8/4 wood, you'll want to test the moisture content before using it. There is a simple method for this. Saw off a small piece of green lumber (taken from the *inside* of the stack) and weigh it. An inexpensive postage scale works well for this purpose. Now put the piece of wood in the oven at 350° for a few hours to dry it thoroughly. Then weigh it again. The difference in the two weights, divided by the original weight of the wood, equals the moisture content. Here's the equation written out:

$$\frac{\text{Original weight} - \text{Dried weight}}{\text{Original weight}} = \% \text{ Moisture content}$$

A *note on measuring moisture content:* You can also measure moisture content the easy way—with a meter. Lignomat U.S.A. Ltd., 14345 N.E. Morris Court, P.O. Box 30145, Dept. B-H, Portland, OR 97230, makes several models of moisture meters. Write to them for more information.

Once the wood has dried sufficiently, bring it into the shop and let it sit for four to six weeks before using it. This will give it time to get acclimated to your shop. A shop is usually drier and warmer than the outside, and the wood needs time to 'breathe'—adjust itself to the change in temperature and humidity. If you cut into the wood right away, the pieces may change shape before you get a chance to assemble them.

Dowels

For the occasional toymaker, dowels can be found in most hardware stores and lumberyards. The quality and the price will vary dramatically, so shop around. Some dowels are made of soft maple. These are okay, but hard maple, beech, and birch are far superior! How do you tell dowels made from softer woods from those made from hard woods? If your thumbnail will easily

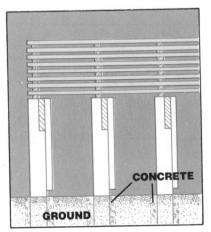

Figure 7. Note that the stickers are directly over each other, and in line with the support posts.

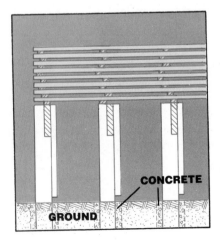

Figure 8. Careless placement of the stickers will result in warped or sagging boards.

make a deep mark in the dowel, it's probably soft maple or an imported light tropical wood.

If you're going to make a lot of toys, it's worth ordering dowels from a dowel manufacturer. There are several such companies, but I usually deal with C.B. Cumming & Sons, P.O. Box 346, Norway, ME 04268. Their dowels are consistently strong, accurately sized, and properly smoothed. Make sure that you specify that you want your dowels bagged, or they'll get dirty during shipping.

Wheels, Pegs, and People

Whether you're planning to build just a few toys or go into production, you should consider buying certain ready-made parts such as wheels, axle pegs, and people. You can turn these parts on a lathe or cut them out with a hole saw, but the process is time-consuming. Often, you can buy a better product than you have time to make. For example, commercially-made toy wheels have an axle hub that protrudes beyond the face of the wheel. This lets you sand the end of a protruding axle flush with the hub without sanding the whole wheel. *(See Figure 9.)*

If you want to buy small quantities of wheels and other toy parts, you can order them from the Wood-craft Supply Corporation, 313 Montvale Avenue, Woburn, MA 01888. They also carry many other supplies and tools that you might need.

If you're planning to go into production, you'll need to purchase larger amounts of these parts. For the past several years, I've been buying wheels, pegs, and 'people' from the Toymakers Supply Company, 105 Weiler Road, Arlington Heights, IL 60005. The more parts you order from these folks, the lower their prices are per part. If you write them, they'll send you their current catalog.

Should you still want to make your own wheels, there are a number of simple methods. Perhaps the easiest is to saw them out on a bandsaw. This technique

Figure 9. A protruding wheel hub will allow you to sand the end of the axle flush without sanding the wheel.

Figure 10. If you use a hole saw to make the wheels, let the blade cut through at least one edge of the board. This lets the sawdust escape. The sawing goes quicker, and it's easier for you to remove the blank from the saw.

is fine for large wheels—4"- 5" in diameter or larger—but it's not accurate enough for small wheels.

There are two relatively inexpensive tools you can mount on your drill press that will turn out perfectly round wheels. The least expensive is a hole saw. *(See Figure 10.)* A circle cutter is somewhat more expensive, but, in my opinion, it's worth it. Circle cutters (or 'fly cutters', as they are sometimes called) are fully adjustable and will make any size wheel. (*See Figure 11.*) These cutters must be kept very sharp or they will bind up, especially in thick wood.

To make a lot of wheels at one time, select a board of the proper thickness and mark the center of all the wheels that you can saw from it. Drill the center points with a bit that is the same diameter as the pilot bit of the hole saw or circle cutter. Select the proper size hole saw or adjust the circle cutter for the size of the wheel you want. Set the blade depth so that the pilot bit enters the wood before the blade does. If you're working with a circle cutter, make sure that the blade is set so that the square side cuts the circumference of the wheel. (*See Figure 12.*)

Set the depth of cut so that the blade goes a little more than halfway through the wood. Cut all the wheels on one side of the board, then flip the board over and cut the rest of the way through. You'll have to stop the drill press after you finish each wheel to pop them off the pilot. Be careful not to try to grab the blade to stop the rotation—let it come to a complete stop by itself. Since you'll be working in hardwood, the edges of the wheels may have friction burns—particularly if you're using a circle cutter. (A circle cutter is a scraping tool and it heats up the wood more than a hole saw.) These burns can be cleaned up on a sander/grinder.

Once you've cut the wheel and sanded the edges, decide how you are going to use the wheel in the toy. If you need an offset axle hole, you'll have to plug the pilot hole with a small dowel and drill a new hole. If you want a centered axle hole, you'll probably have to ream the pilot hole out. Pilot drills are usually no larger than ¼", and often you need a ⅜" axle hole. Use a twist bit to do the reaming.

Abrasives

There's quite a bit of sanding involved in toymaking. You'll find that the right materials make the job go a lot faster.

Hand sanding. The most readily available sandpaper sheets are aluminum oxide grit on 'A weight' paper backing. I find this material next to useless when sanding hardwoods. As you use it, the grit particles round over. In a very short time, the paper will no longer cut. What's more, the lightweight paper often gives way (tears or cracks) before the life of the sanding grit is used up. If aluminum oxide sandpaper is all you have available to you, try to find some on 'C weight' paper. This sandpaper will at least last the life of the grit.

The two best types of sandpaper I've found are

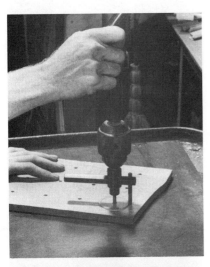

Figure 11. A circle cutter can be adjusted to make wheels of almost any diameter. Always clamp small pieces to the drill press table and keep your hands clear of the spinning cutter arm!

Figure 12. You'll find it easier to cut wheels, if you cut part way through the wood, then turn the blank over and cut through from the other side. Notice how the cutter is arranged—the square side cuts the circumference of the wheel.

garnet and silicon carbide. The grits in these papers don't round over. Instead, they chip away as you use them, constantly creating new cutting surfaces. Because of this, the sandpaper continues to cut evenly throughout its life. Here again, look for grit mounted on 'C weight' paper. If you can't find garnet or silicon carbide paper close to home, you can order it from the Midwest Buff Company, 40 Alpha Park, Highland Heights, OH 44143.

Sanding Belts. As with sanding sheets, most hardware stores carry light-duty belts—aluminum oxide grit bonded to paper loops. These will last for an hour's use—if you're lucky.

Look for resin-bonded grit on X or J weight cloth belts. Here again, the Midwest Buff Company carries an excellent selection of heavy-duty sanding belts. By the way, these folks are primarily a wholesale distributor, but they have agreed to service retail customers who are referred to them through this book. So you can get professional quality abrasives in small quantities at reasonable prices! When you order, specify the grit weight (80#, 120#, etc.), grit type (garnet, silicon carbide, etc.), length and width of belt, and quantity. The belts come in just two types of grit—aluminum oxide (Part # KK711X) and silicon carbide (CK721)—and the sandpaper sheets must be ordered in packages of 50.

Finishes

Perhaps the most important consideration when choosing a finish for your toys is that it be non-toxic. Many natural and synthetic finishes are toxic to one degree or another, and this could be harmful to children. Mineral oil and 'salad-bowl dressing' are two non-toxic finishes that are often recommended, but mineral oil offers little protection for the wood, and salad-bowl dressing is fairly expensive.

I prefer Watco's Danish Oil® to finish indoor toys. Danish oil is made from a combination of oils and resins that soak deep into the wood and polymerize (harden). Even though it does not coat the surface of the wood, it offers a fair amount of protection. After it dries for 30 days, it becomes non-toxic. It also brings out the luster and the grain patterns of hardwoods. Watco Danish Oil is available in most hardware and paint stores. If you can't find it, write the Watco-Dennis Corporation, Santa Monica, CA 90404, and they'll send you a list of suppliers near you.

Color can be a nice touch on some toys. Use a gloss latex paint. This is non-toxic and gives the toys a bright, deep hue. You can buy latex paint in quart containers at a paint store, mixed to any color your heart desires.

Some woodworkers use Luma Dye® water colors to paint woods. Unlike latex, these colors don't coat the wood. They soak in and become transparent, allowing you to still see the wood grain. However, these colors only work well on light colored woods such as poplar or maple. They are available at most art supply stores.

Glue

The best glue that I've found for toymaking is an aliphatic resin glue, commonly called "yellow glue". Yellow glue, when it is used properly, sets up to be stronger than the wood it joins. In particular, I use

Figure 13. Aliphatic resin glue (yellow glue) is sold in a variety of container sizes. If the glue in a large container gets too thick, just add some water.

Titebond® Wood Glue. This is available in most hardware stores and lumberyards in a variety of container sizes, from four ounces to one gallon. (*See Figure 13.*) If you can't find it, write to Franklin International, 2020 Bruck Street, Columbus, OH 43207 and they'll give you a list of suppliers.

Titebond® offers an additional advantage over some other yellow glues: It's freeze-thaw stable. It won't change consistency or spoil if it freezes, then thaws again. This is especially important if you work in a garage or an outbuilding where the temperature sometimes dips below the freezing mark. Just allow the glue to return to room temperature (above 55° F.) before using it.

Yellow glue is also water-soluble. It cleans up with a wet rag. And if it becomes too thick, just add a little water and mix it with a paint stirrer.

To use yellow glue, both surfaces of the wood must be clean and free from oil. (Yellow glue won't hold if the parts have been previously finished with Danish oil.) Spread the glue out evenly, applying extra glue to end grains. The end grains soak up the glue faster than the flat grains, so end-grain joints require more glue if they are to bond properly.

Once you've spread the glue properly, *clamp* the pieces together. This clamping is extremely important. Glue that cures under pressure is much stronger than glue that is allowed to dry without pressure. But don't apply so much pressure that the clamps squeeze the glue out between the boards. This will result in a weak, 'starved' joint.

Pull Handles and Cords

I use macrame beads for pull handles. They come in a variety of finishes: Natural, stained and varnished, or brightly colored and lacquered. As small children will almost certainly chew on these parts, I recommend you buy the unfinished beads, then finish them yourself with a non-toxic finish.

The best cord that I've found for pull toys is acrylic macrame cord. Cotton will fray, but acrylic can be melted at the end so that it won't unravel. Just pass the end of the cord past a candle flame until it begins to shrivel up. This also makes it easier to insert the cords into the toys—the melted ends can be threaded through holes with less frustration than ordinary cut ends. Look for braided cord. Twist cord is not intended for continuous flexing and will eventually lose its twist after extended use. Macrame supplies are available at most department stores and craft shops.

Hand tools

There are a few hand tools that you'll need to make toys. (*See Figure 14.*)

The **dovetail saw** is used to cut off protruding dowel ends during assembly. It's also useful for taking toys apart to make corrections. If you can find a small saw without a stiff back, it will work even better than a dovetail saw, because you can flex it slightly and saw flush to your project without your hand being in the way. (*See Figure 15.*)

The **four-in-hand** is a combination of a flat and curved rasp for coarse work and a flat and curved file for smoothing out rough areas. This is an extremely useful hand tool for a variety of shaping and smoothing tasks. I prefer the smaller size (8″) for most work.

A **rat-tail file** will come in handy from time to time to smooth tight curves.

You'll need a standard **16-ounce claw hammer**. You may think that a rawhide or wooden mallet would be more appropriate for this work. However, a steel hammer is the best. For hammering wheels on axles, you want the metal mass of a hammer to drive them through straight away in just one or two hits. Every time you hit a wheel onto an axle, a little glue squeezes out onto the tool you're hitting it with. Glue can be easily wiped off a metal hammer, but it tends to build up on wood or rawhide. After a time, there is an ugly black mess on the end of your mallet. This, in turn, will leave black marks on the wheels.

In the clamp department, you can get by with two **large C-clamps**, two **small C-clamps**, and two **small bar clamps**. However, if you can afford more clamps, buy them. Often times, you will have several parts glued up and drying in the clamps when you're ready to glue up something else. If all your clamps are in use, you'll find yourself waiting for glue to dry.

You'll need a **chisel** from time to time, but there's no need to buy an entire set. A ½″ or ¾″ straight chisel will work for most situations where you need a chisel.

A **coping saw** is needed for a few of the toys in this book, for cutting out small pieces. You can also use it instead of a bandsaw for cutting out irregularly-shaped parts. This takes a great deal of patience and care, though.

A small **square** of some sort is essential for marking and for keeping the bandsaw blades and sanding belts square to their respective work tables.

A **scratch awl** is useful for marking the center of holes before drilling. You can also use it to mark stock for cutting.

A **glue applicator** is indispensable for gluing wheels on axles, applying glue to small parts, and putting glue inside holes. Keep a piece of wire handy to clean out the long nose, or it will become clogged up. If it does clog, soak it in hot water and ream it out with the wire.

All of these hand tools are available from the Woodcraft Supply Corporation, whose address I mentioned earlier under "Wheels, Pegs, and People". They also sell a few types of hardwood, Danish oil, and several of the products I've mentioned in this chapter. Write them for a free catalog.

All of the suppliers that I've listed in this chapter are listed again in the Appendix, in alphabetical order, for quick reference.

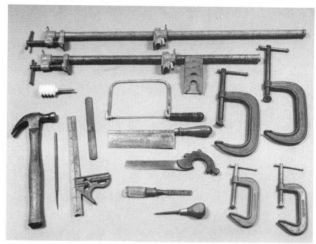

Figure 14. You don't need a lot of tools to make toys, just the few basic cutting, pounding, gluing, clamping, and measuring tools shown here.

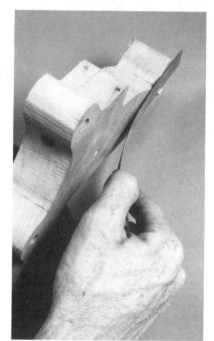

Figure 15. Some small saws can be flexed slightly to cut flush to the project.

DINOSAURS!

PREHISTORIC MONSTERS

TEXT BY KATE BRASCH · PHOTOGRAPHS BY JEAN-PHILIPPE VARIN

Brontosaurus

Designing Animated Toys

This is a book of toy designs. I've published them for your pleasure—it's my hope that you'll take joy in making them and giving them to your friends and family. For most of you that will be enough, but some of you will find making toys so rewarding that you'll want to design your own toys. A few may even wish to pursue toymaking as a profession.

As a toy designer—amateur or professional—one of the first things you'll learn is the value of good design. Design is the essence of this business; anyone can purchase woodworking tools, but not everyone can come up with a good design for a wooden toy. I can't give you concrete instructions for designing, as if I were explaining a toymaking technique or laying out a blueprint, but I can give you a glimpse of how I work out a design for the first time.

A brief aside for budding professionals: As I said, toy designs are valuable. Once you come up with a design that sells well, I strongly suggest that you *copyright* it. All the designs in this book are my copyrighted property, and as such they cannot be reproduced by anyone else *for sale or profit*. The law allows the readers of this book to make my toys for their own enjoyment or for gifts, but the toys cannot be sold without my permission—even for the benefit of a church or other non-profit organization. Protect your designs in the same way. Write the Library of Congress, Washington, D.C. 20559 for the proper forms. It costs a few dollars to register each design, but it's well worth the investment.

Elements of Design

So . . . where do I start? Well, the best way to start is by looking around you. Is there an animal that you're particularly fond of? Or is there some kind of plane, car, or boat that you'd like to make into a toy? Once you've picked the animal or vehicle, think about its appealing characteristics and what movement it has that you can capture in wood. This is the fundamental skill of toy designing; how to convey the character of things through line and movement.

Let's take an example. Say you like butterflies. What is it about butterflies that makes them attractive? The form and color of the wings would probably come to mind first, followed closely by their fluttering movement. These two elements become the focus of your design efforts. Another example would be a beaver. Most people would immediately think of the buck teeth and the slapping tail. So you would try to include both of these features in your design.

Now, how do you actually work out the design? In most cases, you'll want to go to the library and pull out some books with pictures of the animal or machine you want to design. Look for side views to help you draw a silhouette. It's very important to draw a silhouette which includes all the important features you're trying to capture. These silhouettes should either be accurate or somewhat exaggerated to emphasize the character of the animal or machine; for example, look at the down-turned mouth and protruding eye of the Frog, or the big nose and ears of the Hound.

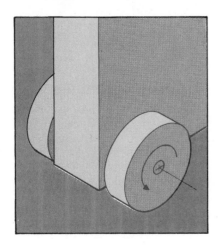

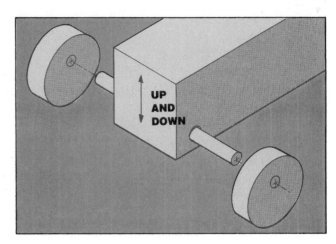

Figure 1. The simplest type of moving toy has rolling wheels.

Figure 2. If you offset the axle from the middle of the wheels, and 'synchronize' the wheels so that the high spots and low spots are identical, the toy will bob up and down.

After you've worked out a rough silhouette, decide what type of movement is appropriate for the animal or machine. There are several different ways that you can make a toy move.

How Do I Make it Move?

Rolling wheels. The easiest toys to design are those that simply roll along, like the Fanciful Beasties and the Panel Truck Collection. Any shape you care to design can be made to roll by adding two axles and four wheels. There's no limit to the number of things that can be made into toys by simply cutting out a silhouette and adding wheels. (*See Figure 1.*)

Synchronized offset wheels. The easiest deviation from the simple rolling toy is to offset the axle in the wheels. To do this, plug the center of the wheels and drill new axle holes slightly off-center. When the wheels are glued onto the axle and set perfectly in 'sync' with each other (both wheels up or down), they will lift the toy up and drop it down as it is pulled along. For an example, see the Rabbit or the Whale. This is a great mechanism for anything that you want to make jump or bob. (*See Figure 2.*)

Opposed offset wheels. This is similar to the synchronized offset wheels, but the wheels are opposed (one wheel up and the other down) so that the toy tips to one side and then the other, as does the Seal, Duck, or Tug. It makes the toy waddle. (*See Figure 3.*) In some cases, this type of toy may require a central wheel as a 'pivot', while the two outside wheels tip the toy back and forth.

Offset drive axle. This mechanism lets the toy roll evenly while the drive axle lifts or pushes something. The Turtle is a good example of this setup. This wheel-and-axle configuration generally needs a hollow area inside the toy to house the offset drive axle. (*See Figure 4.*)

Outside wheel peg. This is a good way to make legs and other parts move. I used this mechanism in the Hound, the Frog, the Bulldozer, and the Front End Loader. Usually, the part that moves is attached to the peg by the peghead. (*See Figure 5.*) Bear in mind that the part must be able to make a full revolution without touching the ground or any other part of the toy.

Figure 3. If the high spots and low spots of offset wheels are opposed, the toy will tip back and forth.

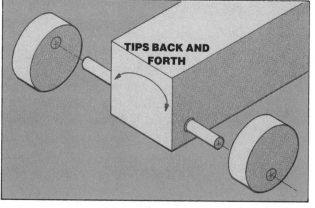

TIPS BACK AND FORTH

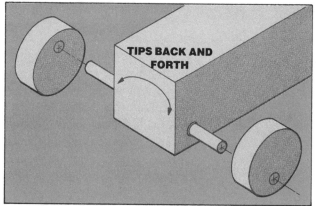

LIFTS

Figure 6. A peg on the inside of a wheel can be used to lift a part of the toy. The part will fall back into place after the peg has rotated out of the way.

Figure 4. An offset drive axle will move part of the toy back and forth, or up and down.

BACK AND FORTH

Figure 5. If you attach a part of a toy to a peg on the outside of a wheel, it will move back and forth.

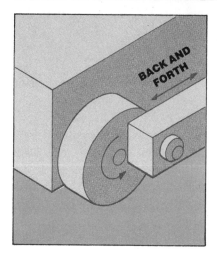

BACK AND FORTH

Inside wheel peg. This mechanism produces the most surprising movements. In most cases, the peg is hidden and the action seems mysterious. *(See Figure 6.)* For example, look at the Hippo or the Lobster. With the peg mounted on the inside of the wheel, the distance between the pivot point on the moving part and the edge that is pushed is quite critical. Take care that the peg can indeed lift the part without too much force. Making the part lightweight will help. You'll also want to make sure that the part doesn't move so far that it doesn't fall back down again. I generally cut out pieces of cardboard and experiment a bit before I finalize the design.

Figure 7. A cam on an axle will lift a part of a toy. The cam is just an offset wheel that doesn't contact the ground.

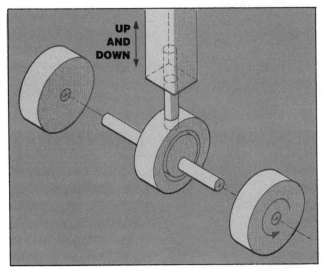

UP
AND
DOWN

Figure 8. A cam in a ring can be used to pull a part back and forth, or up and down, similar to an offset drive axle.

Simple cam. A cam on the axle raises parts up and lets them fall again, as you can see in the Bus or the Tyrannosaurus. It's a fairly easy mechanism to make, but it usually requires cutting a slot or dado under the toy. *(See Figure 7.)* This can be done with a dado cutter, or by chiseling out the material. The cam is really just an offset wheel that doesn't touch the ground. Simply cut it out with a circle cutter, plug the axle hole and drill a new axle hole off center. The cam can be made any width, depending on the application. You'll want to peg the cam to the axle with a ⅛" dowel to prevent it from slipping on the axle.

Cam in ring. This is a combination of a cam and the offset drive axle. It produces the same type of motion, but it eliminates many of their disadvantages. It requires less space than the offset drive axle, and unlike the cam, it will move a part through an entire stroke without the help of gravity. *(See Figure 8.)* When making this mechanism, the outside diameter of the ring should be ⅝" larger than the cam. Drill a hole in the center of the ring that's ¹⁄₁₆" larger than the cam, and drill an offset axle hole in the cam. Holding the ring perpendicular to the drill press, drill a hole in the outside diameter so that you can attach the moving part to the ring. Usually, the axle must be glued to the cam with the ring and other parts in place. This makes it impossible to peg the cam to the axle. To help prevent slipping, put some glue grooves on the axle by giving the axle a squeeze with a pair of pliers.

Engaged wheels. I've used this mechanism in the Sub and the Whirlybird to transfer rotating motion from one direction to another. One wheel should rest on top of the other so that as the bottom wheel moves, the top wheel spins as well. *(See Figure 9.)* If you cut some grooves on the edges that rub, this will increase the friction and help ensure smooth operation. It's a great mechanism—use it to design a merry-go-round or a seal with a ball spinning on his nose.

Engaged axle and wheel. The action of the

Hummingbird depends on this mechanism. Make sure that you drill the axle hole large enough to let the axle spin freely. Also, position the hole behind and below the top center on the drive wheel. *(See Figure 10.)* This way the axle will rest firmly on the wheel and the motion of the wheel will tend to lift the axle as it spins it, rather than pushing it down and binding it.

Rubber band around axles. This is a very simple mechanism that has been neglected for too long. Motion can be easily transferred from one axle to another one some distance away—as long as that distance can be bridged by a rubber band! *(See Figure 11.)* Look at the Monoplane and the Cement Mixer for examples. The direction of the motion can easily be changed by a twist in the rubber band—the possibilities are unlimited. Use this setup for a ferris wheel or mechanical toys like the old wind-driven action toys.

Conclusion

These are just the methods of making toys move that I've managed to discover during my career as a toymaker. I'm sure there are many more that I haven't found yet. Those mechanisms that I have shown here can be combined in many different ways for truly amazing results. An obvious example is the Frog. The offset wheels lift the body while the feet (which are pegged to the same wheels) pull the legs up and down. The Frog really looks as if it is hopping along! Or look at the Hound: Like the Frog, the hound's feet are pegged to wheels. But the feet also push against other parts to make the nose and ears move. Half the fun of playing with these toys is tracing the different motions back to the point of origin and figuring out how everything works together. And all the fun in designing these toys is figuring out how to use or combine these simple mechanisms so that everything works together to produce just the right movements.

All the elements are there for you to experiment with. Don't get discouraged if things don't work out the

way you planned on your first attempts. I have an intimate understanding of the phrase, "Back to the drawing board..." But I also know that once you perfect a toy design, it gives you a wonderful satisfaction to see it rolling along, magically moving.

So...good luck! This world can use all the delight we can muster.

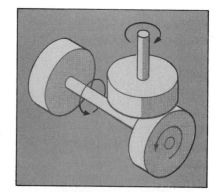

Figure 9. If you set one wheel on top of the other so that they 'engage' or rub against one another, you can transfer the motion from one wheel to the other. Furthermore, you can change the direction of this motion.

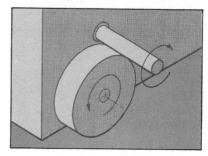

Figure 10. By setting an axle so that it engages or rubs against a wheel, you can transfer motion from one part to another. The axle will spin much faster than the wheel, because of the difference in diameters.

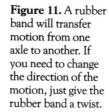

Figure 11. A rubber band will transfer motion from one axle to another. If you need to change the direction of the motion, just give the rubber band a twist.

Active ANIMALS

The Hopping RABBIT and the Bobbing WHALE

The Rabbit and the Whale are so similar that I'll explain their construction together. Both of these toys get their pleasant bobbing motion from an offset axle. The Rabbit has the offset axle in the front and the Whale has it in the back.

These toys can be made with almost any type of wood. Bear in mind, though, that fibrous woods such as poplar and aspen will leave fuzzy holes. You may have to drill the axle holes from both sides to make the holes smooth enough to let the axles spin freely.

Transfer the patterns onto appropriate scraps. The thickness can be adjusted to use the scraps that you have available. Simply adjust the axles accordingly.

Drill the eye and axle holes. Cut the eye (B) slightly longer than the thickness of the body. Glue the eye into place leaving a little extending on each side of the body. When the glue is dry, flat sand the end of B flush on the side of the body that doesn't have the pattern marked on it. This will let the piece sit flat on the bandsaw table as you cut it out.

If you have a ⅛" bandsaw blade, you can cut both toys out. If not, cut the tight curve on each toy by making passes from both directions (*See Figure 1*), or by drilling a hole at the curve (*See Figure 2*) and then cutting them out.

Next, drill the pull cord holes using scraps under the toy, or a block clamped on either side of the toy to hold it at the proper angle on the drill press table (*See Figure 3*).

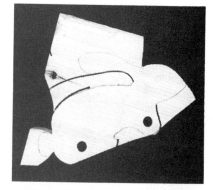

Figure 1. If you don't have an ⅛" blade for your bandsaw, you can cut tight curves by making several cuts with a ¼" blade.

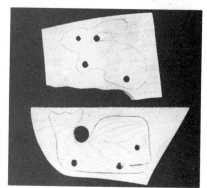

Figure 2. You can drill holes at the tight curves to make bandsawing easier.

Figure 3. Use a scrap under the toy to hold it at the proper angle to drill the pull cord holes.

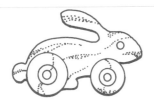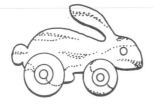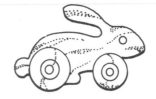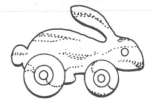

Edge sand with 80# and then 120# sandpaper. The sander/grinder belt will not fit behind the Rabbit's ears or in front of the Whale's tail. Sand these areas with a rat-tail file and a small drum sander, or a dowel wrapped with sandpaper (*See Techniques and Production Procedures, Figure 18*). Flat sand the sides with 80# and then 120#.

These toys are so small that I don't rout the edges. Just break the corners by hand with 120# sandpaper and you're ready to put on the wheels.

Drill the offset axle holes in the rear wheels of the Whale and the front wheels of the Rabbit (E). Plug the original holes and flat sand the protruding plugs when the glue is dry. Glue these wheels onto the appropriate axles, make sure that the wheels are perfectly opposed and parallel or the toy won't move smoothly.

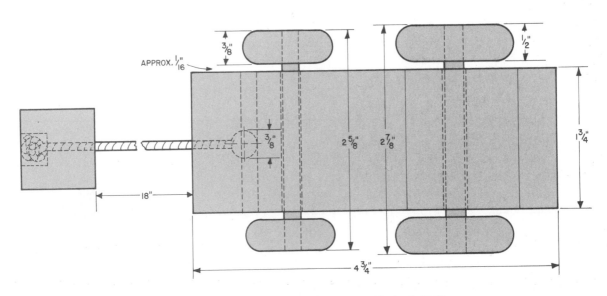

RABBIT/TOP VIEW

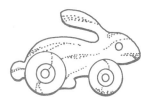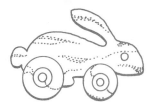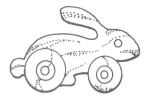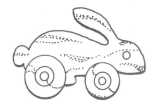

Glue wheels (F) onto the other axles. When the glue is dry, edge sand the ends of both axles.

Apply the finish.

Cut the pull string to length, melt both ends, and insert it through the pull cord hole. Tie several knots on the end of the string under the front of the toy and pull it back through from the front until the knots disappear into the hole under the toy. Feed the free end of the string through a bobble and tie a few knots. You may not be able to find a bobble with a small enough hole for a thin string. They are generally made for macrame cord which is too thick for these small toys.

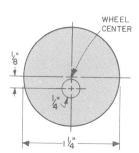

FRONT WHEEL

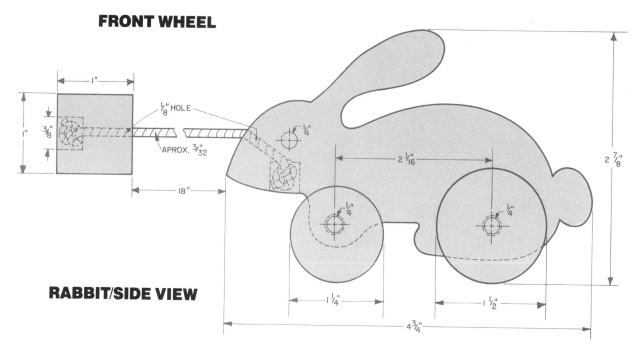

RABBIT/SIDE VIEW

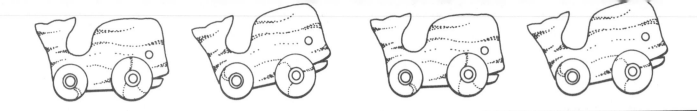

To make a small handle, cut off a 1″ long section of 1″ dowel. Drill a ¼″ hole in one end of the dowel, and another hole that is slightly larger than the string you're using, all the way through the dowel. Flat sand the ends, hand sand the edges, and oil it. Thread the string through from the end with the small hole. Tie several knots and pull them back into the drilled recess. Off go the Rabbit and Whale, hopping and bobbing.

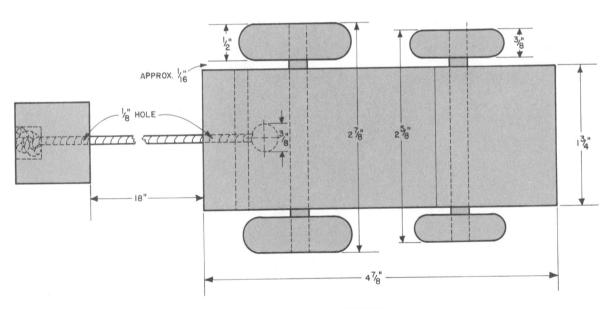

WHALE/TOP VIEW

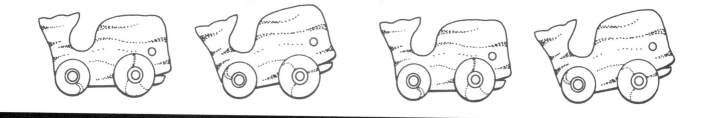

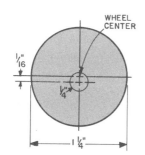

REAR WHEEL

WHEEL CENTER

$\frac{1}{16}$"

$\frac{1}{4}$"

$1\frac{1}{4}$"

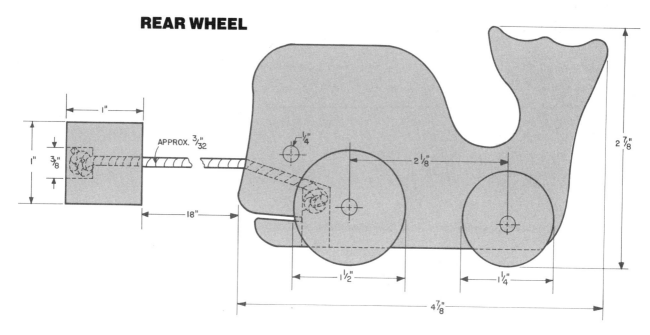

1"

1"

$\frac{3}{8}$"

APPROX. $\frac{3}{32}$"

18"

$\frac{1}{4}$"

$2\frac{1}{8}$"

$2\frac{7}{8}$"

$1\frac{1}{2}$"

$1\frac{1}{4}$"

$4\frac{7}{8}$"

WHALE/SIDE VIEW

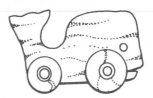
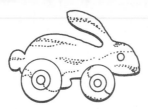
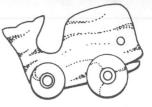

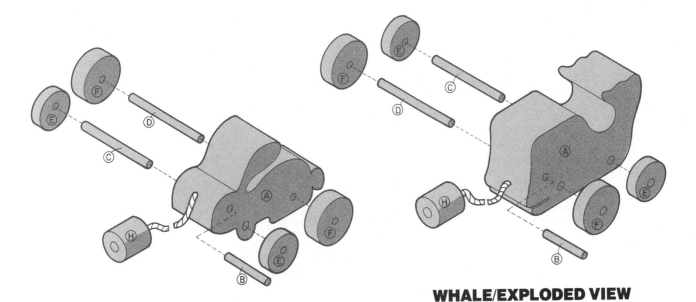

RABBIT/EXPLODED VIEW

WHALE/EXPLODED VIEW

BILL OF MATERIALS

PART	DESCRIPTION	QTY	THICKNESS	WIDTH OR DIAMETER	LENGTH
A	Body	1	1½"-2	2⅞"	4¾"-4⅞"
B	Eye	1		¼" dia.	Body thickness
C	Rear axle (Whale) Front axle (Rabbit)	1	¼" dia.		Body thickness plus ⅞"
D	Front axle (Whale) Rear axle (Rabbit)	1	¼" dia.		Body thickness plus 1⅛"

PART	DESCRIPTION	QTY	THICKNESS	WIDTH OR DIAMETER	LENGTH
E	Rear wheels (Whale) Front wheels (Rabbit)	2	⅜"	1¼" dia.	
F	Front wheels (Whale) Rear wheels (Rabbit)	2	½"	1½" dia.	
G	Pull cord	1		3/32" approx.	18"
H	Handle	1		1" dia.	1"

54

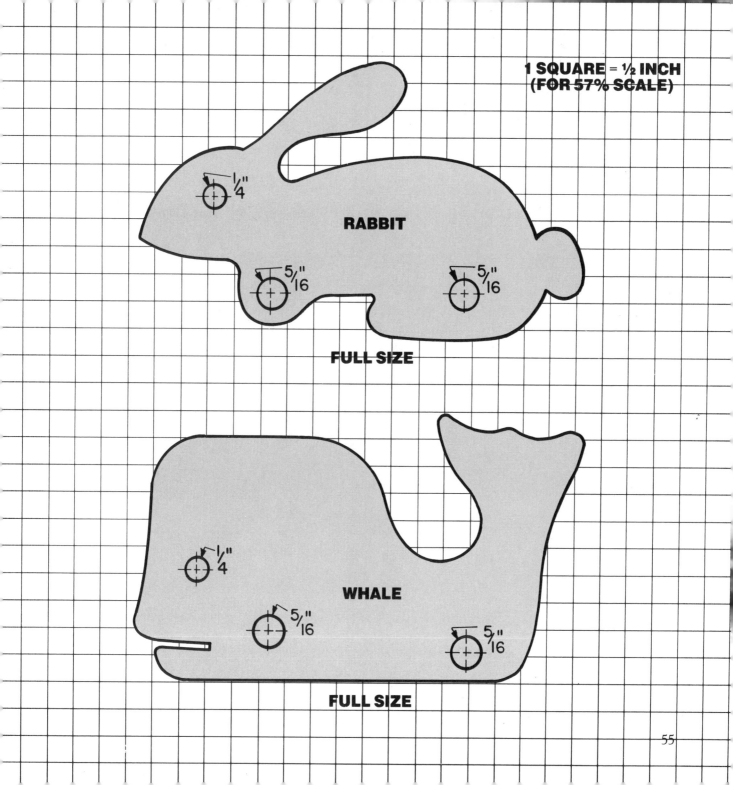

1 SQUARE = ½ INCH
(FOR 57% SCALE)

RABBIT

¼"

5/16"

5/16"

FULL SIZE

WHALE

¼"

5/16"

5/16"

FULL SIZE

55

The Hungry HIPPO

The Hippo's mouth opens and closes with a friendly "chomp" as he's pushed. This movement is accomplished by two ½" dowels that protrude on the inside of each of the front wheels. As the wheels turn, the dowels are alternately pushed against the bottom of the Hippo's jaw. The eye peg acts as the pivot of a lever and, as the back of the jaw is pushed down, the front of the jaw is lifted. As the wheel continues to turn, the dowels no longer support the front of the jaw and it falls down with a chomp.

The Body

The body of the Hippo can be made out of any species of wood. Transfer the body pattern (A) onto a suitable piece of 1¾" wood. The thickness of the body is not critical. Whatever the thickness is, though, the jaw spacer must be ⅛" thicker than the body. So, if you don't have any 1⅞" stock for the spacer, you can make it from 1¾" stock and plane a 1¾" thick piece for the body down to 1⅝" on the jointer. You'll have to adjust the length of the axles accordingly.

Drill the axle and peg holes. Cut the shape out on the bandsaw. Flat sand with 80# and then 120# sandpaper. Edge sand with 80#. Rout all the edges. Edge sand with 120#. Hand sand all the roughness and router burns with 80# and then hand sand all the routed edges with 120#.

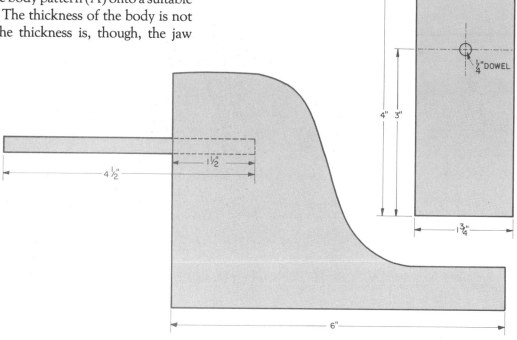

Figure 1. This jig is quite easy to make and can be used for several other toys as well.

57

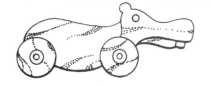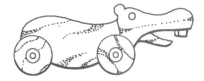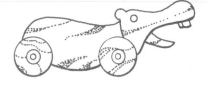

The Head

The head needs to be made from a strong, light wood. Cherry is perfect. Transfer the pattern of the head sides (B) onto two pieces of wood with the grain running lengthwise. Drill the peg holes. Cut the pieces out just outside the line so that you can edge sand them and end up with the exact shape of the pattern. The distance from the eye hole to the bottom of the jaw is critical to the proper opening of the mouth, so drill and cut these pieces out very carefully. Transfer the pattern of the head spacer (C) onto a piece of wood 1⅛" thick and cut it out on the bandsaw. Edge sand the pointed end of the jaw spacer so that it is rounded over. This will make the area stronger and prevent it from chipping later.

To assemble the jaw you'll need to make a jig. It will only take a few minutes and you can reuse it for several of the other toys (*See Figure 1*). The point of this jig is to ensure that the eye holes line up perfectly so that the mouth opens and closes easily.

Clamp the jig to the edge of the workbench and slide the sides of the head onto the dowel with the ears upward. When the surfaces of the spacer are glued, spread the sides far enough apart to position the spacer between them without smearing the glue. Now position

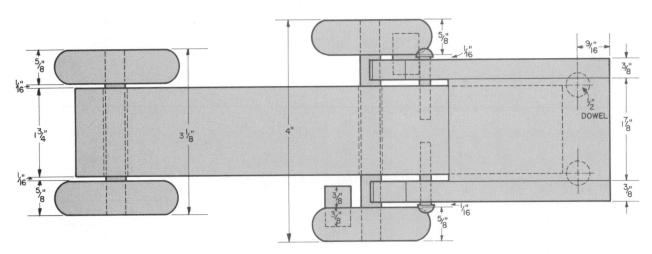

TOP VIEW

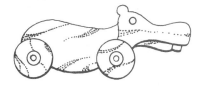
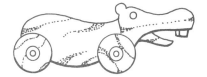
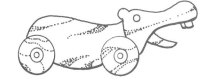

the spacer carefully and press the assembly together (*See Figure 2*). Press the pieces together firmly and make sure that: (1) the side piece next to the jig is flat against it and that, (2) the whole assembly can still move easily on the ¼″ shaft. After you've made any adjustments necessary, apply a clamp across the assembly with its pressure points on the center of the nose. Be careful not to let the assembly shift as you tighten the clamp. Now

Figure 2. Use the jig to line up the head parts and press them firmly together. Make sure the side next to the jig is flat against it and that the whole assembly can slide easily along the ¼″ dowel.

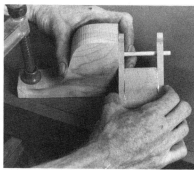

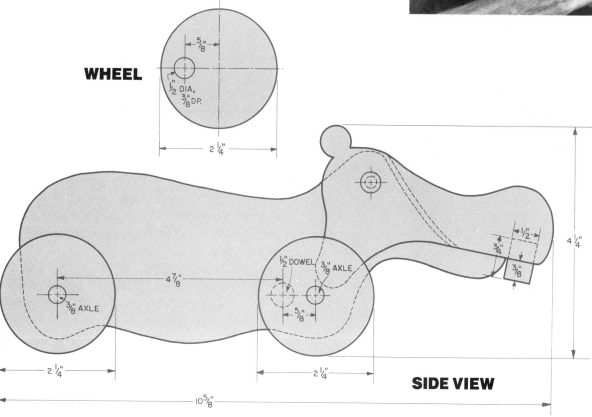

WHEEL

SIDE VIEW

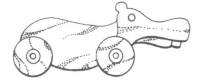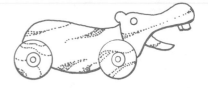

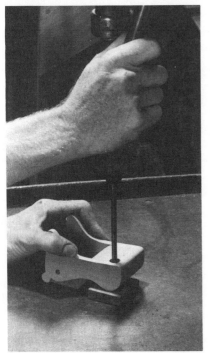

Figure 3. Be careful not to let the parts shift as you apply the clamps. Take the assembly off the jig to position the second clamp.

Figure 4. Use a scrap under the Hippo's nose to support it at the proper angle to drill the teeth holes.

slide the assembly off the jig and apply a second clamp at the upper end of the spacer (*See Figure 3*).

When the head is completely dry (don't rush it), look at how closely the pieces line up. If they're off by more than 1/16″, you should saw off any overhang to save wear and tear on the sander/grinder belt. Now, edge sand the head with 80# sandpaper. If you glued the pieces accurately, there should not be any problems. Just remember not to sand beyond the pencil line on the lower back end of the jaw or you'll reduce the distance that the jaw will open. Be careful around the ears. They're easily messed up when edge sanding. Beware when you pass from the area with the spacer to the thin sides alone. There is a tendency to dig in as the thickness suddenly decreases by 1⅞″. Use easy, smooth passes over these transitional areas.

To drill the teeth holes, rest the nose on a scrap on the drill press so that the surface to be drilled is parallel to the table (*See Figure 4*). The clearance between these holes and the edge of the mouth is so small that the holes will split open unless you either drill the holes slightly oversize (33/64″) or sand down the teeth until they fit in easily. A Forstner bit will be less likely to split out the sides as you drill.

Before you glue the teeth in, edge sand the head with 120# sandpaper. Flat sand the sides with 80# and then 120#. Hand sand all the fuzzy edges with 120#. Cut the teeth (H) to length and round off both ends by hand sanding. Spread glue (not too much) inside the teeth holes and tap the teeth into place. Do this on a smooth surface or you'll mar the top of the nose.

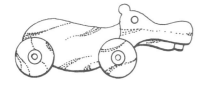
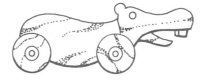
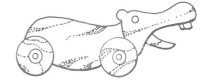

The Wheels

Using the wheel jig (*See Techniques and Production Procedures, Figure 17*), drill the offset holes in the front wheels.

Assembly

Glue each of the eye holes in the body, position the jaw piece, and tap the eye pegs (G) into place, using the clearance gauge (*See Techniques and Production Procedures, Figure 28*). Glue the back wheels on. Glue the ½" dowels into the front wheels, making sure they are perpendicular to the wheel's surface (*See Figure 5*).

The front wheels can be positioned in several different ways (*See Figure 6*). Generally, I put the front wheels on with the dowels diagonally opposed so the mouth opens and closes twice for every revolution of the wheels. If, however, the child tends to push toys quickly, you may want to put the pegs directly opposite each other so the mouth will only open once per revolution. This will give the mouth time to close completely between chomps. If the child is gentle with toys and sensitive to subtlety, you may want to put the pegs halfway between, diagonally opposed, and directly opposite. This will give the Hippo a rhythmic "chomp, chomp…chomp, chomp…chomp, chomp."

When the glue is dry, edge sand the ends of the axles. Let the glue dry thoroughly and then oil the Hippo, and he's ready to look for his first meal!

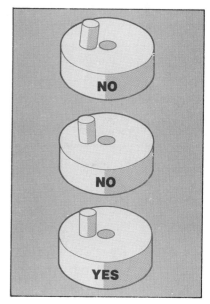

Figure 5. Make sure that the ½" dowel is glued perpendicular to the inside wheel surface.

Figure 6. The front wheels can be lined up in different ways for different effects.

CHOMP.....CHOMP.....CHOMP   CHOMP...CHOMP...CHOMP...CHOMP   CHOMP, CHOMP.....CHOMP, CHOMP

61

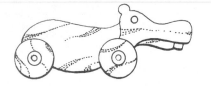
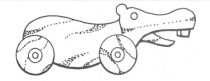
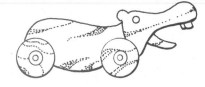

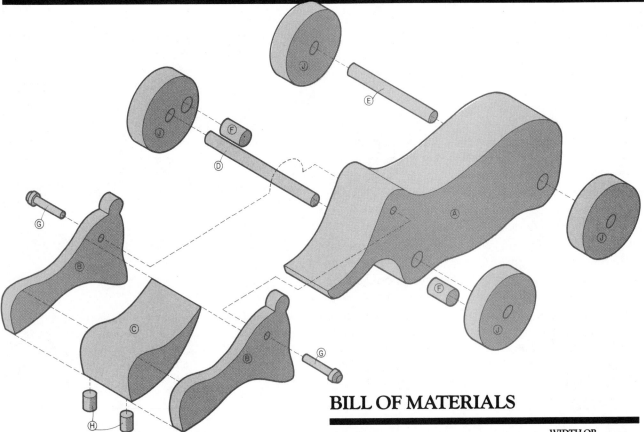

EXPLODED VIEW

BILL OF MATERIALS

PART	DESCRIPTION	QTY	THICKNESS	WIDTH OR DIAMETER	LENGTH
A	Body	1	1¾"	3½"	9½"
B	Head sides	2	⅜"	3"	4⅝"
C	Head spacer	1	⅞"	1½"	3½"
D	Front axle	1		⅜" dia.	4"
E	Rear axle	1		⅜" dia.	3⅛"
F	Wheel plugs	2		½" dia.	¾"
G	Eye pegs	2		7/32" dia.	1 1/16"
H	Teeth	2		½" dia.	¾"
J	Wheels	4	⅝"	2¼" dia.	

62

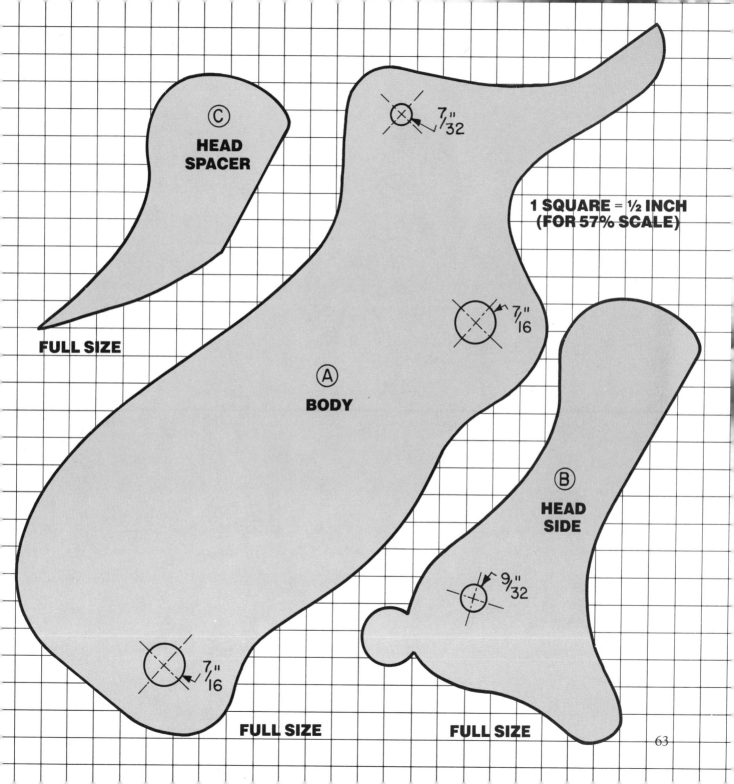

The Carefree KANGA & ROO

I have a special affinity for this toy as I was born in Australia. When you were cuddling with your "Teddy Bear," I was snuggling up with a stuffed "Kanga" and "Roo." This Kanga's great leaps are accomplished by the offset axle on the large front wheels. The feet, being pegged to the wheels, provide the corresponding leg movements. The upper arms are pegged tightly so that they can be positioned to shield "Roo" while running, or to box with enemies. Baby "Roo" can be taken out to play with.

Most of the mass of this toy has to be lifted by the front wheels so it's essential that you use a light wood for the body. The body has no weak areas, so the strength of the wood is not an important factor.

The Body

Transfer the body pattern (A) onto a suitable piece of wood. Drill the axle, eye, and peg holes. Cut the eye dowel (G) slightly oversize and glue it in the eye hole so that it protrudes slightly on both sides of the head. When the glue is dry, flat sand the dowel end flush to the back of the body so that it will pass smoothly over the bandsaw table. Now, cut out the body on the bandsaw. Drill the holes for the baby and the pull cord, using clamps and/or blocks to position the body on the drill press.

The Legs and Arms

Transfer the leg and arm patterns (B, C, D) onto strong wood. The arms should be laid out with the grain running along the length of the forearms to give strength to the paws. Drill all the holes, paying special attention to which holes hold the peg tightly ($7/32''$) and which holes pivot on the axle pegs ($9/32''$). Cut the parts out on the bandsaw.

Flat sand all the parts, including the body, with 80# and then 120# sandpaper. Rout all the edges of the body. Edge sand all the pieces with 120#. Hand sand burns and roughness with 80# and then smooth all the routed edges with 120#.

Roo

To make the baby, transfer the pattern (E) onto a small square of reasonably strong wood so that the bottom of the head lays along one of two parallel end grain edges. The grain should run up through the ear to give it strength (See Figure 1). Drill and plug the eye hole and sand the protruding dowel flush to the back of the blank. Drill the hole for the $1/4''$ dowel (K) on the drill press. Tap a 3" or 4" long dowel into the $1/4''$ hole. Use

Figure 1. Lay out the pattern for "Roo" (E) with the bottom of the head along an end grain edge. Cut out a square that includes the head, and has two parallel end grain edges.

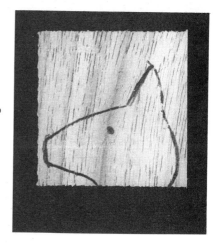

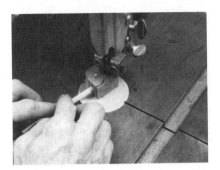

Figure 2. Use a dowel for a handle to cut out baby "Roo."

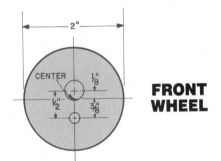

this for a handle to cut out the baby's head (*See Figure 2*). Edge sand with 80# and then 120# sandpaper. You can leave the dowel in place to help with the sanding, too (*See Figure 3*). Flat sand with 80# and 120#. You'll have to remove the dowel to edge sand the bottom of the head. Now, hand sand all the edges with 120#. Cut the ¼" dowel (K) to length and glue it into the bottom of the head. Sand the dowel until it fits snugly into the hole in the pouch.

Front Wheels

Plug the axle holes of the front wheels. When they're dry, drill the new axle holes. Then drill the peg holes (*See Techniques and Production Procedures, Figure 17*).

FRONT WHEEL

TOP VIEW

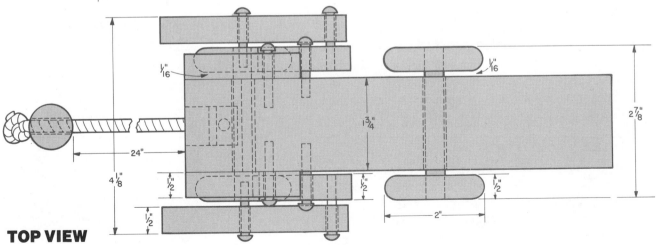

Assembly

Glue the back wheels to the axle. Glue the front wheels on, being careful to get them perfectly opposed. Roll the Kangaroo to make sure it doesn't wobble from side to side, and adjust the wheels if necessary. It won't jump easily at this point, without the pull cord, so don't get upset if it doesn't seem to want to leap smoothly. Check for wheel alignment right now. When the glue is dry, edge sand the axle ends.

Figure 3. You can use the handle for sanding, as well.

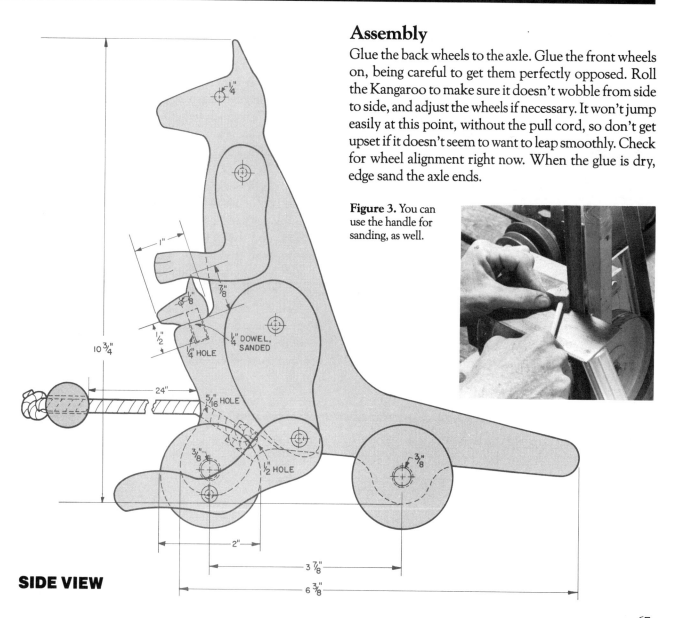

SIDE VIEW

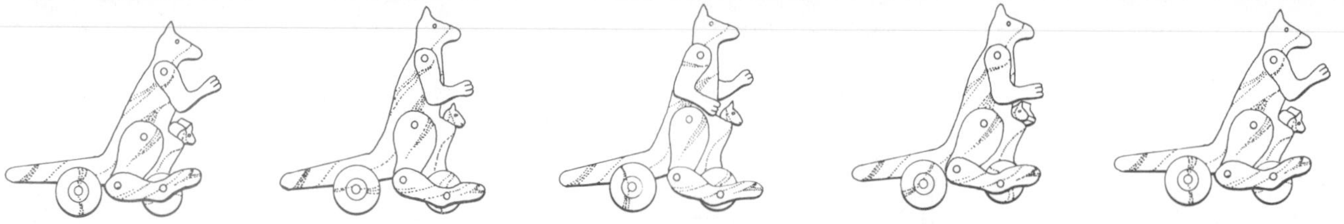

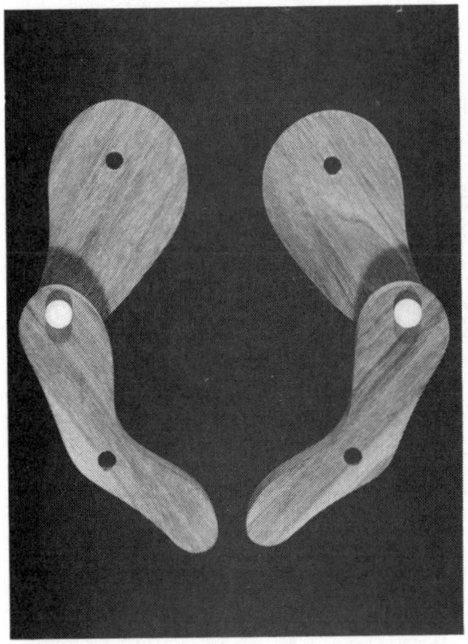

Figure 4. Be sure to assemble the legs so that you end up with two opposing sets. This may seem obvious, but it's easy to make a mistake and it's infuriating to have to cut the legs apart and re-drill them.

Peg the arms in as firmly as possible without splitting the pegs.

Lay the thigh pieces down on some waxed paper, opposing each other. Put glue in the peg holes and attach the corresponding leg pieces, using the clearance gauge (*See Techniques and Production Procedures, Figure 28*). Be careful. It's easy to mix these assemblies up. Visualize both legs on the Kangaroo before you glue them (*See Figure 4*).

Let both assemblies dry. Flat sand the peg ends and glue off the inside surfaces of the thighs.

Now peg the legs to the body, using the clearance gauge. Round the tips by hand with sandpaper. Using these pegs and the clearance gauge, glue the feet to the wheels. Use the edge of the workbench to support each wheel as you drive the pegs home.

When the glue is dry, you can oil the Kangaroo. When the oil is dry, attach the pull cord and bobble and away you go! Now you can teach your children how they leap over "down under."

BILL OF MATERIALS

PART	DESCRIPTION	QTY	THICKNESS	WIDTH OR DIAMETER	LENGTH
A	Body	1	1¾″	6⅜″	10¾″
B	Arms	2	½″	2¾″	2½″
C	Upper legs	2	½″	2″	3½″
D	Lower legs	2	½″	1½″	4½″
E	Roo's head	1	¾″	1″	⅞″
F	Roo's eye	1		⅛″ dia.	¾″
G	Kanga's eye	1		¼″ dia.	1¾″
H	Front axle	1		⅜″ dia.	2⅞″
J	Rear axle	1		⅜″ dia.	2⅞″

PART	DESCRIPTION	QTY	THICKNESS	WIDTH OR DIAMETER	LENGTH
K	Roo's locating pin	1		¼″ dia.	½″
L	Pegs	8		7/32″ dia. ⅜″ head	1 1/16″ to head
M	Wheels	4	½″	2″ dia.	
N	Acrylic cord	1		¼″ dia.	24″
P	Bobble	1		⅞″ dia. with ¼″ dia. hole	

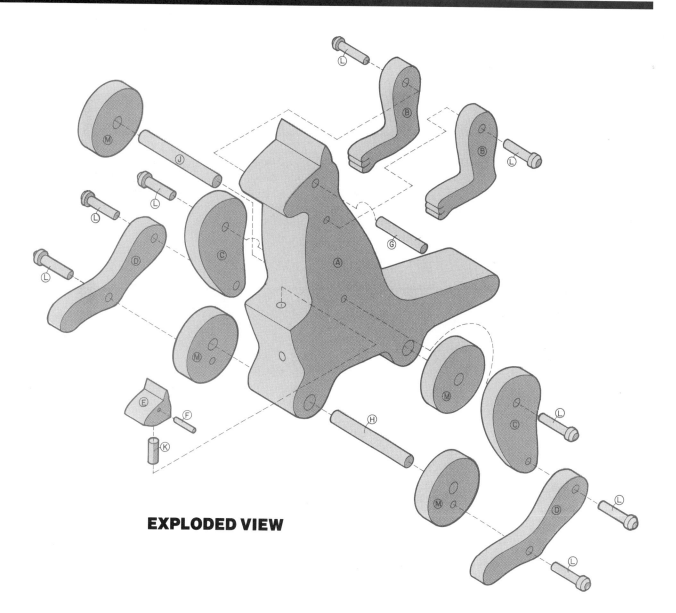

EXPLODED VIEW

69

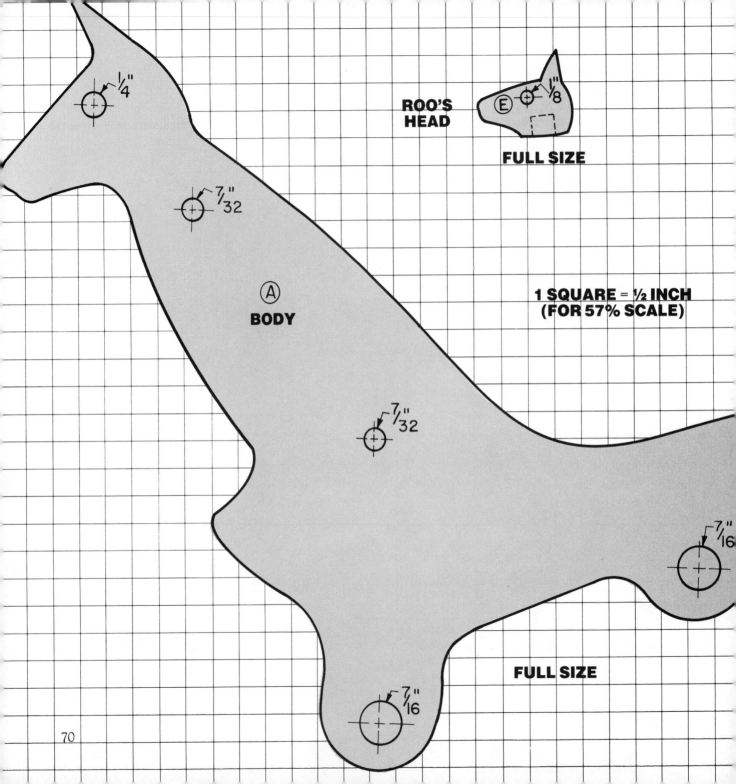

ROO'S
HEAD

(E)   1/8"

FULL SIZE

1 SQUARE = ½ INCH
(FOR 57% SCALE)

1/4"

7/32"

(A)
BODY

7/32"

7/16"

7/16"

FULL SIZE

70

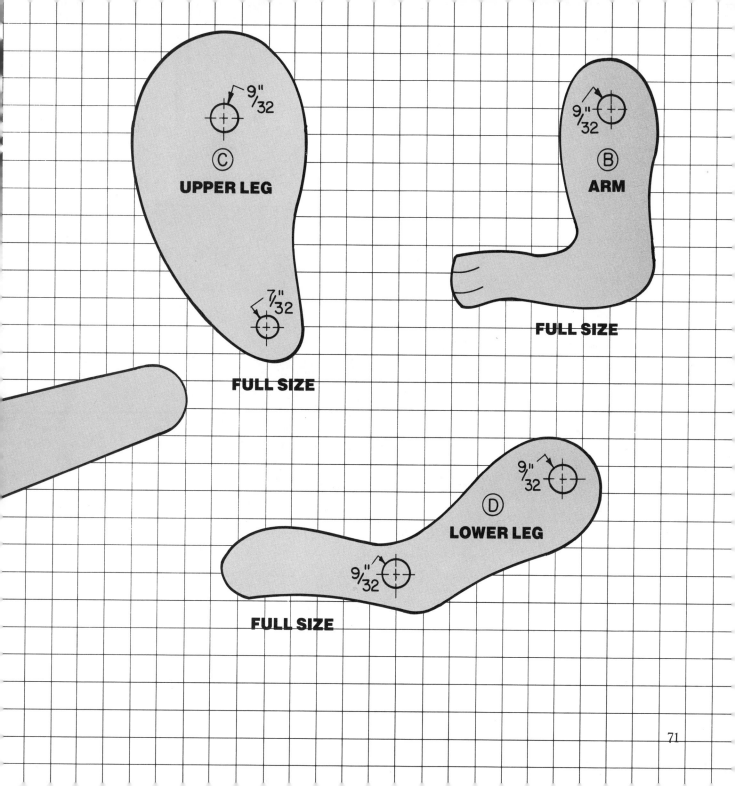

9"/32

© C
UPPER LEG

7"/32

FULL SIZE

9"/32

® B
ARM

FULL SIZE

9"/32

Ⓓ D
LOWER LEG

9"/32

FULL SIZE

71

The Gallivanting GORILLA

Don't get between this fellow and his banana, or you may get hurt. Parallel, offset wheels in the front give him that ape-like gait. His hands are pegged to the wheels to give him the appropriate arm motion. This toy isn't hard to make, but it calls for some careful bandsaw work.

The Body

I suggest that you use walnut for this toy for two reasons. Firstly, most of the weight must be lifted by the front wheels so it must be fairly light. Secondly, walnut is the perfect color (next to grey, which is a hard color of wood to find, to say the least).

Transfer the body pattern (A) onto a suitable piece of wood. Drill the eye, axle, and peg holes. Glue the ¼" dowel (D) into place and sand it flush to the back of the block. Cut the silhouette out on the bandsaw, using a ⅛" blade, or a coping saw, to cut the tight curves. Edge sand the whole body with 80# sandpaper, being especially careful on the face outline. You may want to sand this area by hand with sandpaper wrapped around a dowel (*See Figure 1*). Drill the pull cord holes on the drill press, using blocks to support the piece at the proper angle. Flat sand the body with 80# and then 120#. Rout the entire outline on both sides. Try not to slow down on the curves of the face area or you'll burn the edges. Edge sand the outline with 120# again using a dowel and sandpaper if necessary.

The Legs

Lay out the leg pieces (B, C) with the grain running lengthwise. Drill the holes, being careful to drill the pivoting holes to ⁹/₃₂" and the peg holes to ⁷/₃₂". When you saw the legs out, you can use a coping saw to saw out the toes. This little line conveys the curled knuckle that is so clearly an ape's hand, so cut it carefully. Edge sand all the pieces with 80# and 120# sandpaper. Flat sand with 80# and 120#. If these small pieces make you nervous on the belt sander, you can rub them back and forth on sandpaper on the workbench. I think that the toes lose their definition if you rout the legs, so just break the edges with 120#.

Wheels

To prepare the front wheels (H), first plug the axle holes. Then, using the drilling jig (*See Techniques and Production Procedures, Figure 17*), drill the ⁷/₃₂" and ¼" holes all the way through the wheels.

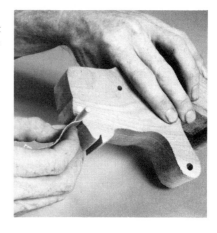

Figure 1. The sander/grinder won't work too well for the face outline, so use a ¼" dowel wrapped with sandpaper.

Figure 2. Hold the arm assembly firmly and touch it down lightly to remove any glue off the inside of the elbow.

Assembly

Lay out the legs in sets before gluing, choosing the best sides to show and making sure that you will have two opposing sets. Then, on waxed paper, spread glue in the peg holes in the upper arm pieces and peg the two sets together. When they're dry, flat sand any glue off the inside of the upper arms (*See Figure 2*). Glue the back axle (E) and wheels together. Glue the front axle (F) and wheels together, making sure they are perfectly opposed. Line the pieces up before you tap the wheel on because they won't twist (without breaking the ¼″ axle) after they're driven home. When they're dry, edge sand the axle hubs to remove any glue or fuzz. Next, put glue in the shoulder peg holes of the body and, using the clearance gauge (*See Techniques and Production Procedures, Figure 28*). peg the shoulders to the body. Now put glue in the peg hole of one wheel, rest it on the

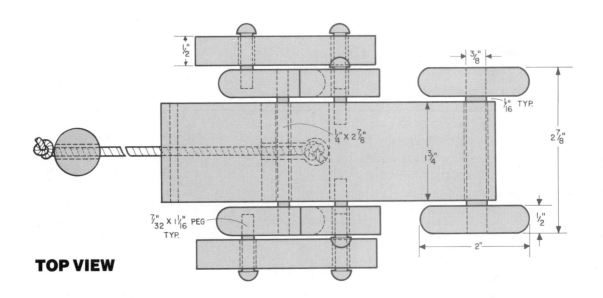

TOP VIEW

edge of the workbench for support, and peg the foot to the wheel using the clearance gauge. Be careful to wipe any excess glue off the inside of the wheel before it smears onto the body. Repeat this process on the other side.

Now, when the glue is thoroughly dry (overnight), oil your ape and then attach the pull cord. One more mountain Gorilla on the loose.

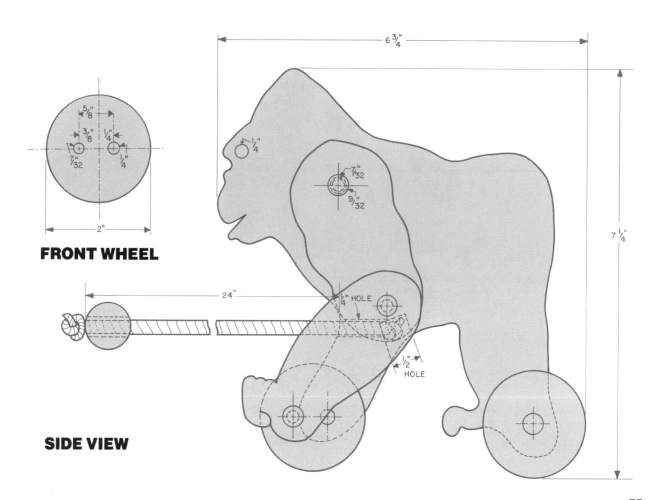

FRONT WHEEL

SIDE VIEW

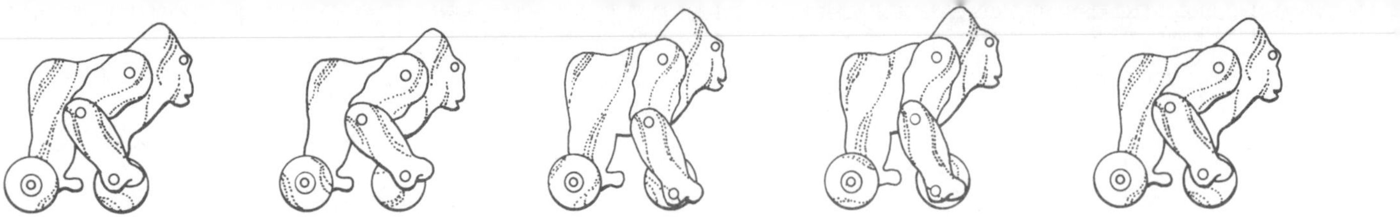

EXPLODED VIEW

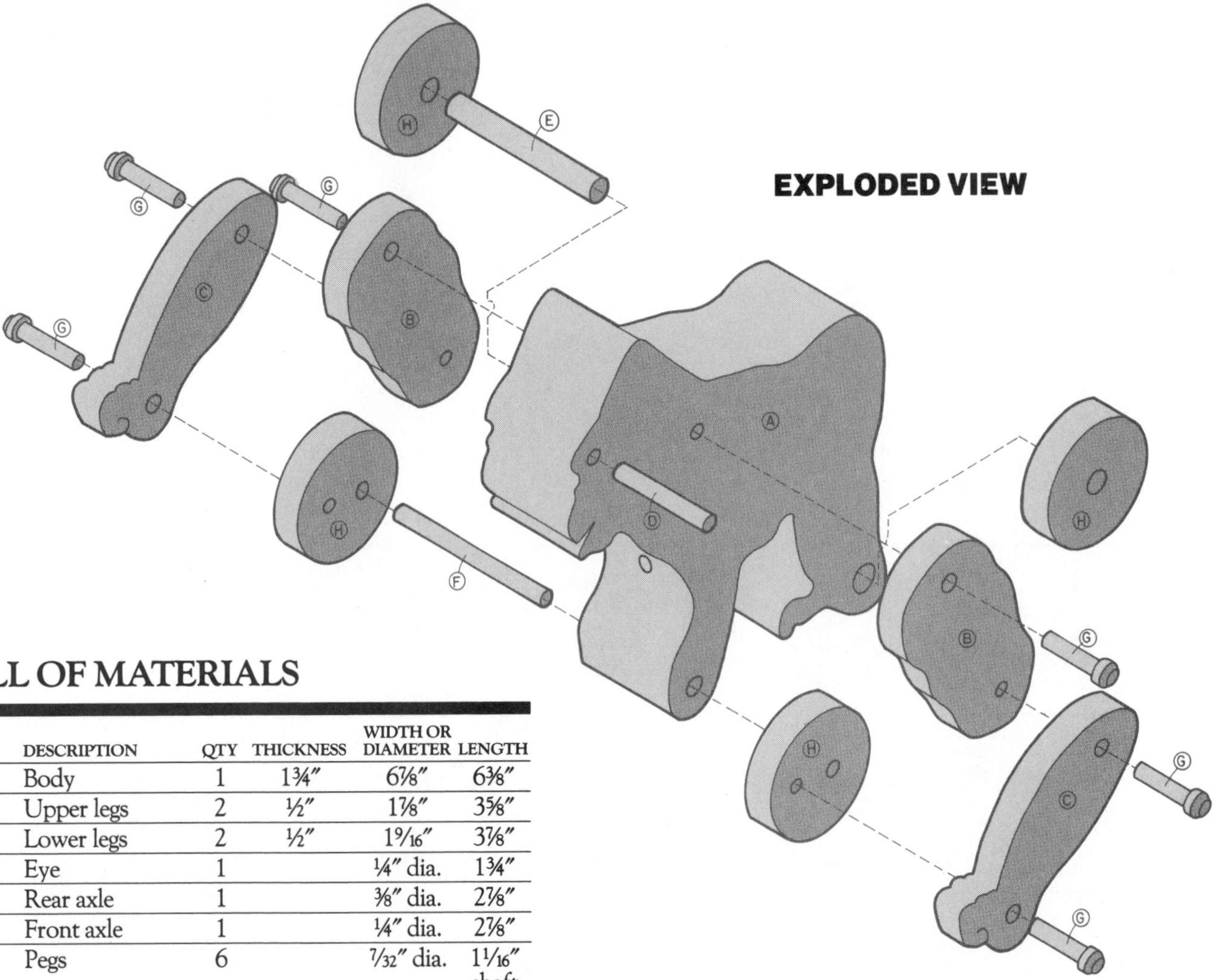

BILL OF MATERIALS

PART	DESCRIPTION	QTY	THICKNESS	WIDTH OR DIAMETER	LENGTH
A	Body	1	1¾″	6⅞″	6⅜″
B	Upper legs	2	½″	1⅞″	3⅝″
C	Lower legs	2	½″	1 9/16″	3⅞″
D	Eye	1		¼″ dia.	1¾″
E	Rear axle	1		⅜″ dia.	2⅞″
F	Front axle	1		¼″ dia.	2⅞″
G	Pegs	6		7/32″ dia.	1 1/16″ shaft
H	Wheels	4	½″	2″ dia.	
J	Acrylic cord	1		¼″ dia.	26″
K	Bobble	1		⅞″ dia.	

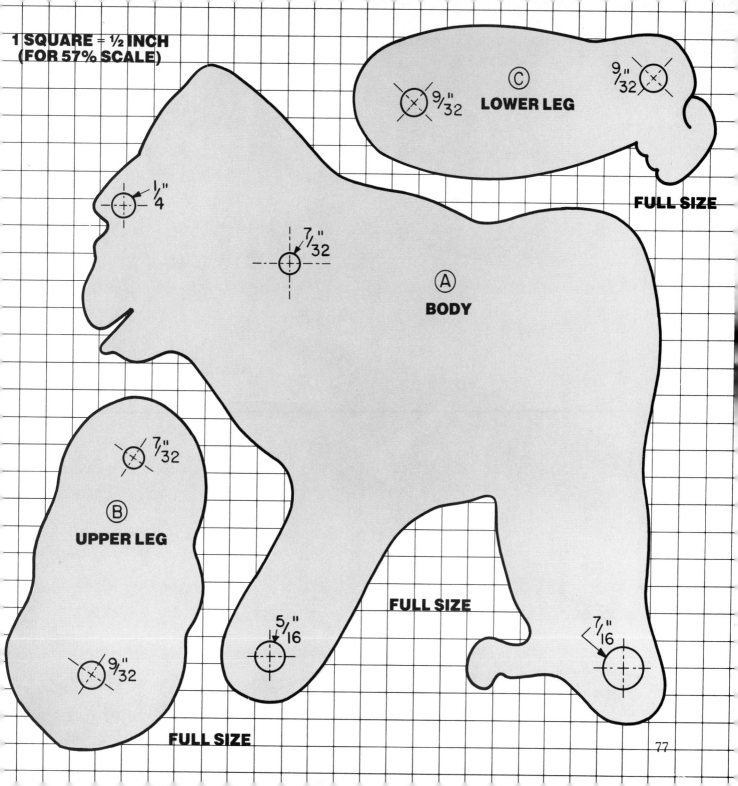

The Ruby-Throated HUMMINGBIRD

I think this little toy is truly amazing. With its bright colors and whirring wings, it looks exactly like its living counterpart. It's so small and delicate and yet full of life that it will fill a child with that sense of wonder that we often yearn for as adults.

I suggest cherry for this toy because it is strong enough for the delicate parts, and yet light enough to allow the wings to spin freely.

The Body

Mark the body silhouette onto a piece of suitable stock. Square the ends of the piece perpendicular to the beak line to enable you to drill the beak hole on the drill press (*See Figure 1*). Drill the eye hole, the wing axle hole, and the wheel axle hole. Plug the eye hole and sand the unpatterned side flush after the glue is dry. (Don't bother with eye hole and dowel (D) if you plan to paint the Hummingbird.) Mark the beak location on the front of the block. Stand the block up on its end and drill the beak hole to the proper depth and glue the beak into place. Don't put too much glue in the hole or the beak won't go in all the way. Now cut out the silhouette and the tail slot. Leave the tail slot a bit small to ensure a tight fit. Be careful to cut right up to the beak without cutting into the beak itself. Drill the pull cord holes. Edge sand with 80# sandpaper and flat sand with 80#. It's easier to rest the body on its back on the bandsaw, so mark the top view on the bottom of the body and cut it out on the bandsaw. Again, be careful to cut right up to the beak without cutting into it. Edge sand the newly sawn areas with 80#. Next, rout the unsawn edges. The other areas will have to be rounded over by hand with a four-in-hand rasp and sandpaper.

Try to round the nose so that it meets up perfectly with the beak. Edge sand what you can with 120#. Hand sand all the rough edges with 80#. Go over the whole body with 120#, sanding *with* the grain to remove all the sander/grinder scratches.

Wings and Tail

Mark out the wings (B) so that the axle holes can be drilled on the drill press. Drill the holes to 9/32" so they will slip on the axle without splitting. Be very careful to center the holes perfectly with respect to both the width and the thickness or they will be weak, or won't spin properly. Cut out the wings on the bandsaw. Flat sand and edge sand them with 80# and 120# sandpaper. Break the edges by hand with 120#.

Mark the tail with the grain running front to back to give strength to the tail feathers. Flat sand it and edge sand it with 80# and 120# sandpaper. Break the edges by hand with 120#. Fit the tail in the tail slot. If it's too tight, enlarge the tail slot until it fits snugly. Then put glue in the tail slot and insert the tail. When it's dry, drill the 1/8" hole and glue the 1/8" dowel (G) in place. Saw off any excess and hand sand it flush. Now the body and wings are ready to paint.

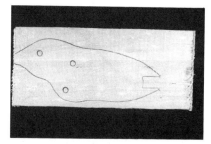

Figure 1. As you lay out the Hummingbird, position it so that the beak will be perpendicular to the two parallel end grain edges. This will enable you to drill the beak hole on the drill press.

Wheels

This is one toy where manufactured wheels won't work as well as homemade wheels. The spinning of the wing relies on the friction of the wheels' tread, so a handmade wheel with its flat tread will work better than the rounded surface of a manufactured wheel. So make two wheels.

Painting

If you plan to paint the Hummingbird, it will be much easier before assembly. When you paint the wings, be careful not to get paint in the holes or it will weaken the glue joint. Do not paint the wing axle (F) or the treads of the wheels (J) as the paint will interfere with the friction drive.

Assembly

Glue the front wheels and axle (J, H) together. Edge sand the ends of the axles with the grain of the wheels. Glue the wings onto axle (F) with the axle in place. Don't put too much glue on the inside of the wing holes or they won't seat properly. Position the wings perpendicular to each other as in the top view. When all the glue is dry, oil the toy (if you didn't paint it). Attach the pull cord.

You may not be able to find a bobble with a hole small enough to accommodate the Hummingbird's thin cord. To make one, cut a ¾″ long section of ¾″ dowel. Drill a ⅜″ hole in the end grain. Then drill the rest of the way through with a bit slightly thicker than the pull cord. Flat sand both ends and round the edges over by hand. Oil the bobble before assembly.

Feed the pull cord through the bobble, entering through the smaller of the two holes and exiting through the ⅜″ hole. Tie several knots and then pull the cord until the knots disappear into the recess in the bobble.

There you are. A delicate and delightful little Hummingbird.

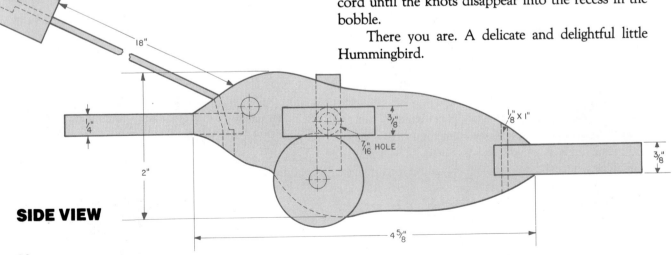

SIDE VIEW

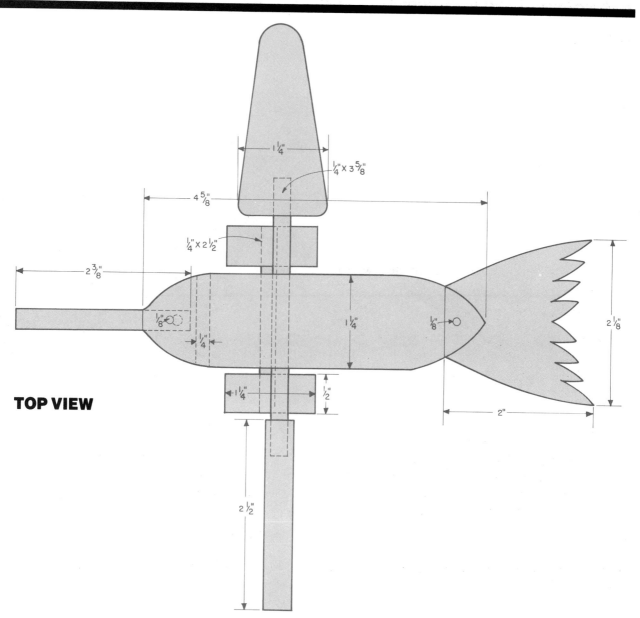

1 1/4"

1/4" x 3 5/8"

4 5/8"

1/4" x 2 1/2"

2 3/8"

1/8"

1/4"

1 1/4"

1/8"

2 1/8"

TOP VIEW

1 1/4"

1/2"

2"

2 1/2"

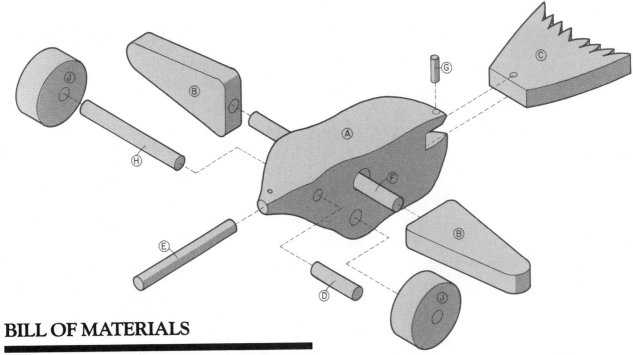

BILL OF MATERIALS

PART	DESCRIPTION	QTY	THICKNESS	WIDTH OR DIAMETER	LENGTH
A	Body	1	1¼"	2"	4⅝"
B	Wings	2	⅜"	1¼"	2½"
C	Tail	1	⅜"	2⅛"	2"
D	Eye	1		¼" dia.	1¼"
E	Beak	1		¼" dia.	2⅜"
F	Wing axle	1		¼" dia.	3⅝"
G	Tail pin	1		⅛" dia.	1"
H	Wheel axle	1		¼" dia.	2½"
J	Wheels	2	½"	1¼" dia.	
K	Pull cord	1		⅛" dia.	20"
L	Bobble	1		¾" dia.	1"

EXPLODED VIEW

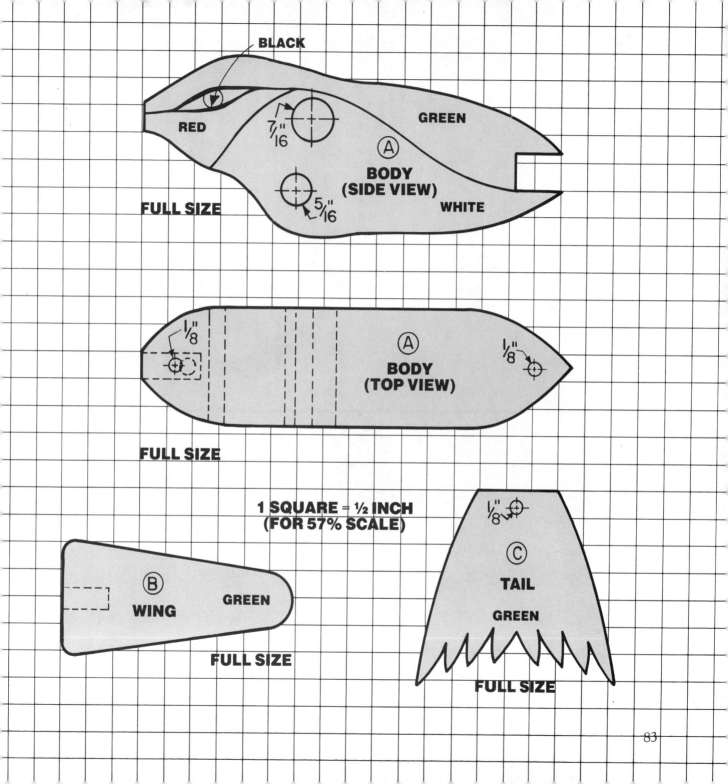

BLACK

RED

7/16"

GREEN

Ⓐ
BODY
(SIDE VIEW)

5/16"

WHITE

FULL SIZE

1/8"

Ⓐ
BODY
(TOP VIEW)

1/8"

FULL SIZE

1 SQUARE = ½ INCH
(FOR 57% SCALE)

1/8"

Ⓒ
TAIL

GREEN

Ⓑ
WING

GREEN

FULL SIZE

FULL SIZE

The Touted TOUCAN

The Toucan silently opens and closes his huge colorful beak as he's pulled along. He's fairly simple to make, but still has quite a bit of character. I recommend that you make the body fairly heavy, and the beak as light as possible to keep him from being top heavy and to help the beak open easily.

The Body

Lay out the body piece (A) so that the slot (to be removed) is parallel to a jointed edge of the board. This will give you a square surface for removing the slot with a wobble or dado blade. Draw a straight line down through the center to position the dowel (F) that will lift the beak (See Figure 1). Drill the holes for the axles and the eye peg. Cut out the slot for the cam on the table saw. Now cut out the Toucan's shape on the bandsaw. Make sure the table on the bandsaw is perfectly square so that the body will stand up straight as you drill the hole for the dowel (F).

Stand the Toucan on his tail and drill the pull cord hole in his chest. Now, using a square, put a scrap under the front of the Toucan to support it at the proper angle to drill the hole for the lifter dowel (F) (See Figure 2). Carefully center the bit and drill all the way through (See Figure 3). Flat sand both sides with 80# and then 120# sandpaper. Edge sand the outline with 80#. Rout the outline and edge sand with 120#. Hand sand the routed edges with 80# and then 120#.

Figure 2. Use a scrap and a square to position the body on the drill press.

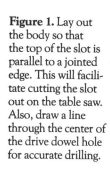

Figure 1. Lay out the body so that the top of the slot is parallel to a jointed edge. This will facilitate cutting the slot out on the table saw. Also, draw a line through the center of the drive dowel hole for accurate drilling.

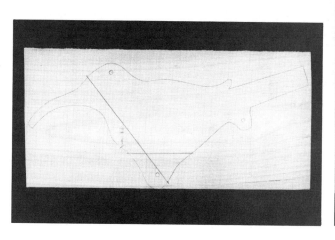

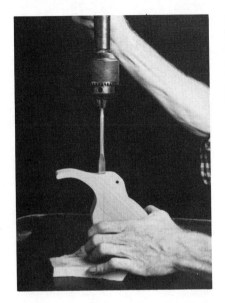

Figure 3. Holding the body firmly, drill the hole for the drive dowel (F). You may want to clamp the piece for this operation.

The Head

Cut out the beak sides (C). Lay one on top of the other and drill the 9/32" holes to make sure they are identically placed. Cut out the 1⅞" beak spacer (B), making sure the table is perfectly square on the bandsaw. Glue up the beak assembly using the jig for the Hippo's head (*See Techniques and Production Procedures, Figures 20, 30, 31, 32*). When the glue is dry, if there is more than a ¹⁄₁₆" discrepancy in the way the pieces line up, saw the excess off on the bandsaw. Edge sand with 80# sandpaper, flat sand with 80# and then 120#, and rout the outline. Hand sand any roughness or burns with 80#. Edge sand with 120#, and then hand sand all the edges with 120# to smooth them out.

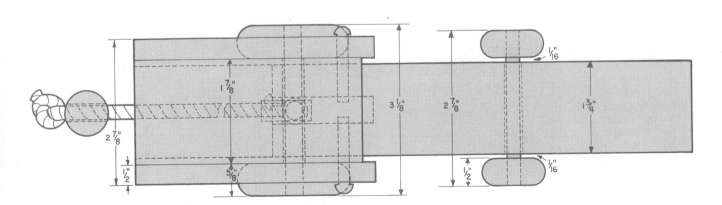

TOP VIEW

Painting

Transfer the painting lines onto the beak assembly and the body, and paint them both. You could paint the eye pegs black at this point and touch them up after assembly. Don't get any paint in the peg hole for the eye, or on the shaft of the eye peg, or it will interfere with the strength of the glue bond later on. Don't paint the tread of the cam or the ends of the drive dowel or they will not work smoothly.

Assembly

Make a 1″ wheel for the cam (D). Plug the ¼″ hole. Let the glue dry. Use a Forstner bit to avoid splitting the cam and drill the ⅜″ axle hole off center. Now cut the front axle to length (a little long). Position the cam in the slot and slip the axle through the body and the cam. With the Toucan on its back on the drill press, the cam perfectly centered in the slot, and the mass of the cam hanging below the axle, drill the ⅛″ hole. Cut the ⅛″ dowel to length (⅞″) and, with a bit of glue in the hole, tap the ⅛″ dowel into place. Wipe off any excess glue. Glue the front wheels on. Glue the back wheels on. Edge sand the axle hubs after the glue is dry.

$\frac{7}{32}$″ HOLE IN BODY

$\frac{9}{32}$″ HOLE IN BEAK

½″ HOLE

24″

⅜″ DOWEL

4 ⅞″ APPROX.

1 ½″

⅜″

1″

2 ¼″

¼″

1 ¼″

SIDE VIEW

1″

¾″   ¼″

CAM

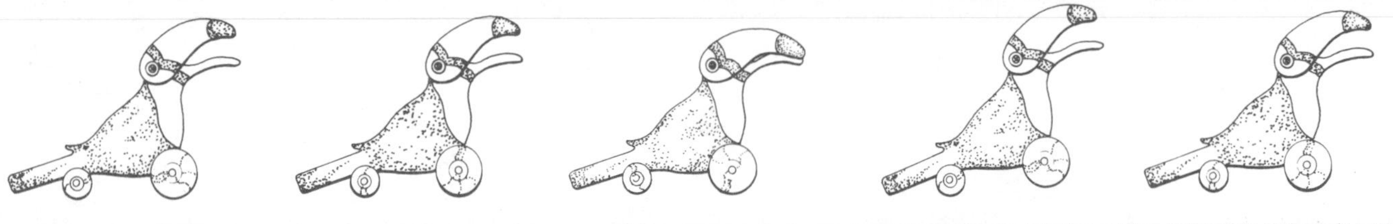

Cut the pull cord peg to length *(See Techniques and Production Procedures, Figure 14)*. Put glue on the end of the pull cord and inside the pull cord hole. Position the end of the cord in the hole (no more cord than the depth of the hole). Tap the peg into place, making sure not to drive any more of the cord into the hole. If the cord sticks out into the drive dowel hole after the glue has dried, ream the hole out again.

Glue the beak assembly onto the head using the clearance gauge if necessary *(See Techniques and Production Procedures, Figure 28)*. Attach the (oiled or painted) pull handle (P) on the end of the cord. With the beak closed and the back of the head facing you, see what the clearance is between the drive dowel hole and the underside of the beak assembly *(See Figure 4)*. Measure the clearance; it'll be anywhere from 0″ to ⅜″, depending on the accuracy of your sawing and assembly. With the beak open, slip a ⅜″ dowel into the drive hole. Put the cam in the down position and mark the dowel where the beak sat when it was closed. (Remember the clearance that you just measured.) Now cut the dowel to this length *(See Figure 5)*. Round over both ends *(See Techniques and Production Procedures, Figure 24)*. You can either paint or oil this piece and then slip it into the hole again. (Don't paint the tips though. It makes too much friction.) There you are, ready to watch your Toucan walking without squawking.

Figure 4. With the beak closed, look from the back of the head to see how far above the drive hole the beak sits at rest.

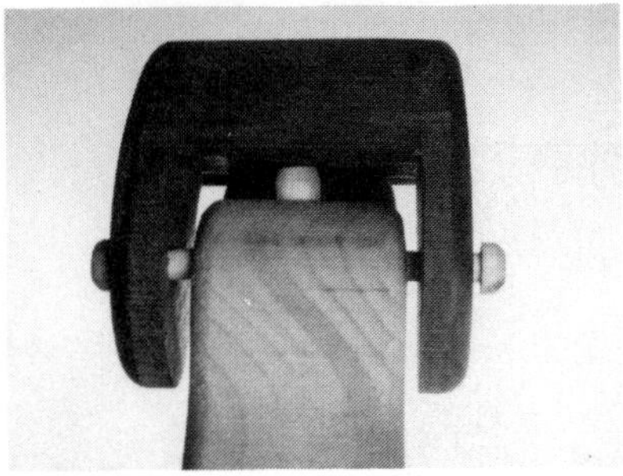

Figure 5. This is where you'll want the drive dowel to end when the cam is in the down position.

BILL OF MATERIALS

PART	DESCRIPTION	QTY	THICKNESS	WIDTH OR DIAMETER	LENGTH
A	Body	1	1¾″	5⅛″	12½″
B	Beak spacer	1	1⅞″	1⅛″	4½″
C	Beak sides	2	½″	2″	4⅞″
D	Cam	1	⅜″	1″ dia.	
E	Front axle	1		⅜″ dia.	3⅛″
F	Drive dowel	1		⅜″ dia.	4⅞″
G	Rear axle	1		¼″ dia.	2⅞″
H	Pin for cam	1		⅛″ dia.	⅞″
J	Pegs	2		7/32″ dia.	1 1/16″ shaft
K	Peg (short)	1		7/32″ dia.	⅜″ shaft
L	Front wheels	2	⅝″	2¼″ dia.	
M	Rear wheels	2	½″	1¼″ dia.	
N	Acrylic cord			¼″ dia.	26″
P	Bobble			⅞″ dia.	

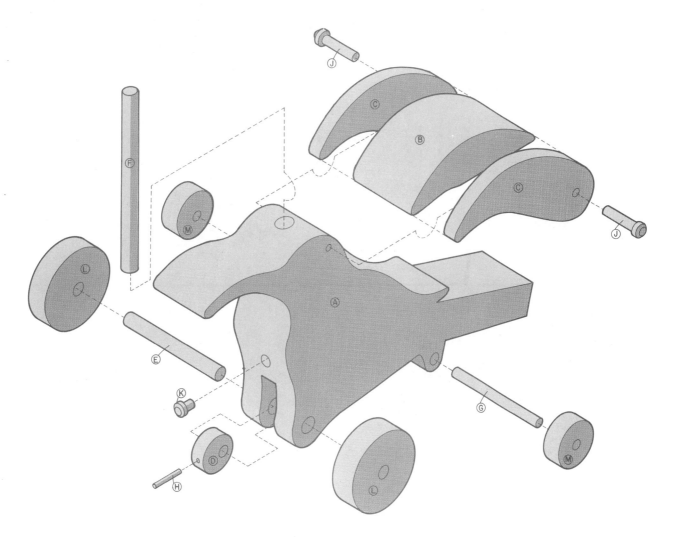

EXPLODED VIEW

89

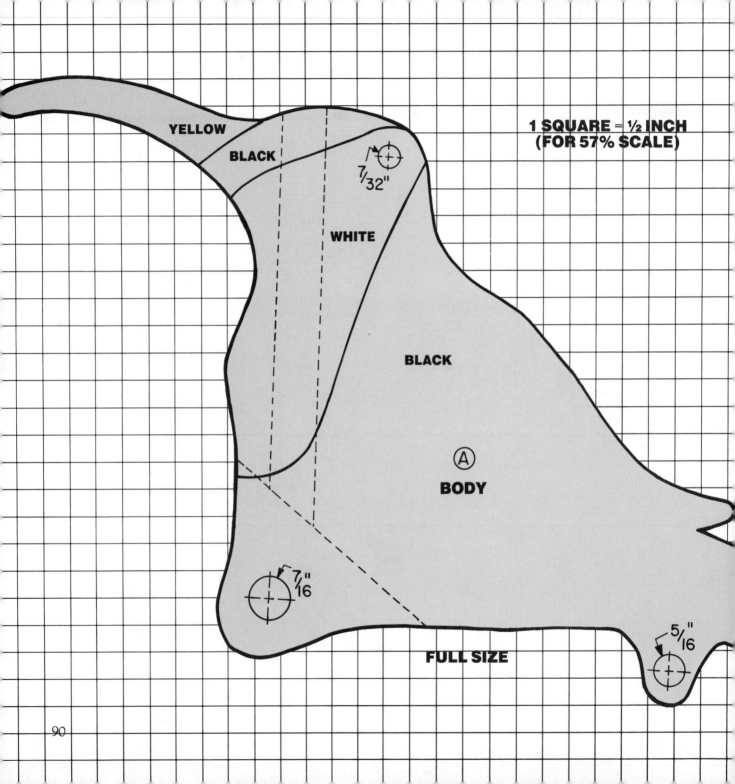

YELLOW

BLACK

$\frac{7}{32}$"

WHITE

1 SQUARE = ½ INCH
(FOR 57% SCALE)

BLACK

Ⓐ
BODY

$\frac{7}{16}$"

$\frac{5}{16}$"

FULL SIZE

90

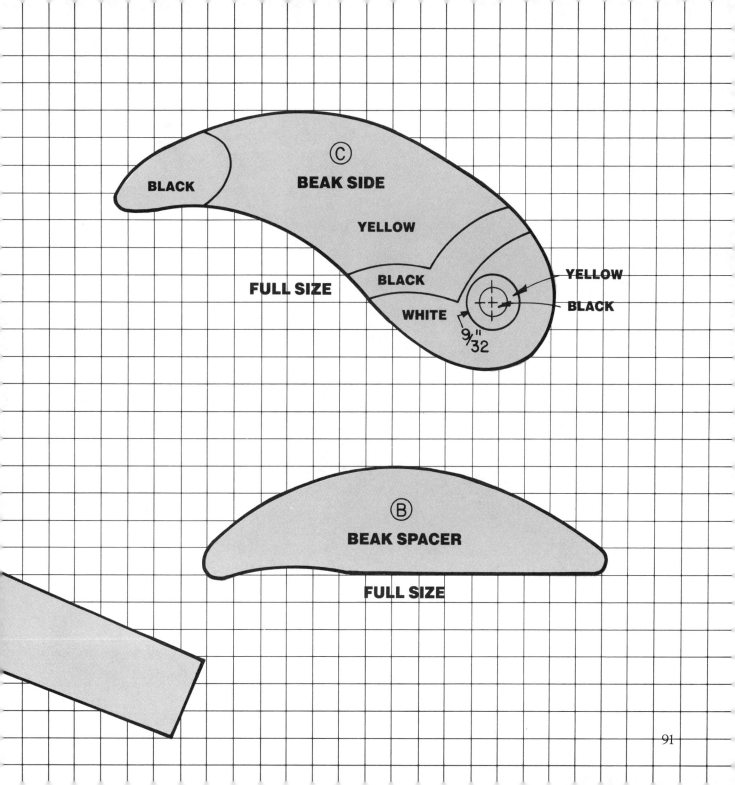

BLACK

Ⓒ

BEAK SIDE

YELLOW

FULL SIZE

BLACK

WHITE

YELLOW

BLACK

$\frac{9}{32}''$

Ⓑ

BEAK SPACER

FULL SIZE

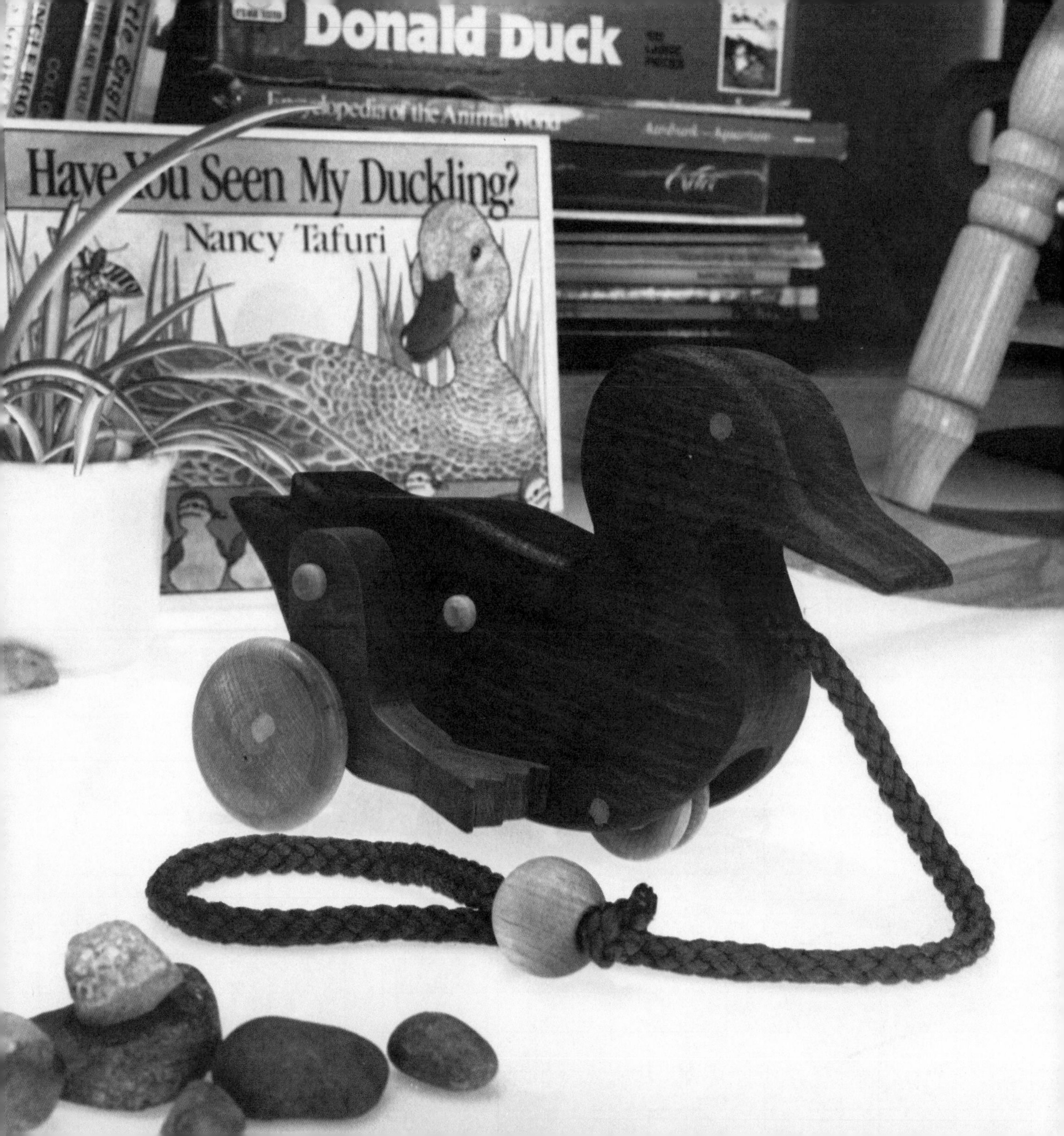
Donald Duck
Have You Seen My Duckling?
Nancy Tafuri

The Waddling DUCK

The Duck combines two types of movement to accomplish that convincing waddle. The back wheels have offset axle holes, and are assembled in a diagonally opposed fashion so that the Duck tips first to one side and then to the other. As the wheels make the Duck tip from side to side, the ½" dowels on the inside of the wheels kick the webbed feet forward one at a time. The combined effect is an endearing "waddle."

The Body

This body does not need exceptional strength, so weaker woods such as poplar can be used. Transfer the body pattern (A) onto a suitable piece of wood. Drill the eye, axle, and peg holes. Cut the dowel for the eye (C) slightly long. Glue it into the eye hole so that it protrudes slightly on each side. Flat sand the protruding dowel end off the unpatterned side when the glue is dry.

Cut out the body on the bandsaw. To drill the big hole for the front wheel, position the Duck on the drill press at the proper angle to drill the foremost of the two holes. Use clamps and/or blocks to secure it while you drill. If you have a multispur bit, you can drill to the full depth of the hole, reposition the Duck and drill the second hole.

If you use a spade bit, drill the first hole to the full depth. Reposition the Duck and drill the second hole, stopping before you intercept the first one. If you break through into the first hole, the drill bit will bind up and yank the Duck out of your hands.

Chisel out the remaining material. File the insides of the hole and round over the lip of the hole with a four-in-hand rasp. Hand sand the lip and sides of the hole with 80# sandpaper, and then hand sand the lip with 120#. Using the same setup on the drill press, drill the cord holes. Drill the ½" hole first. Reposition the Duck with its chest up and carefully drill the smaller hole until it meets the ½" hole.

Flat sand the body with 80# and then 120# sandpaper. Edge sand the body with 80#. The throat and the back of the neck will have to be sanded by hand or with a drum sander. Now rout the entire outline of the Duck, except for those edges on either side of the front wheel hole. Round these edges over with the four-in-hand rasp and sandpaper. Edge sand the body with 120# again, and hand sand the throat and the back of the neck. Hand sand all the routed edges with 80# to remove any roughness, burns, or splinters. Hand sand all these edges with 120#.

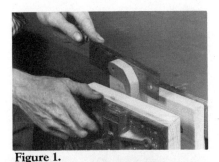

Figure 1.

Figure 2.

Figures 1 & 2. You can saw out the legs with a back saw or dovetail saw if the bandsaw operation makes you uncomfortable.

The Legs

The legs should be made of a strong wood so that the webbed areas of the feet won't break off. Transfer the leg pattern (B) onto two suitable pieces of stock. Drill the $9/32''$ hole in both legs. If the following directions for cutting out the leg on the bandsaw make you uncomfortable, clamp the foot in the vise and make the cuts with a back saw or dovetail saw (*See Figures* 1, 2). Set the rip fence on the bandsaw $3/4''$ to the left of the blade to

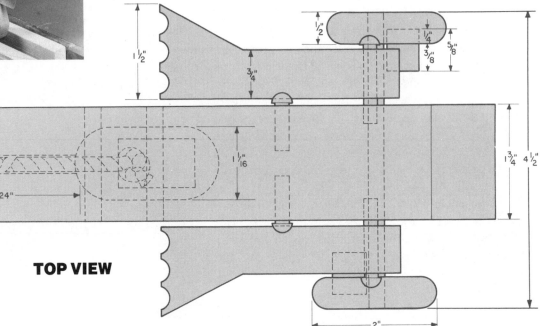

TOP VIEW

cut the upper section of the left leg. Set the roller guides 3" above the table. Face the top of the leg toward the blade with the back of the upper leg flat on the bandsaw table and the foot pointing up (*See Figure 3*). Hold the foot firmly against the fence at all times. Pass the leg by the blade until you reach the first crook in the leg.

Figure 3. To cut the top of the left leg, set the bandsaw rip fence ¾" to the left of the blade and position the leg flat on its back, with the foot pointing upward.

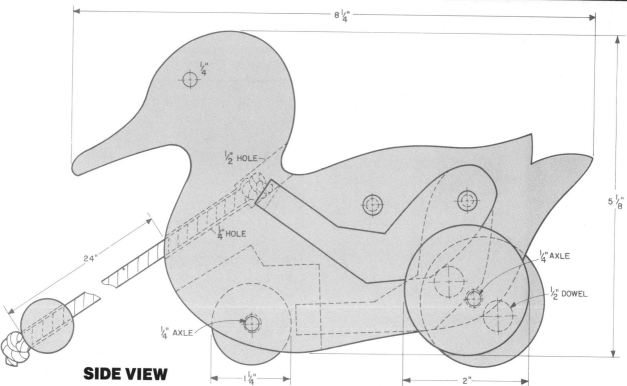

SIDE VIEW

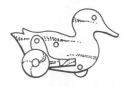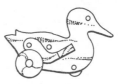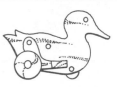

Figure 4.

Figure 5.

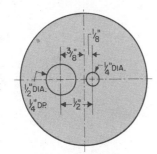

REAR WHEEL

¹⁄₈"

³⁄₈"

¼"DIA.

½"DIA.

¼"DP.

½"

Figures 4 & 5.
Carefully tip the leg at each bend to keep the back of the leg flat on the table.

Slowly tip the leg until the next section is flat on the table (*See Figure 4*). Saw until you get to the ankle. Tip the leg again until the ankle is flat on the table, and saw till you reach the foot (*See Figure 5*). Now, very carefully, retrace the steps backwards to withdraw the leg.

Reset the fence approximately 1″ to the left of the blade, so it will leave ¾″ of material to the right of the blade. Repeat the previous cutting steps to cut the upper section of the right foot.

Mark the foot pattern on the top of each foot. Remove the rip fence. Hold the foot flat on the table saw, from the outside corner of each foot to the point where the ankle cut begins, and cut out the webs. Use a ⅛″ blade on the bandsaw or a coping saw.

Edge sand both legs with 80# and then 120# sandpaper on all surfaces, except the flat surfaces on the inside of the legs and the web. Flat sand the inside of both legs with 80# and then 120#. Smooth out the webs with a rat-tail file and sandpaper wrapped around a dowel. Hand sand all the fuzzy edges with 120# and the feet are ready.

Wheels

The front wheel can be made in two ways:

1. Glue two commercially manufactured 1¼″ x ⅜″ wheels together, using a dowel in the axle holes to line them up. Make sure the dowel doesn't get glued in the hole.

2. Make a wheel from scratch out of ¾″ hardwood using a circle cutter, or a hole saw.

In either case, enlarge the axle hole of the finished wheel to ⁵⁄₁₆″.

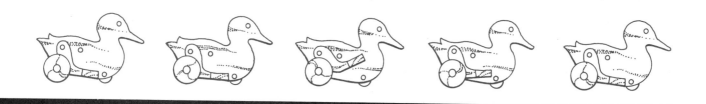

To prepare the back wheels, plug the original axle holes and drill the ½″ holes for the dowels. Glue the dowels in place, making sure they are perpendicular to the inside face of the wheels (*See Figure 6*). When they are dry, locate and drill the new axle holes (*See Techniques and Production Procedures, Figure 17*).

Assembly

Clamp the Duck, belly up, in the wood vise with the front axle hole exposed. Spread glue inside the ¼″ hole on the far side of the big hole. Position the wheel and tap the axle (cut a bit oversize) through the nearest axle hole until it passes through the wheel and just starts into the glued hole on the far side. Now spread a thin coat of glue on the end of the dowel which protrudes toward you. Tap the axle all the way in so that it sticks out a bit on both sides of the body. Let the glue dry and flat sand the dowel ends flush with 120# sandpaper. Glue the two pegs (K) in place.

Now glue and peg the legs to their respective sides, using the clearance gauge to set the depth of the peg (*See Techniques and Production Procedures, Figure 28*).

Glue the rear axle to one of the wheels, making sure the ½″ dowel faces inward. Slip the axle through the body. Put glue in the axle hole on the other rear wheel. Position the wheel so that the ½″ dowels are diagonally opposed (one up, one down), and hammer the wheel onto the axle. When the glue is dry, edge sand the axle ends.

Oil the Duck and attach the pull cord when the oil is dry. Your Duck's ready to waddle gently through a lucky child's imagination.

Figure 6. Make sure that the ½″ dowel is glued perpendicular to the wheel's surface.

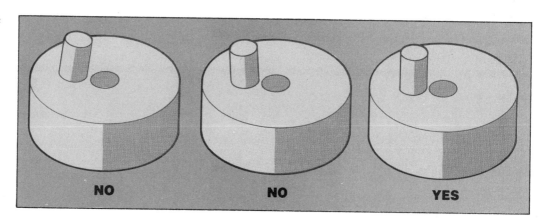

NO   NO   YES

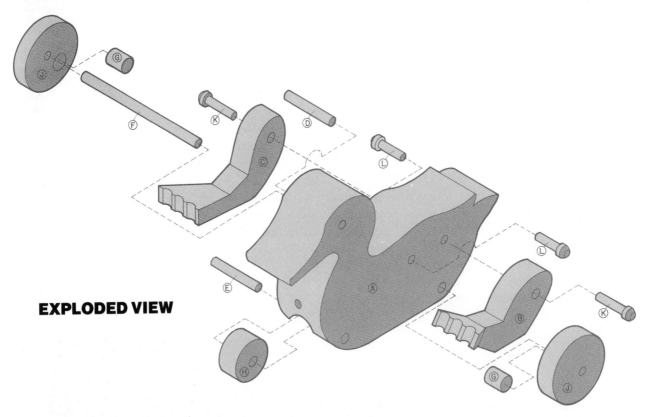

EXPLODED VIEW

BILL OF MATERIALS

PART	DESCRIPTION	QTY	THICKNESS	WIDTH OR DIAMETER	LENGTH	PART	DESCRIPTION	QTY	THICKNESS	WIDTH OR DIAMETER	LENGTH
A	Body	1	1¾"	5⅛"	8¼"	H	Front wheel	1	¾"	1¼" dia.	
B	Left leg	1	1¾"	2"	4"	J	Rear wheels	2	½"	2" dia.	
C	Right leg	1	1¾"	2"	4"	K	Leg pegs	2		⁷/₃₂" dia.	1¹/₁₆"
D	Eye	1		¼" dia.	1¾"	L	Stopper pegs	2		⁷/₃₂" dia.	¾"
E	Front axle	1		¼" dia.	1¾"	M	Acrylic cord	1		¼" dia.	26"
F	Rear axle	1		¼" dia.	4½"	N	Bobble	1		⅞" dia.	
G	Wheel plug	2		½" dia.	⅝"						

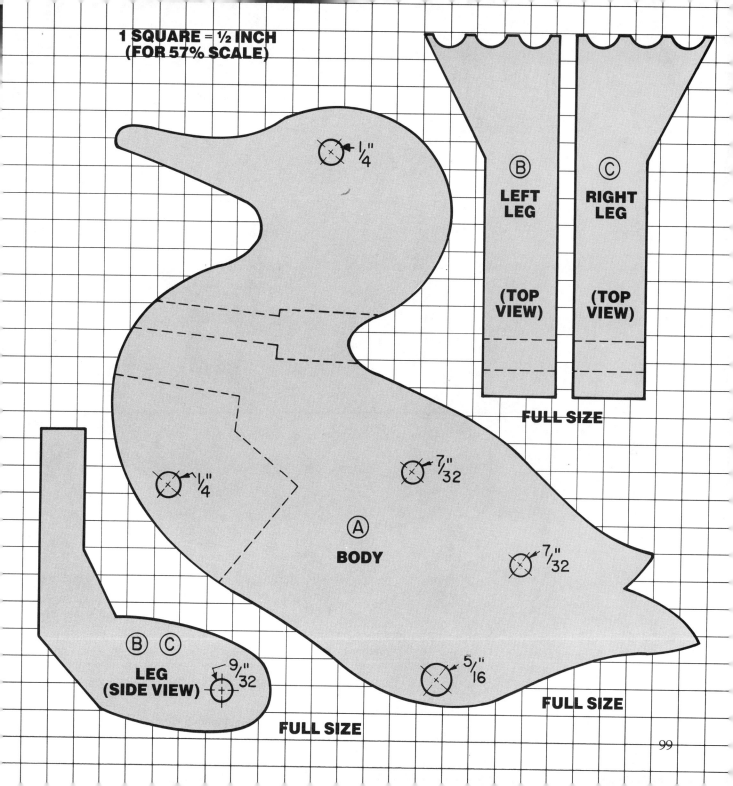

1 SQUARE = ½ INCH
(FOR 57% SCALE)

Ⓑ LEFT LEG

Ⓒ RIGHT LEG

(TOP VIEW)

(TOP VIEW)

FULL SIZE

¼"

⁷⁄₃₂"

Ⓐ BODY

¼"

⁷⁄₃₂"

Ⓑ Ⓒ
LEG (SIDE VIEW)

⁹⁄₃₂"

⁵⁄₁₆"

FULL SIZE

FULL SIZE

99

The Timid TURTLE

This is one of my earlier designs and also one of my favorites. On the surface it appears to be quite a complicated toy and indeed, it does take quite a bit of work to make. However, the *simplicity* of the working mechanisms (and the solid construction) ensure that it will work smoothly for years. It will give a great deal of pleasure to generations of children.

This Turtle is designed to be so strong that not only can small children pull it around indefinitely, but they can actually ride on it and pull each other around. I hope you will appreciate the Turtle as a challenge and a joy.

The Shell Pieces

When you're choosing a piece of wood for the shell, remember that this toy is going to take a bit of work, so choose something special. The angles of the shell will accentuate the grain patterns.

Lay out the pattern for the shell (A) so the grain runs lengthwise on the piece of wood you've chosen. Transfer the pattern to the bottom of this piece.

Tilt the bandsaw table to 40°. Cut the shell out very carefully, following the lines *exactly*. Keep the lines perfectly straight or you will distort the octagonal shape of the shell when you sand the sides flat.

These next two cuts are the most difficult, so take special care. Transfer the pattern for the head and tail holes onto the shell. Leave the bandsaw table set at 40° and cut out these holes using a sharp blade (*See Figures 1, 2, 3*). The trickiest part of the cut is the last half of the curve, from the top of the arc to the end of the cut. To successfully execute this cut, you have to anticipate the curve and stay ahead of it. In other words, turn the

Figures 1, 2, & 3. This is a difficult cut, so use a sharp blade and take your time. Once you pass the top of the arc, anticipate the curve and try to keep ahead of it as you saw or you'll be forced off the line.

Figure 1.

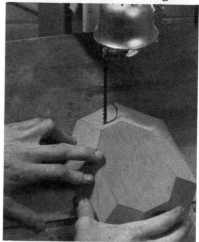

Figure 2.

Figure 3.

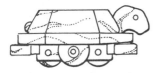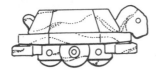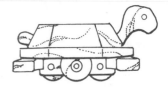

piece beyond the cutting line as you go. You might want to try this cut on a scrap before you go for the shell.

The next step is to flat sand all the surfaces, including the top and underside, on the stationary belt sander with 80# sandpaper. Do this very slowly, looking at the surfaces often to make sure you aren't deviating from the actual sawn surface. Sand slowly, with a light touch.

The front and rear surfaces, where the head and tail come out, need a little more attention. Left as they are, they will be too thin where they meet the shell base. Holding these surfaces flat on the belt sander, rock the shell toward you and away from you, smoothly, to slightly round the bottom where it will meet the shell base (*See Figure 4*).

Repeat the entire belt sanding process with 120# sandpaper. Don't bother with 120# on the underside of the shell. Now, hand sand all the corners with 120#.

Sigh... now, on to some easier steps. To make the shell base (B), take two pieces of wood of the same species as the shell, and joint the edges that will be glued together.

Transfer the pattern of the shell base (B) onto both pieces, make sure the inside edges lay along the jointed edges. Cut them out on the bandsaw. Edge sand the

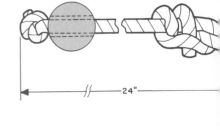

Figure 4. To round over the bottom of the head-hole and tail-hole sections of the shell, hold these surfaces lightly on the belt sander, one at a time, and rock them smoothly toward you and away from you.

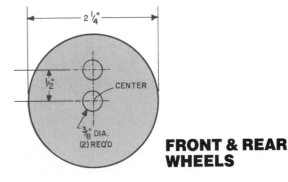

FRONT & REAR WHEELS

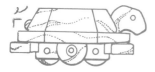 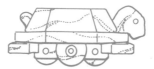 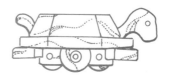 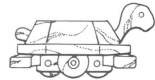

inside edges with 80# sandpaper. Glue and clamp the two pieces together; be careful that they lay flat in the clamps. When the glue is thoroughly dry, flat sand B first with 80# and then with 120#. Now sand all the outside edges on the stationary belt sander, being careful to hold it perfectly vertical. Check the surfaces often to avoid distorting the octagonal shape. A smooth sweep around each corner as you go will gently round the corners of the octagon (*See Figure 5*). Then rout all the edges, inside and out, top and bottom.

Figure 5. Holding the shell base vertically on the belt sander, sweep around each corner to gently round them.

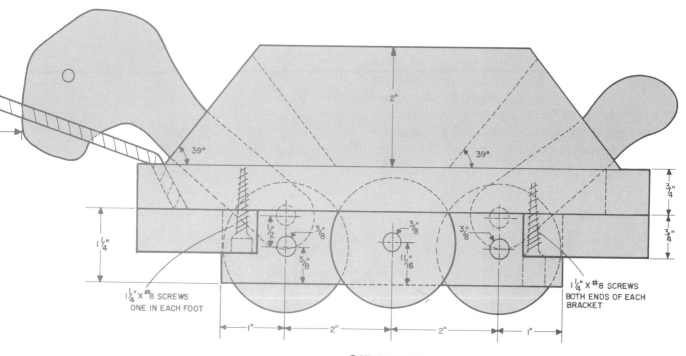

SIDE VIEW

103

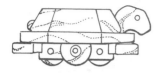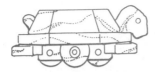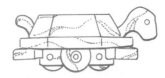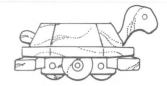

Head, Tail, and Feet, etc.

Transfer the patterns for the head, tail, and feet (C, D, F) to wood that will compliment the shell. Note that the feet are cut out in sets of two to enable you to rout them later. Cut the axle support pieces (E) out of the same wood as the shell.

Drill all the holes in the head, tail, and axle supports. Glue the ¼″ dowel (slightly long) into the eye hole in the head. Sand it flat enough on the unmarked side to pass smoothly over the bandsaw table.

Now cut out the head, tail, and feet (in sets of two). Edge sand the head, tail, and feet with 80# sandpaper. Edge sand the ends of the axle supports with 80# and then flat sand all the remaining surfaces with 80#. Be sure that the edges of E remain perfectly square to ensure free movement of the axles in the holes when the Turtle is assembled. Flat sand the head, tail, and feet with 80# and then 120#. Rout all the edges of the head, tail, and feet. Rout all the edges of the axle supports except the edges that will be glued to the underside of the shell base (*See Figures 6, 7*). When the Turtle is assembled, the inner axle is slightly higher than the others. The inner wheels act only as a means of balance, leaving the weight of the Turtle riding on the other four wheels to move the head and tail. So make sure you leave the proper edges unrouted.

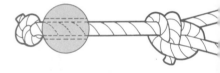

Figure 6. Rout the bottom corners first…

Figure 7. …then you can rout around the corners as you rout the sides.

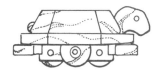
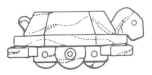
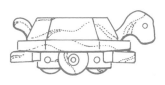
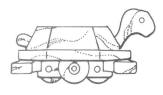

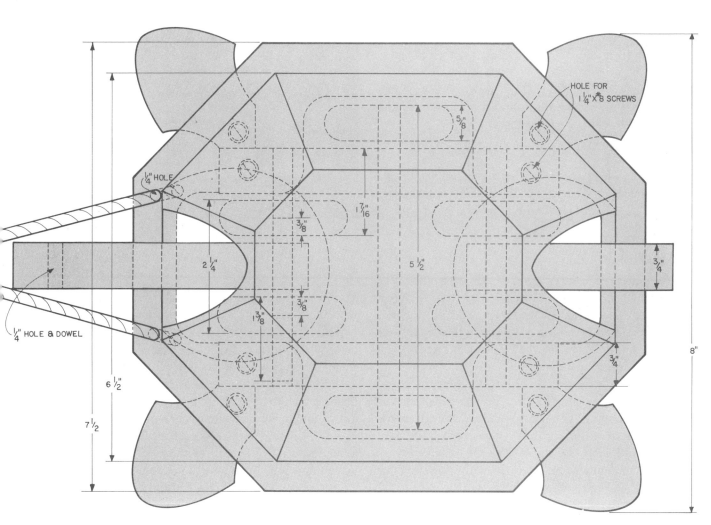

HOLE FOR
1 1/4" X 8 SCREWS

5/8"

1/4" HOLE

1 7/16"

3/8"

2 1/4"

5 1/2"

3/4"

3/8"

1 3/8"

1/4" HOLE & DOWEL

3/4"

8"

6 1/2"

7 1/2"

TOP VIEW

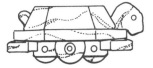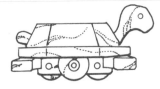

Edge sand all the edges of the head, tail, and feet with 120# sandpaper. Flat sand all the surfaces of the axle supports with 120#, except the ends which can be edge sanded with 120#.

Finally, hand sand all of these parts with 80# sandpaper to remove burns and roughness, and then with 120# on all the routed edges.

Wheels

Using the wheel drilling jig *(See Techniques and Production Procedures, Figure 17)*, drill the ⅜″ holes on the inside of the four 2¼″ wheels for the head and tail assemblies.

Assembly

Cut the four ⅜″ outer drive axles (H) to length. With waxed paper on the workbench, lay the four wheels out with the outside of the wheels facing up. Spread glue in the inner axle hole and drive home the ⅜″ dowels. When the glue is dry, use the flat sander to remove glue from the inside of the wheels.

Cut the two inner drive axles (J) to length. Spread glue in the hole on the inside of one of the wheels that you just doweled. Be especially careful not to put too much glue in the hole or it will prevent the dowel from seating properly. Use the edge of the workbench for support under the wheel as you drive the dowel in as far as you can. Make sure that this dowel is square to the wheel surface and parallel to the dowel sticking out through the center of the other side of the wheel. Leave the wheel on the edge of the workbench and slip the Turtle's head onto the offset axle you just glued. Spread

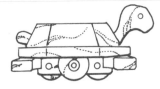

NOT PERFECTLY OPPOSED

Figure 8.

Figures 8 & 9.
Make sure the wheels are perfectly parallel and directly opposite each other.

glue in the hole on another wheel. Locate this second wheel so that the axle starts into the hole, and the two wheels are positioned in perfect opposition. Now hammer the wheel onto the axle, again being careful the wheel is perpendicular to the axle. Look over the assembly before it dries. It is *essential* that this assembly be strong and true for the proper functioning of the Turtle, and to ensure its long life *(See Figures 8, 9)*.

Look at the front and see if the wheels are parallel; adjust accordingly. Look at the side and see if the wheels are directly opposed to each other; make any adjustments necessary. Now roll the assembly on the workbench. If it rocks or waddles at all, the wheels still aren't perfectly opposed. Give them a little twist and try again. If the two protruding axles aren't spinning in a straight line, with no up or down motion, then the

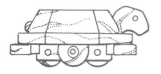
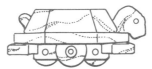
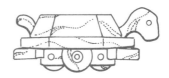
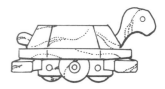

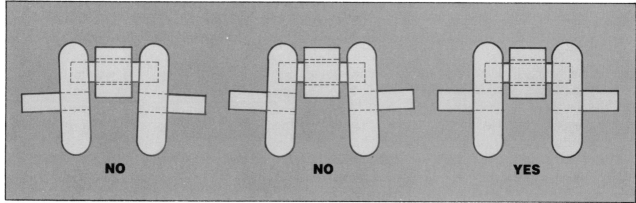

Figure 9.

wheels still aren't parallel. Adjust them by hand or by tapping them with a hammer. When you're sure that the assembly is perfect, repeat the entire procedure for the tail assembly.

Cut the balance axle (K) ¹⁄₃₂″ longer than the specified finished length to allow for sanding the axle ends off after assembly. Glue the axle to one of the 2¼″ wheels. Slip one of the axle supports (E) onto the axle using the central hole in E. Position E so the unrouted surface is up. Put the head and tail assemblies into place, being careful to position them correctly. This may seem like a silly precaution, but it's quite easy to make a mistake here, especially with the tail, and it's infuriating to have to take the assembly apart. Slip the second E piece onto the axle in the same position as the first. Make doubly sure that everything is correct and

glue on the second wheel (*See Figure 10*). When the glue is dry, edge sand the axle ends.

Clamp the shell base in the wood vise with the bottom up. Position the head and tail assembly so the head and tail go through the center of the shell base. The whole assembly should look like the Turtle is

Figure 10. Axle supports should have unrouted edge up.

107

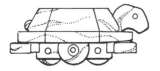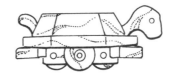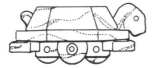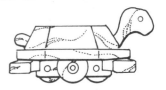

simply upside down. Position the axle supports so that all the parts move freely, including the balance axle. The inside faces of the axle supports should line up with the edge of the head and tail holes in the shell base. This will leave enough of the shell base exposed to glue the feet on securely. Now, clamp them into place, tentatively, to make sure there are no problems (*See Figure 11*). Make sure the assembly is perfectly centered from front to back, as well as from side to side. A good way to judge this is to check the distance from either side of the balance wheels to their respective wheel wells. When you are satisfied with the assembly, mark the positions of the axle supports with a pencil, and unclamp them. Now glue and clamp them in position, watching for any slippage as you tighten the clamps. Once again, make sure that all the axles are perfectly perpendicular to the axle supports, and that they all move freely. Make any adjustments that are necessary.

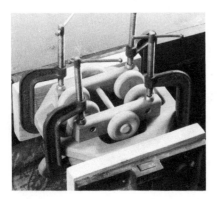

Figure 11. Clamp the entire sub-assembly to the shell base before gluing to make sure that all the parts will move freely when assembled.

When this assembly is thoroughly dry, remove the clamps and position it in the vise so that the surface of the shell base is just above the jaws and the surface of the workbench. Cut the feet out to their final shape. Glue and clamp them to the shell base, one at a time. As you glue them, align them (with each other) from front to back, and from side to side. The more similar the positions of the feet, the better they will look.

From this point until the feet are screwed into place, be careful not to knock them off because it's almost impossible to re-glue them after the shell is glued on.

To attach the shell, clamp a block (1¾″ x 1¾″ x 4″) sideways in the wood vise. Open the jaws 1¾″ and position the block so that it protrudes 1″ above the vise jaws. Set the assembly on the block so the head faces you; both axle supports should be resting on the block with the balance wheels on either side.

Position the shell on top of the shell base, shift it until it is centered and the head and tail can move freely. Note its position. Take it off and apply a moderate amount of glue to the portions of the shell base where the shell will touch. Work glue away from the outer edges to avoid squeeze-out. Use two large C-clamps, with pads or scraps to protect the shell's surface, and clamp the shell in place (*See Figure 12*). Watch for shifting as you tighten the clamps. If the position of the shell is even slightly off, it can bind up the movement of the head and tail.

Let all the glue dry thoroughly and then remove the clamps. With the Turtle on its back on the drill press table, drill the four holes to fasten the axle supports to the shell base, and the four holes to screw the

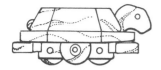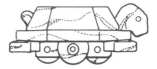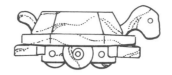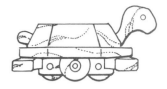

feet to the shell base. Note the depth to which these holes are countersunk on the side view. Clean out *all* of the waste material from the holes and set the Turtle on its back on a piece of carpet. This will prevent marring of the shell as you screw in all eight #8 x 1¼″ screws. You can rub a little paraffin on the screw threads to help them screw in more easily. Don't use soap, it will eat away at the screws. Make sure that the screws go in all the way so their heads press tightly against the bottom of the holes. Screws partially set will not hold firmly.

Cord

Clamp the Turtle head-up in the wood vise with the top of its head facing you. Use an awl or center punch and tap two small holes where the cord holes will be drilled. With a ¼″ brad point bit in the electric drill, use these holes to position the drill bit and drill the cord holes. These holes are drilled at an angle toward the back and the sides *(See Figure 13)*. Check the top and side views to get this angle right.

Now is the time to oil the Turtle to avoid getting oil on the pull cord.

When the finish is dry, feed the cord through both holes from the top. Tie an overhand knot on both ends of the cord and pull it tight. Make a loop in the middle of the cord and attach the second cord with a bolen knot *(See Figure 14)*. Adjust this knot until it is perfectly centered. Attach the bobble with an overhand knot and there you are.

This timid creature was difficult to make, but I'm sure you'll think it was well worth the effort when you watch a small child playing with it.

Figure 12. Use a block (1¾″ x 1¾″ x 4″) in the wood vise to clamp the shell to the shell base.

Figure 13. These holes are drilled at a compound angle, toward the side and back, as well as through the shell base.

Figure 14. Make a loop in the center of the first cord, and attach the second cord to it with a bolen knot.

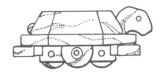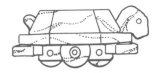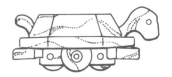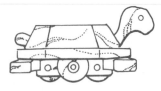

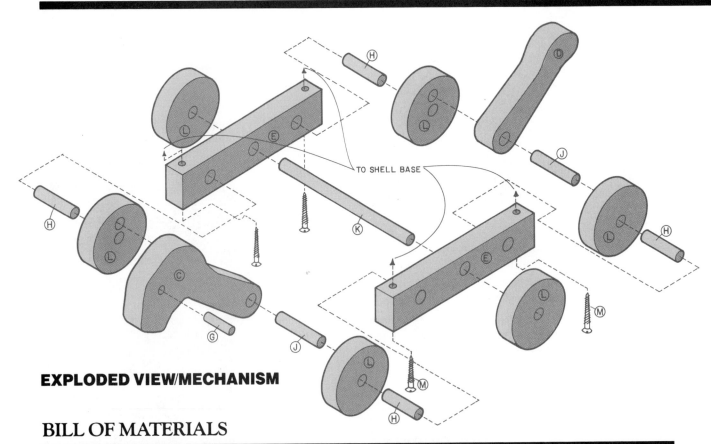

TO SHELL BASE

EXPLODED VIEW/MECHANISM

BILL OF MATERIALS

PART	DESCRIPTION	QTY	THICKNESS	WIDTH OR DIAMETER	LENGTH
A	Shell	1	1¾"	6½"	8"
B	Shell base	2	¾"	3¾"	9"
C	Head	1	¾"	2⅛"	5¾"
D	Tail	1	¾"	1⅛"	4¼"
E	Axle supports	2	¾"	1¼"	6"
F	Feet	2	¾"	2"	5¾"
G	Eye	1		¼" dia.	¾"

PART	DESCRIPTION	QTY	THICKNESS	WIDTH OR DIAMETER	LENGTH
H	Outer drive axles	4		⅜" dia.	1⅜"
J	Inner drive axles	2		⅜" dia.	1¾"
K	Balance axle	1		⅜" dia.	5½"
L	Wheels	6	⅝"	2¼" dia.	
M	Flathead wood screws	8	#8		1¼"
N	Acrylic cord	2		¼" dia.	14"
P	Bobble	1	⅞" approx.		

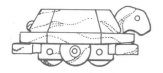
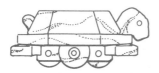
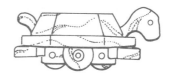
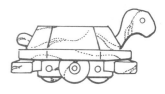

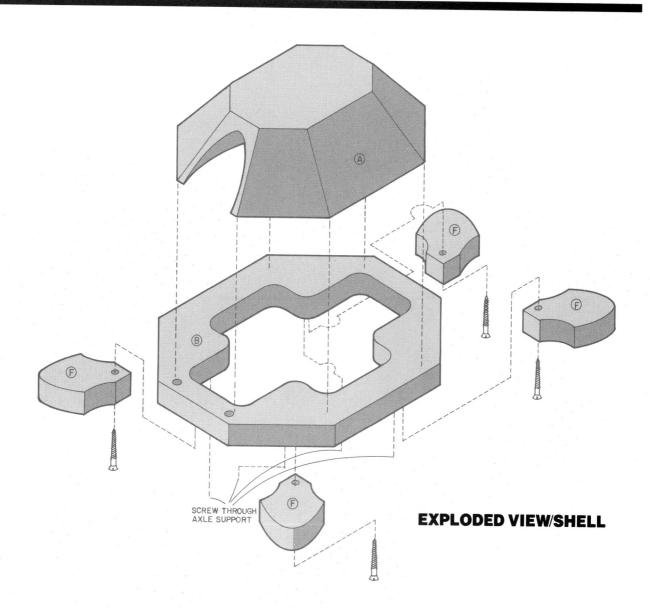

SCREW THROUGH
AXLE SUPPORT

EXPLODED VIEW/SHELL

111

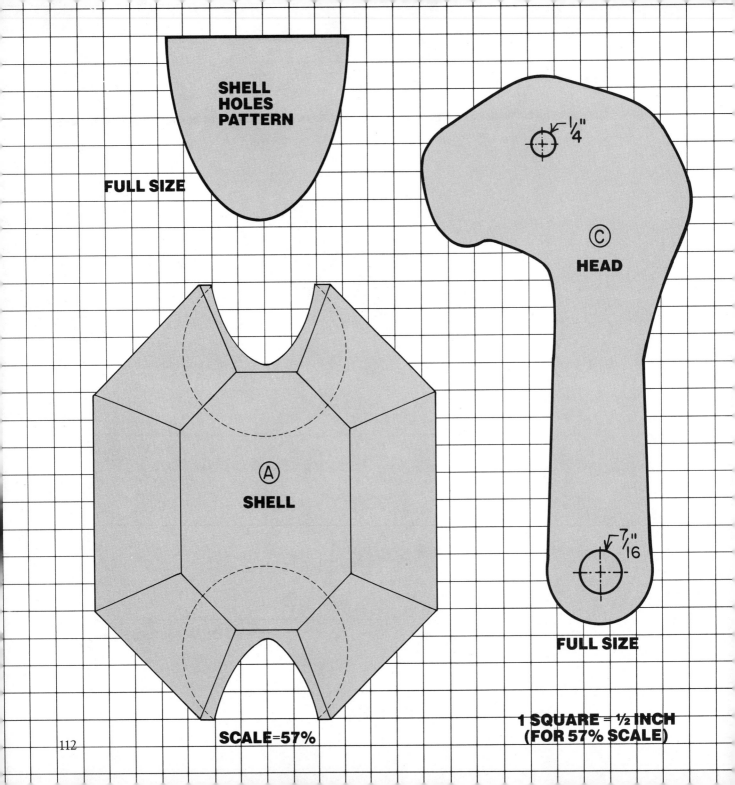

SHELL
HOLES
PATTERN

FULL SIZE

¼"

© HEAD

Ⓐ

SHELL

7⁄16"

FULL SIZE

SCALE=57%

1 SQUARE = ½ INCH
(FOR 57% SCALE)

112

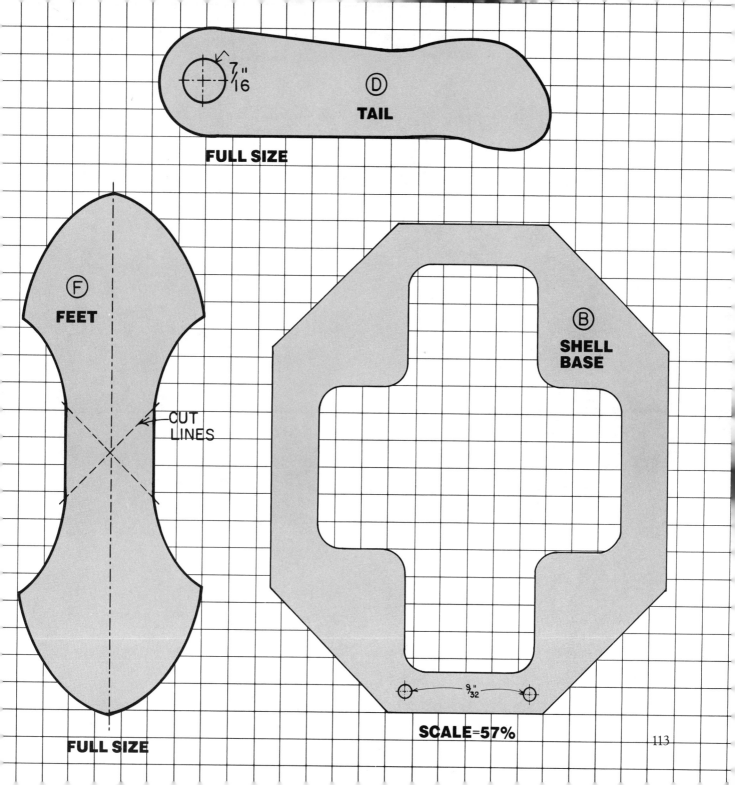

D TAIL

$\frac{7}{16}$"

FULL SIZE

F FEET

FULL SIZE

CUT LINES

B SHELL BASE

$\frac{9}{32}$"

SCALE=57%

113

The Ornery LOBSTER

Every child needs at least one "bad guy" toy, and here he is! When the dowel pegs on the inside of the wheels pass by the edge of the claw, they push that end of the lever down, lifting the rest of the claw up in a threatening manner. As the peg continues around, one claw snaps shut in a nasty fashion as the other claw opens. I don't mean to give this toy "bad press"; it's a great creature and an endless source of fascination.

Wood Considerations

The body of the Lobster must be made of a strong wood. This will give the toy forward momentum which helps the claws open. The arms need to be strong to withstand the constant stress of the falling claws. The claws need to be tough but not too heavy, so they'll lift properly. Looking at all the requirements, it seems that cherry, with its natural red color, is the best choice.

The Body

Lay out the body pattern (A) with the bottom of the body running along a jointed edge. This will enable you to use the rip fence on the bandsaw to cut an accurate tail slot (*See Figure 1*), and will give you a stronger glue joint. Drill the 1″ hole and cut the body out on the bandsaw. Edge sand with 80# sandpaper. Use clamps and/or blocks to hold the body at the proper angles on the drill press, and drill the eye peg holes and the hole for the handle.

Flat sand the sides with 80# and then 120# sandpaper. Rout all the edges except those around the tail joint. Edge sand with 120# and hand sand all the routed edges with 80# and then 120#.

The Arms

Transfer the arm pattern (B) to two pieces of stock with the grain running lengthwise. Drill the 1″ holes with a spade bit. Use the spade bit point hole as a centering device and drill the rest of the way with a 7/16″ twist drill. Don't forget a piece of scrap under the arm to avoid tear-out. Drill the peg holes. Edge sand and flat sand the arms with 80# and then 120# sandpaper, and hand sand all the fuzzy corners and edges with 120#.

The Claws

Lay out the pattern for the claw spacers (C) on a piece of wood, 1/8″ thicker than the arms, and cut them out on the bandsaw. Transfer the claw sides pattern (D) to four pieces of 3/8″ hardwood. Cut out enough of the claw

Figure 1. Lay out the pattern with the bottom of the body along a jointed edge; use the rip fence on the bandsaw to cut a clean tail slot for a strong glue joint.

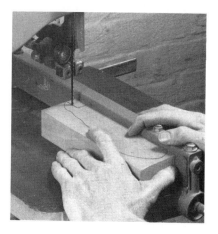

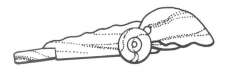
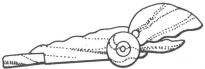
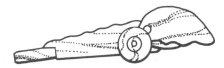

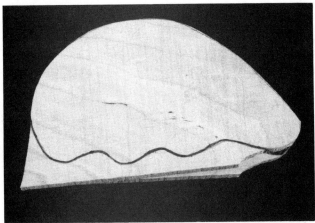

parts to line up the top edges while gluing, but don't cut out the bottom edges (*See Figure 2*). Glue up both claws. When the glue is dry, mark the pattern on them again. This will allow you to accurately locate the peg holes in relationship to the lower back edge of the claw, so the peg in the wheel will hit the claw. This distance is critical to the proper functioning of the claws. Cut the claws out on the bandsaw and drill the peg holes. Edge sand all the way around both claws with 80# sandpaper. Flat sand both sides of each claw with 80# and then 120# and rout all the way around both claws. Edge sand each claw with 120# and hand sand all the routed edges with 80# and then 120#.

The Tail

Transfer the tail pattern (E) to a ¾″ piece of wood with the grain running front to back (the back of the tail will be end grain). Cut the tail out on the bandsaw; edge sand with 80# sandpaper. Flat sand with 80# and then 120#. Rout all edges except the forward (end grain) edge where it will join the body. Edge sand with 120#. Hand sand any router burns or roughness with 80# and then hand sand all the routed edges with 120#.

The Axle Housing

Cut the 1″ dowel for the axle housing (F) to length. To drill the axle hole, you'll need to make a simple jig to keep the dowel perpendicular on the drill press. Take a 2 x 4 that's long enough to clamp securely to the drill press. Put it on edge and drill a 1¹⁄₁₆″ hole most of the way through the center of the board. Now insert the axle housing dowel into the hole. Clamp the board to the drill press table with the axle housing centered

Figure 2. Cut out enough of the claw sides to position the spacer, and glue both claw assemblies. This will enable you to position the peg holes perfectly after they are dry.

Figure 3. Drill a 1¹⁄₁₆″ hole about 2½″ deep in middle of 2 x 4. Clamp it to drill press table with the hole centered under the bit and grip the 1″ dowel with a piece of inner tube and pliers as you drill the axle hole through the center.

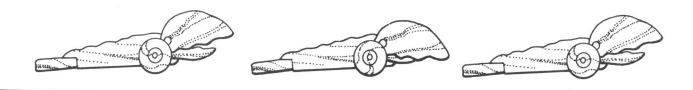

under the 7/16″ bit. You can use pliers with a piece of inner tube as padding to hold the dowel and keep it from spinning as you drill *(See Figure 3)*. Drill a little more than halfway through (about 3″); flip the axle housing over and repeat the drilling procedure. Hand sand the outside of the dowel if it needs it and round over the ends slightly so they'll slip into the arm holes.

Wheels

Prepare the wheels by using the wheel jig *(See Techniques and Production Procedures, Figure 17)* to drill ½″ holes on the inside of the wheels (Q). Cut the ½″ work dowels (M) to length, round over the ends and glue them into place; make sure they're perpendicular to the wheel surface *(See Figure 4)*.

WHEEL

SIDE VIEW

5/8″ X 18″ DOWEL

7/32″ X 1 1/16″

5/16″

1/4″ PEG

1/4″ DOWEL

2 1/4″

2 7/8″

2 1/4″

3/4″

8 1/4″

13 1/4″

5/8″

1/2″

3/8″

2 1/4″

1″

3″

117

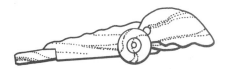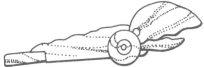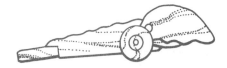

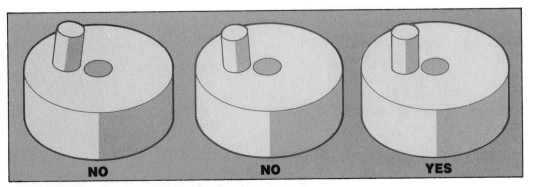

Figure 4. Make sure the work dowels are glued perpendicular to the wheels' surfaces.

NO   NO   YES

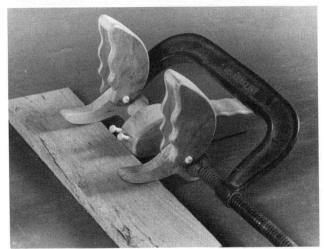

Figure 5. Make sure you clamp both claws at the same angle (side view drawing). If they're too high, they'll flop back and won't close again. If they're too low, the dowel pegs won't be able to open them.

Assembly

First, glue in the eye pegs. Then cut four pegs (P) to length using a piece of hardboard *(See Techniques and Production Procedures, Figure 14)*. Round off the ends of the pegs with sandpaper. Spread glue in the peg holes in the arms. Position the claws one at a time and peg them to the arms, using the clearance gauge *(See Techniques and Production Procedures, Figure 28)* if necessary. While these dry, insert the axle housing (F) into the body and center it. Drill the ¼″ hole from the bottom on the drill press, glue and insert the axle housing pin (K). If necessary, clean out the 7/16″ hole through the axle housing after the glue is dry.

Now glue and clamp both claw assemblies onto the ends of the axle housing. Use a scrap under both claws to set the height as you clamp them. Be sure they are set at the same angle *(See Figure 5)*. If they are too high, the claws will flip too far open and won't close. If they are too low, the claws will be hard to lift.

Next, glue and clamp the tail in position. When it's dry, drill the dowel hole through it from the top,

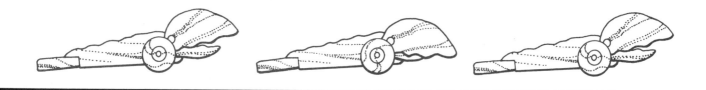

with a piece of scrap underneath. Cut the tail pin (L) a little long and glue it in place with both ends extending out slightly. When the glue is dry, saw off the excess and hand sand smooth with 80# and 120# sandpaper. Ream out the 7/16″ axle hole again to remove any glue squeeze-out from the claw assemblies.

Now glue the axle (G) to one of the wheels. Position the other wheel so that the ½″ pegs are on alternate sides of the axle housing (one above, one below) and tap the second wheel onto the axle. When these are dry, edge sand the axle ends. At this point, roll the Lobster and see if the claws are working properly. The relation-

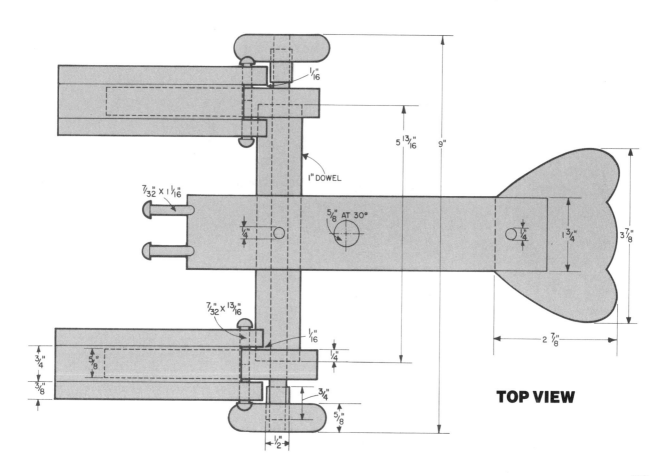

TOP VIEW

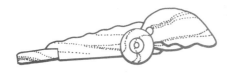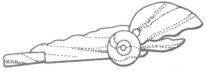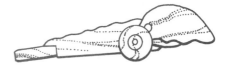

ship between the dowels inside the wheels and the back edge of the claw is critical. If the claws aren't working perfectly, you can remake the wheels, adjusting the position of the dowel pegs. If the dowel peg is too close to the claw edge, you can move it back, closer to the axle. If the peg is too far from the edge of the claw, move it out a little further from the axle. Be patient. These fine adjustments are sometimes necessary to make sure that such a complex toy works properly.

Handle

Cut the handle rod (H) and the handle (J) to length. Drill the ⅝″ hole in the handle (J) using the jig you made for the axle housing hole. If the hole is too deep to leave enough of the dowel protruding to grab with pliers and a piece of inner tube, put a small piece of ¾″ dowel in the bottom of the hole to raise the handle up. Now, drill the ⅝″ hole. Flat sand the ends of the handle.

Figure 6. When hammering the handle into place, use a block under the body to lift it up off the wheels and support it.

Round over the ends of both H and J by holding them diagonal to the stationary belt sander and spinning them (*See Techniques and Production Procedures, Figure 24*).

Spread glue in the hole in J. Don't use too much glue or the handle rod (H) won't go all the way into the hole. Tap them together. Spread glue in the hole in the Lobster's back. Now drive the handle all the way into the hole; use something under the body so the force of the hammering doesn't damage the wheels (*See Figure 6*). Now apply some Danish oil and the Lobster will be ready to chomp his way into infamy.

BILL OF MATERIALS

PART	DESCRIPTION	QTY	THICKNESS	WIDTH OR DIAMETER	LENGTH
A	Body	1	1¾″	2¼″	8¼″
B	Arms	2	⅝″	2¼″	5″
C	Claw spacers	2	¾″	1½″	4⅝″
D	Claw sides	4	⅜″	2½″	4⅛″
E	Tail	1	¾″	2⅞″	3⅛″
F	Axle housing	1		1″ dia.	5¹³⁄₁₆″
G	Axle	1		⅜″ dia.	9″
H	Handle rod	1		⅝″ dia.	18″
J	Handle	1		1″ dia.	3″
K	Axle housing pin	1		¼″ dia.	¾″
L	Tail pin	1		¼″ dia.	1⅝″
M	Work dowel	2		½″ dia.	¾″
N	Eyes	2		⁷⁄₃₂″ dia.	1¹⁄₁₆″
P	Pegs	4		⁷⁄₃₂″ dia.	¹³⁄₁₆″
Q	Wheels	2	⅝″	2¼″ dia.	

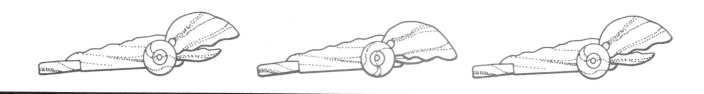

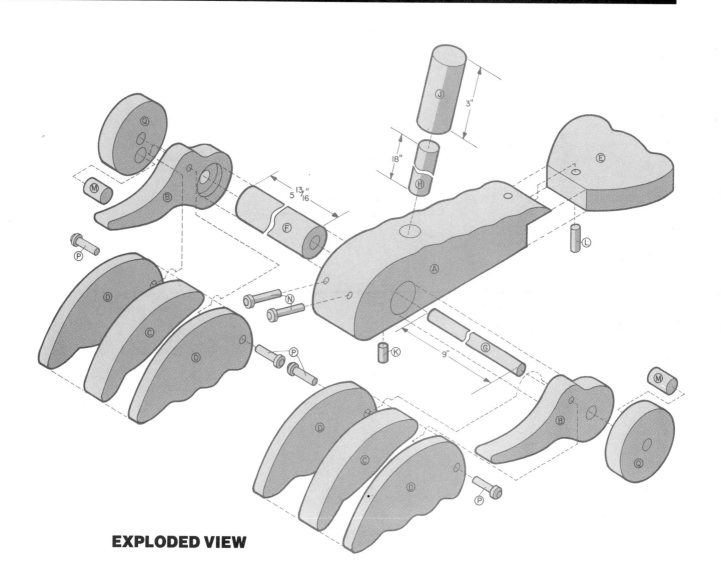

EXPLODED VIEW

121

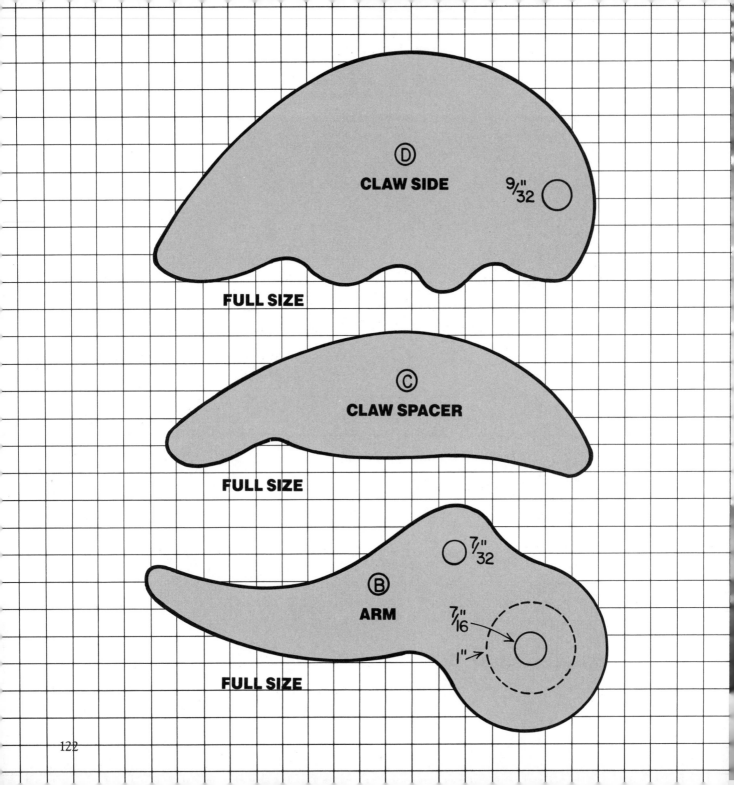

Ⓓ
CLAW SIDE
9/32"

FULL SIZE

Ⓒ
CLAW SPACER

FULL SIZE

7/32"

Ⓑ
ARM

7/16"
1"

FULL SIZE

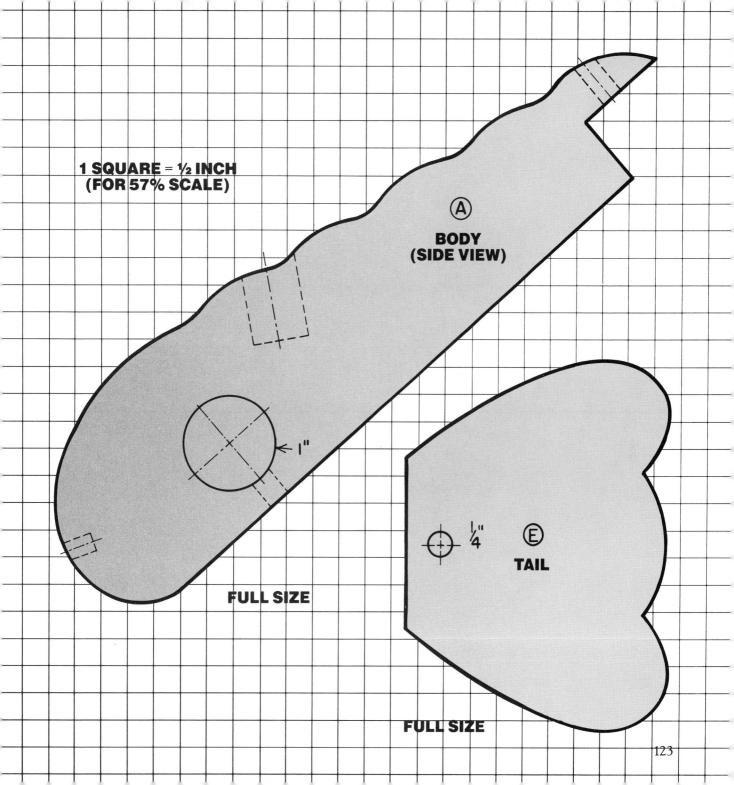

1 SQUARE = ½ INCH
(FOR 57% SCALE)

A
BODY
(SIDE VIEW)

1"

FULL SIZE

¼"

E
TAIL

FULL SIZE

123

The Leaping FROG

This toy is one of my favorites. To my mind it's the consummate frog, replete with amazing leaps and dour expression. The offset axle in the back actually lifts the body; while the feet, being pegged to the wheels, give his leaps the appropriate leg action.

The Body

The Frog's body does not need to be particularly strong, but it does need to be light to jump smoothly. Transfer the body pattern (A) onto a suitable piece of wood. Drill the eye, axle, and peg holes. Cut the eye dowel (D) a little longer than the finished length. Glue it in the eye hole so it protrudes slightly on both sides. Flat sand the protruding dowel off the unpatterned side after the glue has dried.

Now cut out the shape of the body. Make several short cuts around the eye to maintain its spherical outline. Be careful not to cut too close to the rear axle hole or you will weaken it.

To drill the pull cord holes, use clamps and/or blocks to hold the body in the proper position on the drill press table. Drill the ½" hole first and then reposition the body and drill the smaller hole in the chest until it joins the first hole. Now edge sand the body with 80# sandpaper. Sanding around the eye is tricky. Use the edge of the 1" belt to cut into the corners behind and in front of the eye (*See Figure 1*). Then gently smooth out the rest of the curve. Take your time; it's details like the eye that give the Frog a convincing outline. Now flat sand the body and round the edges. Don't forget to sand inside the mouth and to break the edges of the mouth line (*See Figures 2, 3*).

Figure 1. Use the edge of the 1" belt sander to sand the tight corners around the eye. Be careful to maintain the spherical outline of the eye.

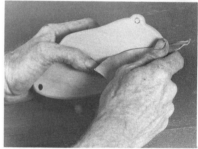

Figures 2 & 3. Sand inside the mouth and break the edges of the mouth line by pulling sandpaper through the mouth upward and then downward.

Figure 2.

Figure 3.

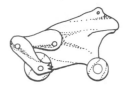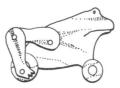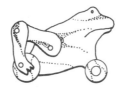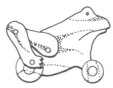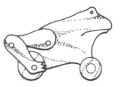

Legs

The legs should be made from a strong wood that compliments the body. Lay out the legs with the grain running lengthwise. Drill all the peg holes, keeping in mind which holes pivot on the pegs (9/32″ holes) and which holes have the pegs glued into them (7/32″ holes). Be careful to keep to the lines as you cut out the feet. If too much material is left below the foot holes, they may touch the ground as the Frog rolls. This will interfere with the Frog's smooth movement. If you remove too much material, the area will be weak. Keep this in mind as you edge sand the leg parts with 80# and then 120# sandpaper.

Flat sand the legs with 80# and then 120# sandpaper. This is a delicate operation. Hold the legs firmly, one at a time, with your fingertips so that the tips of your fingers don't touch the belt (*See Figure 4*). This may seem crazy if you're new to the belt sander but, with time, it will become quite easy. A little moisture on the fingertips will help you grip the wood. If you don't feel comfortable with sanding the legs this way, you can rub them back and forth on a piece of sandpaper on the workbench (*See Figure 5*). With 120#, hand sand the fuzz off the corners where the surfaces meet the sides.

Wheels

Using the wheel jig (*See Techniques and Production Procedures, Figure 17*), drill the offset axle holes and peg holes in the back wheels. Plug the original axle holes and, when the glue is dry, sand off the dowel ends the same way you flat sanded the legs.

Figure 4. Sanding small pieces on the belt sander is easier than it looks. A little water on your fingertips will help you grip the wood. Use a firm grip and a light touch and watch your fingertips.

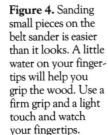

Figure 5. Small pieces can also be sanded by rubbing them back and forth on a piece of sandpaper.

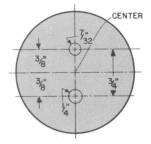

REAR WHEEL

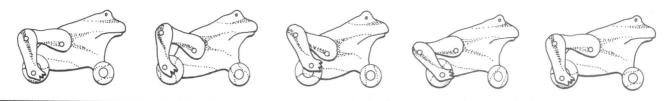

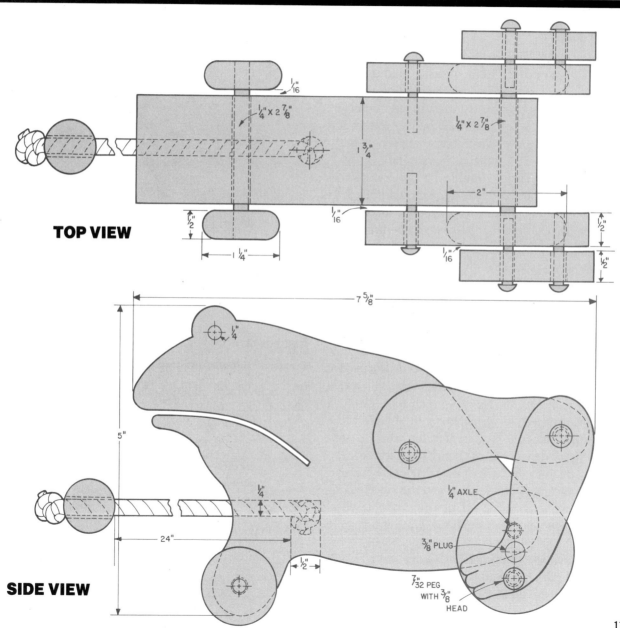

TOP VIEW

$\frac{1}{16}$"

$\frac{1}{4}$" X 2$\frac{7}{8}$"

$\frac{1}{4}$" X 2$\frac{7}{8}$"

1$\frac{3}{4}$"

2"

$\frac{1}{2}$"

$\frac{1}{2}$"

$\frac{1}{2}$"

$\frac{1}{16}$"

1$\frac{1}{4}$"

$\frac{1}{16}$"

7$\frac{5}{8}$"

5"

$\frac{1}{4}$"

$\frac{1}{4}$"

24"

$\frac{1}{2}$"

$\frac{1}{4}$" AXLE

$\frac{3}{8}$" PLUG

$\frac{7}{32}$" PEG
WITH $\frac{3}{8}$"
HEAD

SIDE VIEW

127

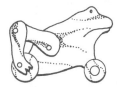

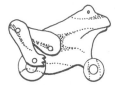

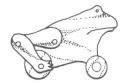

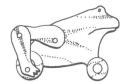

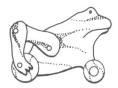

Assembly

Cut the two axles (E, F) to length, leaving them slightly oversized. Glue on the front wheels. Glue the back wheels on, being sure to line up the peg holes so that they are directly opposite each other. Inspect the alignment of the back wheels carefully before you let the glue dry, and make any adjustments that are necessary. When the glue is dry, edge sand the axle ends.

The next step is to assemble the legs. Before you glue the legs together, lay them out on the workbench to make sure you are making two opposite assemblies. Slip a peg through the foot piece and glue it into the bottom of the thigh piece. Repeat for the second leg. When the glue is dry, sand off the axle tip and glue the same way you sanded the individual leg pieces, on the belt sander or on a sheet of sandpaper.

Now, using two pegs, glue and fasten the thighs to the body above the rear wheels. Make sure you're gluing the correct leg on each side. Use the clearance gauge to set the peg depth *(See Techniques and Production Procedures, Figure 28)*, so that the legs will move freely but not sloppily. Now peg each foot, one at a time, to its respective wheel. Put a little glue in the wheel hole. Hold the Frog so that the wheel is supported by the edge of the workbench *(See Figure 6)*. Tap the peg in flush to the back of the wheel, make sure to keep clearance between the foot and the wheel. *Carefully* wipe the excess glue off the back of the wheel before it gets smeared on the body. Glue and peg the second foot.

When all the glue is *thoroughly* dry, your Frog is ready to oil. When the oil is dry, attach the pull cord and there you are. One more Frog on the loose.

Figure 6. Support the wheel on the edge of the workbench as you tap the peg into place.

BILL OF MATERIALS

PART	DESCRIPTION	QTY	THICKNESS	WIDTH OR DIAMETER	LENGTH
A	Body	1	1¾″	5″	6¾″
B	Upper legs	2	½″	1½″	3⅝″
C	Lower legs	2	½″	1½″	3⅝″
D	Eye	1		¼″ dia.	1¾″
E	Rear axle	1		¼″ dia.	2⅞″
F	Front axle	1		¼″ dia.	2⅞″
G	Front wheels	2	½″	1¼″ dia.	
H	Rear wheels	2	½″	2″ dia.	
J	Pegs	6		7/32″ dia.	1 1/16″ shaft
K	Acrylic cord	1		¼″ dia.	26″
L	Bobble	1		⅞″ dia. approx.	

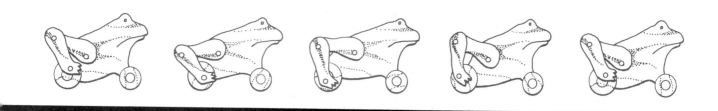

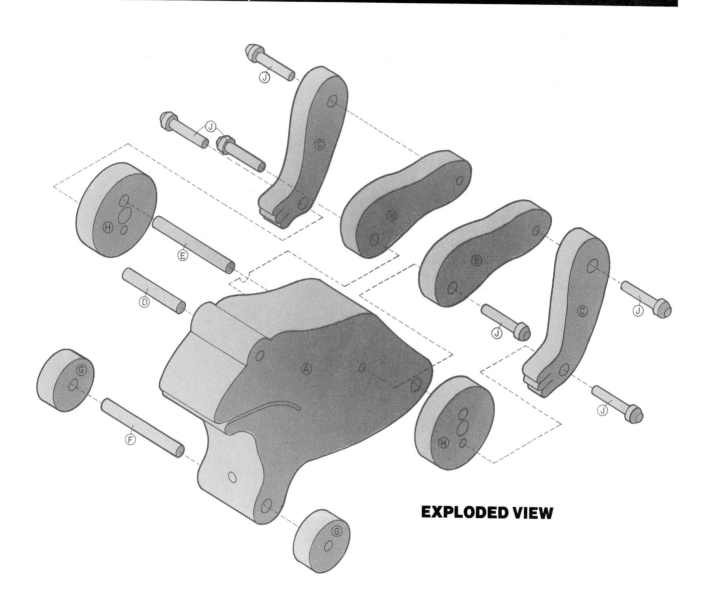

EXPLODED VIEW

129

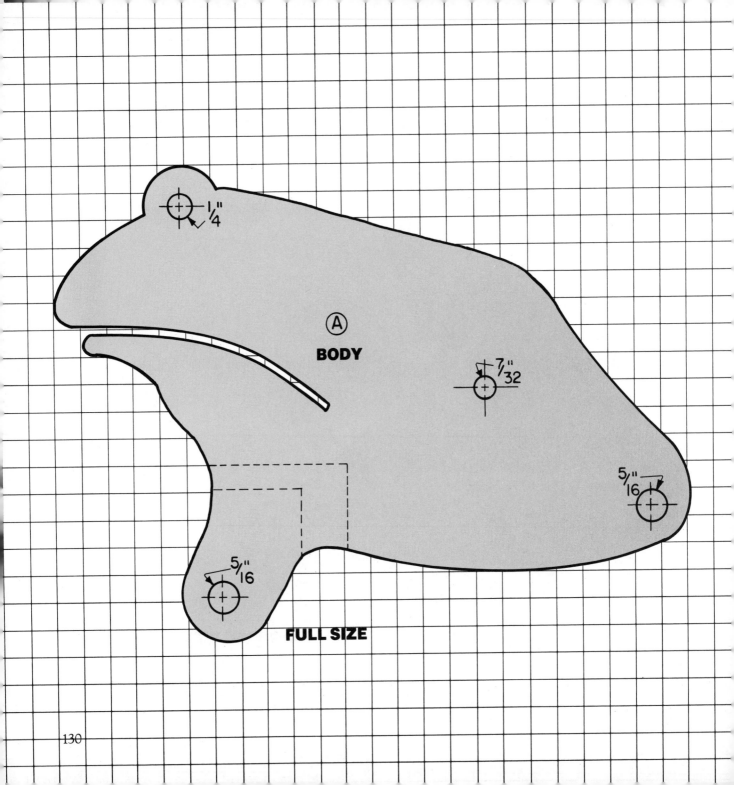

A
BODY

$\frac{1}{4}$"

$\frac{7}{32}$"

$\frac{5}{16}$"

$\frac{5}{16}$"

FULL SIZE

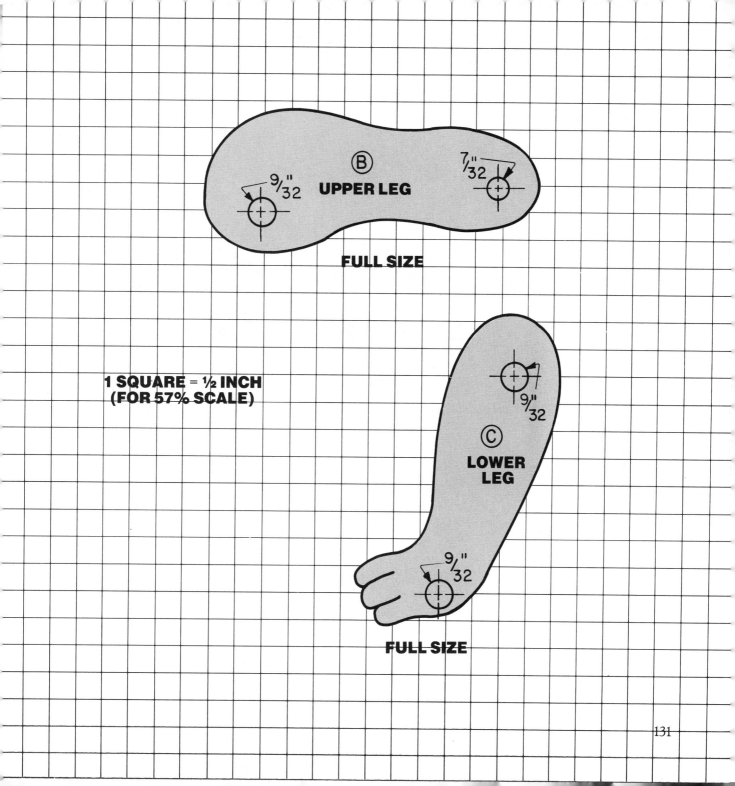

(B) UPPER LEG

9/32" 7/32"

FULL SIZE

1 SQUARE = ½ INCH
(FOR 57% SCALE)

(C) LOWER LEG

9/32"

9/32"

FULL SIZE

131

The Saucy SEAL

When you pull this toy, its simple shape comes to life. It gets its convincing waddle by means of the diagonally opposed offset wheels and its flippers that spin on the ends of the axle.

The Body

There are no special requirements to consider when you're choosing a piece of wood for the Seal's body. Just about anything will do. Transfer the body pattern (A) to a piece of 1¾″ stock. Drill the axle and eye holes. Glue the ¼″ dowel (D) into place, leave it protruding a bit on both sides. When the glue is dry, flat sand the end of the dowel till it's flush to the body on the unpatterned side of the piece.

Next, cut out the body shape. Edge sand it with 80# sandpaper. Flat sand it with 80# and then 120#. Using a block to support the body, position the body at the proper angle on the drill press table and drill the ½″ hole in the back of the Seal's neck. Drill the hole slowly, cleaning it out just before you gently break through. Edge sand the body with 120#. Rout all the edges.

Now, transfer the tail pattern onto the upper surface of the Seal's tail *(See Figure 1)*. Cut the slices out on the bandsaw and round the back corners of the tail. Edge sand the newly sawn areas with 80# and then 120# sandpaper. Smooth out the areas where the new saw cuts meet the previously flat sanded areas *(See Figure 2)*. Now clamp the Seal in your vise with the tail sticking up. Using the curved side of the four-in-hand rasp, round over the edges so that they resemble the routed edges. Smooth these areas with the curved file on the four-in-hand rasp and hand sand the corners with 80# sandpaper. Hand sand all the routed and filed

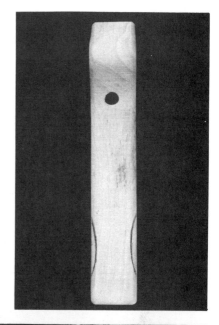

Figure 1. Transfer the tail pattern onto the upper surface of the Seal's tail.

Figure 2. Smooth out the juncture of the already flat sanded sides and the newly sawn areas.

areas with 120#. Hand sand the sawn areas on the tail with 80# and then 120# *with* the grain to remove the vertical sanding marks from the sander/grinder.

Pull Cord

With this particular toy it's necessary to attach the pull cord before assembling the toy. The plug that covers the pull cord must be edge sanded before the flippers are attached. Feed the cord through the hole. Tie an overhand knot in the end sticking out of the ½″ hole. Pull the cord back through the body until the knot seats at the bottom of the hole.

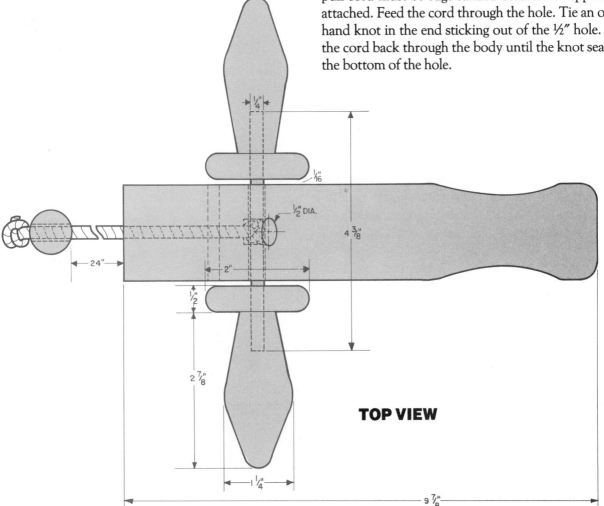

TOP VIEW

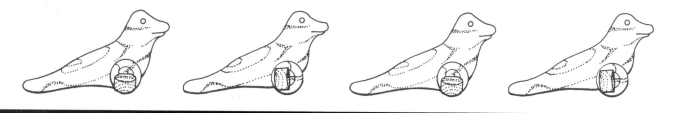

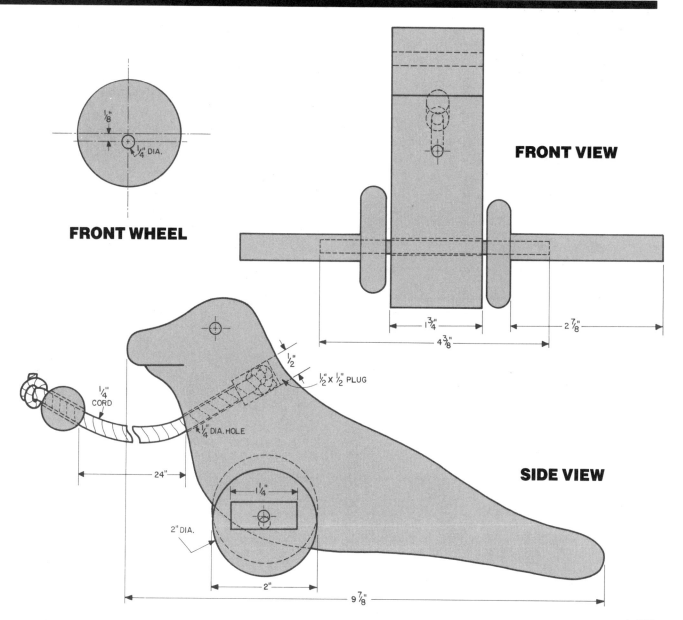

FRONT WHEEL

$\frac{1}{8}$"

$\frac{1}{4}$" DIA.

FRONT VIEW

$1\frac{3}{4}$"

$2\frac{7}{8}$"

$4\frac{3}{8}$"

$\frac{1}{2}$"

$\frac{1}{2}$" X $\frac{1}{2}$" PLUG

$\frac{1}{4}$" CORD

$\frac{1}{4}$" DIA. HOLE

SIDE VIEW

24"

$1\frac{1}{4}$"

2" DIA.

2"

$9\frac{7}{8}$"

135

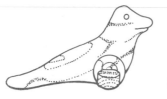 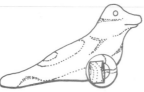  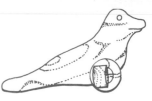

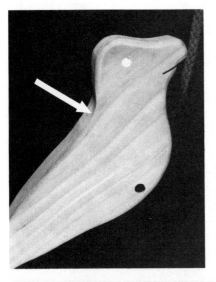

Figure 3. Stop edge sanding the neck area as soon as the dowel is flush with the surface or you'll ruin the finished edge.

Figure 4. Lay out the flippers perpendicular to the end grain. The end that is to be drilled should be flush against the end grain edge.

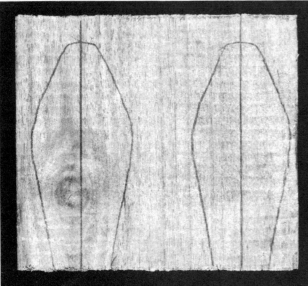

Measure the depth of the hole to the knot. Cut the ½″ dowel (E) to that length. Spread glue on the inside of the hole. Drive the plug in so that it protrudes slightly. When the glue is dry, edge sand the plug end with 80# and then 120# sandpaper, so that it smoothly conforms to the shape of the neck. Don't sand too hard or you'll cut into the routing (*See Figure 3*).

The Flippers

The flippers should be made out of a strong wood. Cut out a perfectly square 3″ x 3″ piece of ½″ stock. Lay out two flippers with the grain running lengthwise. The end of the flipper that is to be drilled should be flush against an end grain edge, and the flippers should be perfectly perpendicular to that edge (*See Figure 4*). Using a center punch or an awl, mark the position of the ¹⁷/₆₄″ holes to be drilled.

Clamp a square-edged 2 x 4 to hold the flipper blank perfectly vertical on the drill press table as you drill the holes (*See Figure 5*). I make these holes slightly oversize to prevent splitting the flippers during assembly. If you don't have a ¹⁷/₆₄″ bit, you can use a ¼″ bit and sand the ¼″ dowel down some before assembly.

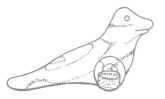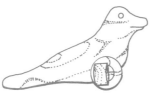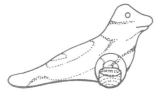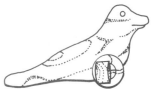

The Wheels

Because the axle location overlaps the true center of the wheel, you'll have to plug the original axle hole and sand it flush before you drill the offset axle hole (*See Techniques and Production Procedures, Figure 17*).

Assembly

Put glue on the inside of one of the flipper's holes. Don't put too much glue in or the dowel won't seat properly. Slip one wheel onto the axle. The outside of the wheel should go first. Put a little glue around the axle next to the flipper. Look at the side view and front view drawings to position the wheel correctly, and slide it up against the flippers. Slip the axle through the body. Holding the whole assembly, carefully put some glue a little further out on the axle than where the wheel should end up. Keep in mind the 1/8" clearance between the body and the wheel. Again consulting the drawings, position the second wheel and slip it on the axle. Remove any glue from the inside of the wheel with a paper match or something similar. Put a little glue on the inside of the other flipper hole. Position it so that both flipper surfaces are perfectly parallel and slip it on. Before the glue dries, roll the Seal and make any adjustments necessary. When the glue is dry, oil the Seal, be careful not to get any oil on the cord. Now tie the bobble on the end of the cord and waddle away!

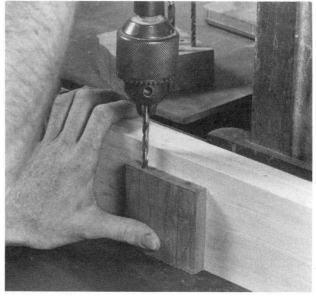

Figure 5. Use a square block to hold the flippers perpendicular to the drill press table as you drill the 17/64" holes.

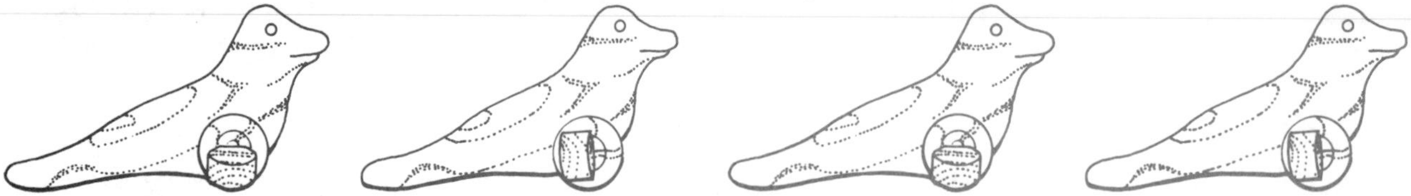

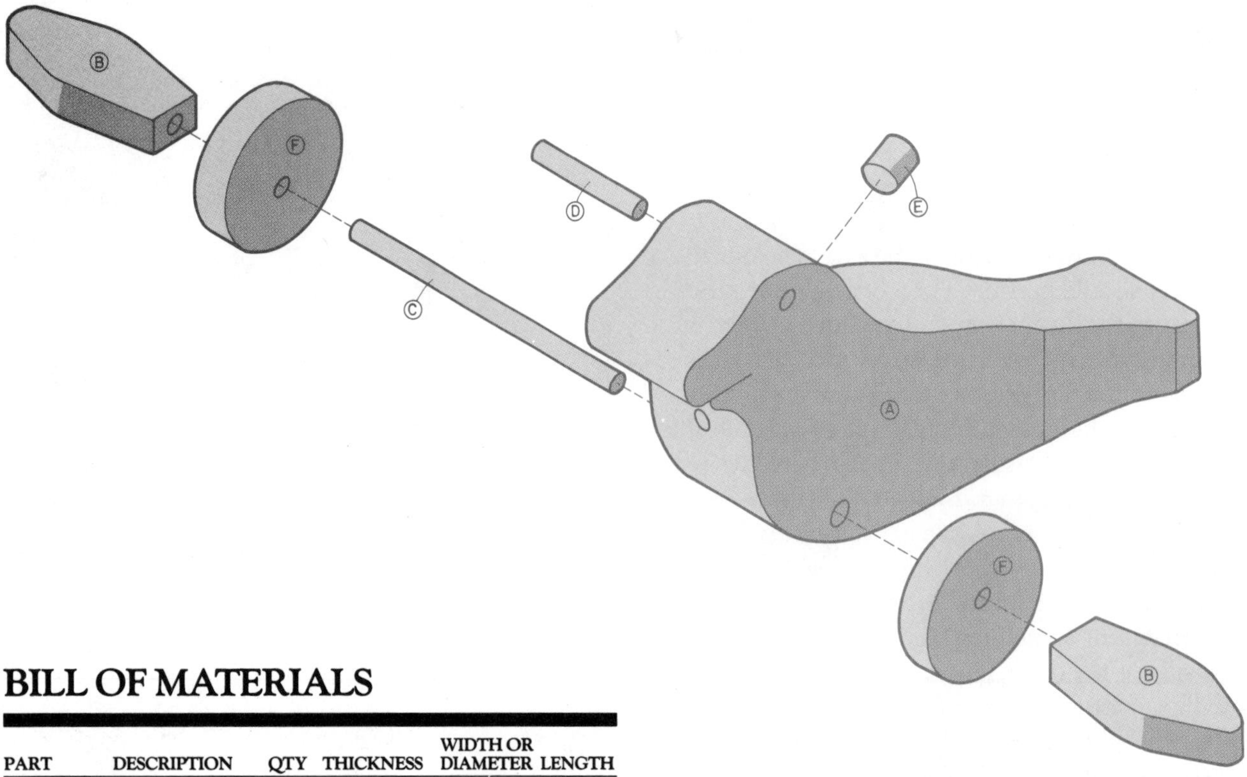

EXPLODED VIEW

BILL OF MATERIALS

PART	DESCRIPTION	QTY	THICKNESS	WIDTH OR DIAMETER	LENGTH
A	Body	1	1¾″	3½″	9⅞″
B	Flippers	2	½″	1¼″	2⅞″
C	Axle	1		¼″ dia.	4⅜″
D	Eye	1		¼″ dia.	1¾″
E	Cord plug	1		½″ dia.	½″ approx.
F	Wheels	2	½″	2″ dia.	
G	Acrylic cord	1		¼″	26″
H	Bobble	1		⅞″ dia.	

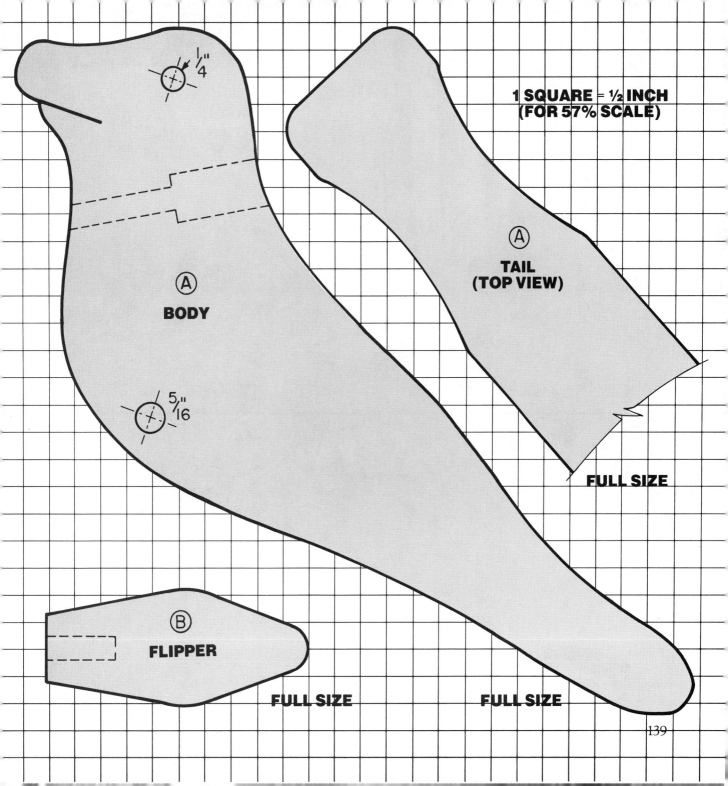

1 SQUARE = ½ INCH
(FOR 57% SCALE)

Ⓐ
TAIL
(TOP VIEW)

FULL SIZE

¼"

Ⓐ
BODY

5/16"

Ⓑ
FLIPPER

FULL SIZE

FULL SIZE

139

The HOUND on the Hunt

The combination of the appearance and the movement of this toy makes it a true classic. The feet, which are pegged to alternate sides of the front wheel, make the Hound trot along as he's pulled.

The feet also push forward on the ears as they pass, lifting the head and giving it that wonderful sniffing motion. The spots are an extra that give the Hound the look of a blue tick hound.

Body

The body (A) can be made out of almost any wood. It doesn't have any critically weak areas, or any need to be particularly heavy or light. Transfer the body pattern (A) onto a suitable piece of wood and drill all the axle, peg, and dowel holes (spots). Do not drill the ⅜" and ½" holes where the hind legs attach; they will be drilled after the hind legs are glued in place.

Glue dowels into all the spot holes. After the glue is dry, flat sand the back of the body to allow the body to sit flat on the bandsaw table. Now cut out the body on the bandsaw. Use blocks and clamps to position the body on the drill press table and drill the pull cord holes. Before you drill the tail hole, cut out the leather for the tail with a mat knife and wrap it around a ⅜" dowel. You will now be able to determine what size hole you'll need to fit the tail and the ⅜" dowel plug snugly (See Figure 1). The hole size will vary according to the thickness of the leather you use (the stiffer the leather the better). Now drill the hole.

Flat sand the body with 80# and then 120# sandpaper. Edge sand it with 80#. Rout all the edges and edge sand with 120#. Hand sand all the routed surfaces with 80# and then 120#.

Legs and Feet

Transfer the patterns for B, C, and D onto a moderately strong piece of wood that will go well with the body. Drill all the axle peg holes and dowel holes, except the two holes on each of the hind legs for attaching them to the body. The holes in the hind legs will be drilled after assembly.

Plug all the "spot" holes. Sand off the back of the dowel ends after they're dry and cut out the parts on the bandsaw. Edge sand all the parts with 80# and 120# sandpaper. Flat sand all the parts with 80# and then 120#, and then hand sand the roughness off all the edges of the front leg parts with 120#. Now rout and sand the hind legs with 80# and 120#.

Peg the front legs in alternate sets, using a clearance gauge (See Techniques and Production Procedures, Figure 28) if necessary. When they're dry, sand off the inside of the shoulder pieces to remove any glue.

Figure 1. Wrap the leather for the tail around a piece of ⅜" dowel and measure how big to make the tail hole. Make the hole just a bit smaller than the actual diameter of the dowel and the leather in order to hold the tail firmly in place.

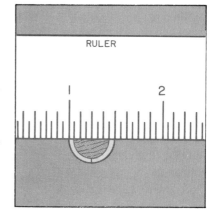

RULER

1   2

The Head

Lay out the patterns for E, F, and G on pieces of strong wood. Cut out the nose (G). Cut out both ears (F), being careful to follow the line perfectly and keep them identical. Drill the peg holes in the head sides (E). Cut out one E piece and lay it on the other E piece to make sure the peg hole location is the same on both pieces, and that they are identical. Flat sand both pieces with 80# sandpaper. Now glue the nose (G) and the two head sides (E) together using the gluing jig *(See Techniques and Production Procedures, Figures 30, 31, 32).* When the assembly is dry, hand sand away excess material, if necessary, and edge sand with 80# and 120#. Flat sand the outsides with 80# and then 120#; make sure to remove any dents from clamping. Hand sand all the edges with 120#.

To attach the ears, make a template (out of hardboard or plywood) of the head with the overlap of the ears removed *(See Figure 2).* Cut this out very carefully. Now using this template, glue on the ears one at a time, making sure that they are perfectly opposed to each other.

Assembly

Peg the head to the body using the clearance gauge *(See Techniques and Production Procedures, Figure 28).* Prepare the front wheels by drilling the peg holes using the drilling jig *(See Techniques and Production Procedures, Figure 17).* Now glue one wheel on the axle. Slip it through the body and glue on the second wheel. Make sure that the peg holes are diagonally opposed, so that one foot will be forward when the other is back. Set the wheels as close to the body as possible so they will fit inside the ears and let the head fall all the way down between sniffs. If they won't fit, file away some of the inside of the ears until they do.

Figure 3. Leave extra material around back of template so it won't break. Use template to position first hind leg, and then line up second leg perfectly with first. Make sure axle is square and spins freely, and then clamp legs, using pads or scraps to protect the surface of the legs.

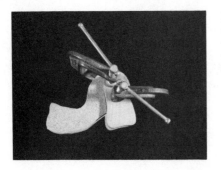

Figure 2. Use this template to position the ears, one at a time, as you glue them.

142

Front Legs

Peg both shoulders to the body using the clearance gauge. Peg the feet to the wheels; use the edge of the workbench to support the wheels as you drive in the pegs. Carefully wipe any excess glue off the inside of the wheels before it gets smeared on the body. To determine the rear axle length, position the rear legs and measure the total distance across both feet, add the thickness of both wheels plus 1/8" clearance, and cut the rear axle to that length.

Attach the rear axle to one of the rear wheels. Run the dowel through both rear feet and glue on the second wheel. When they're dry, edge sand the dowel ends.

Rear Legs

To attach the rear legs, you need to make a template similar to the one used to position the ears. Cut out the shape of the rear of the body with the rear leg overlap removed. Leave a little extra around the back so that the template won't break (*See Figure 3*). Now glue and clamp the rear legs using the jig you've made to align

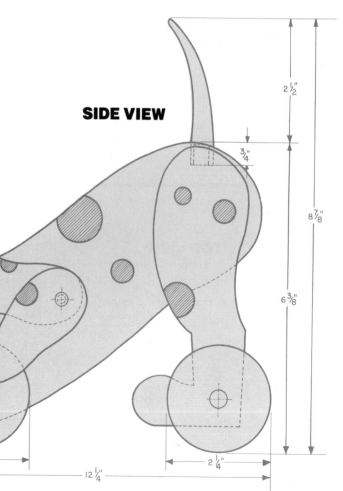

SIDE VIEW

143

them properly. Make sure the nose is just off the ground as you glue the legs or it will rub the floor when it's finished. Check to be sure the axle is perpendicular and lets the wheels spin freely. When the glue is dry, drill the holes through the body and both legs. Remember to put a scrap under your work to avoid tear-out when the bit breaks out the back. Now glue the dowels into place. Sand off the ends of the dowels by hand with 80# and then 120# sandpaper.

The Tail

Spread glue in the tail hole. Next, spread glue ¾" up from the bottom of the tail leather, on both inside and outside. Roll up the leather and place it in the tail hole.

Carefully place the ⅜" plug inside the leather in the hole. Now drive the plug home using another piece of ⅜" dowel to avoid squishing the leather with the hammer. When you oil the Hound, don't get oil on the tail as it will get stiff when the oil dries.

Now attach the pull cord and there you go. A child's best friend!

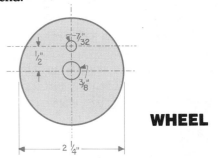

WHEEL

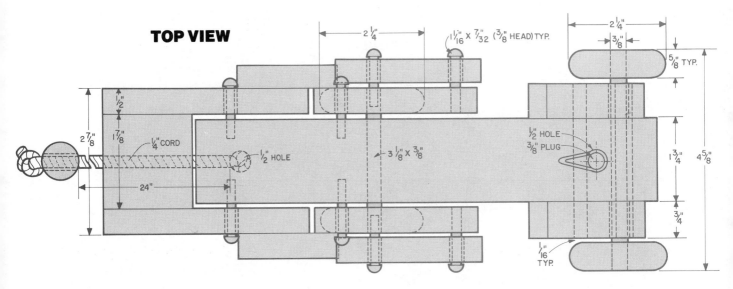

TOP VIEW

144

EXPLODED VIEW

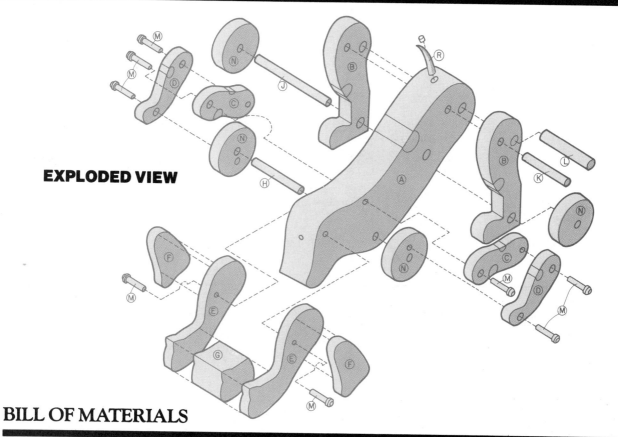

BILL OF MATERIALS

PART	DESCRIPTION	QTY	THICKNESS	WIDTH OR DIAMETER	LENGTH
A	Body	1	1¾″	4″	11½″
B	Rear legs	2	¾″	2½″	6″
C	Upper front legs	2	½″	1½″	3¾″
D	Lower front legs	2	½″	1½″	3¾″
E	Head sides	2	½″	2½″	6″
F	Ears	2	½″	2″	3¼″
G	Head spacer	1	1⅛″	1¾″	2″
H	Front axle	1		⅜″ dia.	3⅛″

PART	DESCRIPTION	QTY	THICKNESS	WIDTH OR DIAMETER	LENGTH
J	Rear axle	1		⅜″ dia.	4⅝″
K	Rear leg dowel	1		⅜″ dia.	3¼″
L	Rear leg dowel	1		½″ dia.	3¼″
M	Pegs	8		7/32″ dia.	1 1/16″
N	Wheels	4	⅝″	2½″ dia.	
P	Acrylic cord	1		¼″ dia.	26″
Q	Bobble	1	⅞″ approx.		
R	Leather	1		1¼″	3-¼″

145

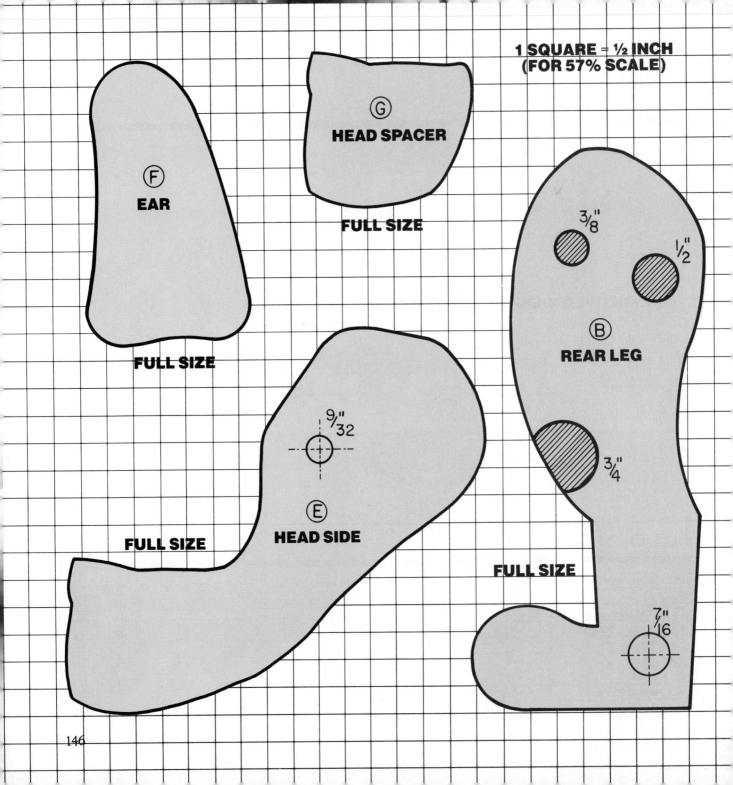

1 SQUARE = ½ INCH
(FOR 57% SCALE)

Ⓖ
HEAD SPACER

FULL SIZE

Ⓕ
EAR

FULL SIZE

3/8"

1/2"

Ⓑ
REAR LEG

9/32"

Ⓔ
HEAD SIDE

FULL SIZE

3/4"

FULL SIZE

FULL SIZE

7/16"

146

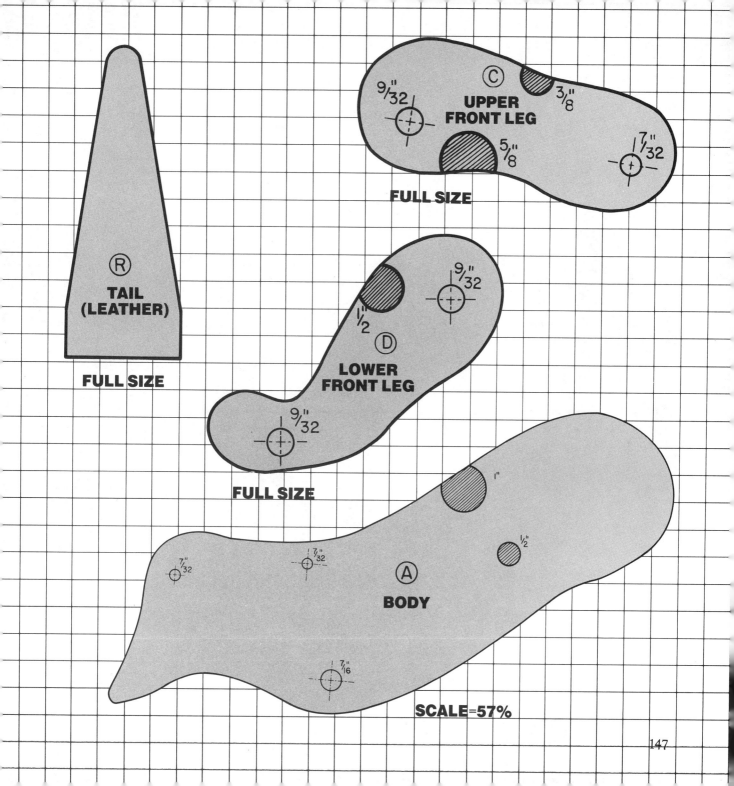

TAIL
(LEATHER)

Ⓡ

FULL SIZE

Ⓒ
UPPER
FRONT LEG

9/32"

3/8"

5/8"

7/32"

FULL SIZE

9/32"

1/2"

Ⓓ
LOWER
FRONT LEG

9/32"

FULL SIZE

1"

1/2"

7/32"

7/32"

Ⓐ
BODY

7/16"

SCALE=57%

147

Fanciful BEASTIES

These anachronistically Fanciful Beasties are simple to make and a great way to use up scraps. You can experiment to see which species of wood you prefer to burn on, but most any wood will give good results, except dark woods such as walnut.

Find a scrap big enough to fit the creature you've chosen. I use ¾" stock because it seems proportionate, but also because it's what I have the most of. Any thickness within reason will do.

Flat sand the scrap piece (A) on both sides with 80# and then 120# sandpaper. Use carbon paper and a stylus to transfer the image onto one side of A. Drill the axle holes. Use the axle holes to locate the pattern on the reverse side and transfer the image onto A. Using your woodburning tools, burn the image into both sides of A. Now cut the Beast out on the bandsaw leaving an even border (see side view). Edge sand with 80# and 120#. Hand sand all the rough edges with 120#. Glue the wheels to the axles. When the glue is dry, edge sand the dowel ends. Oil the Beast and "let 'er roll!"

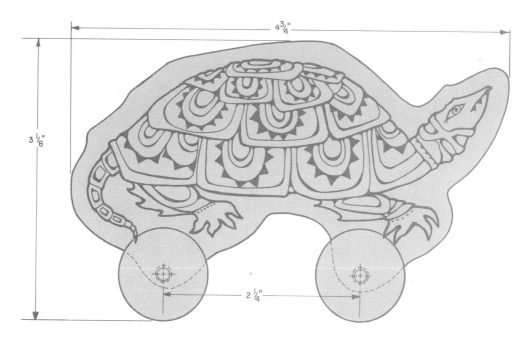

SIDE VIEW

149

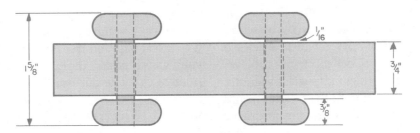

TOP VIEW

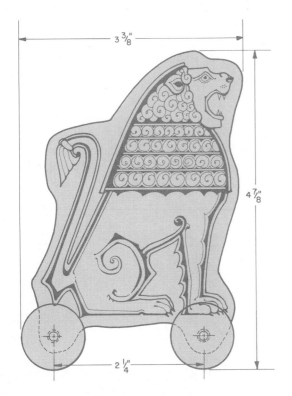

SIDE VIEW

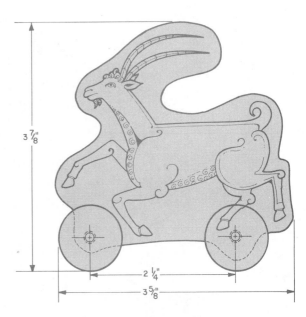

SIDE VIEW

150

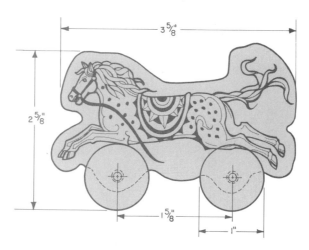

SIDE VIEW

NOTE: All wheels are 1″ x ⅜″. Axles are ¼″, with ⁵⁄₁₆″ holes in bodies.

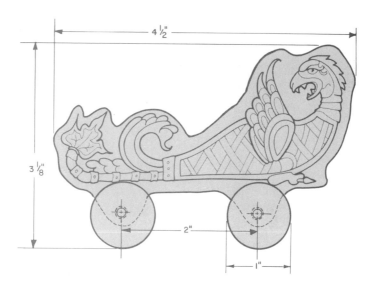

SIDE VIEW

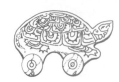

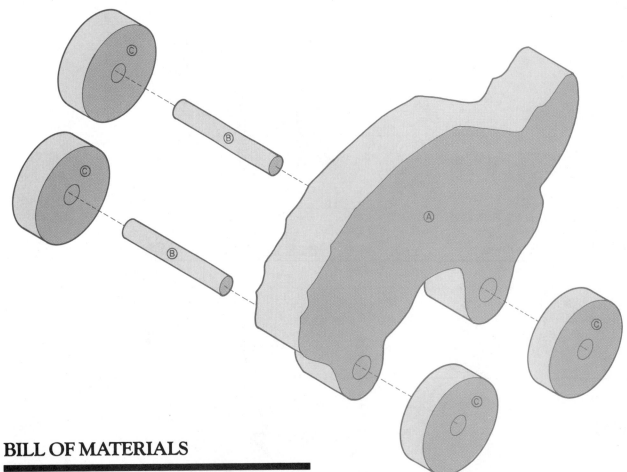

BILL OF MATERIALS

PART	DESCRIPTION	QTY	THICKNESS	WIDTH OR DIAMETER	LENGTH
A	Body	1	½"–1"	Variable	Variable
B	Dowels	2		¼" dia.	Body thickness plus ⅞"
C	Wheels	4	⅜"	1" dia.	

EXPLODED VIEW

1 SQUARE = ½ INCH
(FOR 57% SCALE)

FULL SIZE
IMAGE PATTERNS

Woodburn drawings by Alexandra Eldridge.

153

A Variety of VEHICLES

The Bouncing BUS

This is a fairly simple toy to make but the results are quite pleasing. A cam on both the front and rear axles lifts a hidden piece of wood which bounces the passengers and driver up and down as the Bus is pulled or pushed. The passengers and driver are removable and the window holes make for easy gripping by small fingers. It's a great toy for little crawlers.

Most woods will do for this toy. Don't use a fibrous wood like poplar or aspen, however, as the large holes will end up fuzzy and rough.

Transfer the body pattern (A) onto a suitable piece of wood. Cut it out in the shape of a rectangle rather than following the curves (*See Figure 1*). The final shape will be cut out after the two small fillers (B, C) are in place. Locate the 1″ holes in the top of the Bus and drill them with a spade bit, making sure you drill them deeper than the top of the slot that is to be cut in the bottom.

Locate and mark the centers of the 1$\frac{1}{16}$″ holes so that they correspond perfectly with the 1″ holes that you've drilled. Clamp the body down securely and drill the 1$\frac{1}{16}$″ window holes with a multispur bit to cut smoothly through the other holes. Drill the axle holes.

Now, cut the ¾″ x 1⅞″ slot in the bottom of the Bus. This can be done on the table saw with a dado blade or with several passes over a rip or combination blade (*See Figure 2*).

Cut out the filler pieces (B, C). If you're going to attach a cord to your Bus, drill the pull cord holes in the end grain surface of B. Now, glue and clamp these pieces in place, making sure that B is in the front with the ½″ hole facing inward. When they're dry, cut out the exact shape of the Bus.

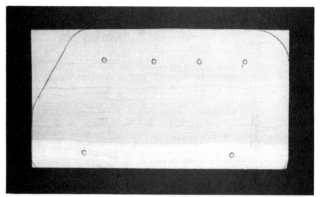

Figure 1. Cut out a rectangle which encompasses the Bus body. The final shape will be cut out after B and C are glued in place.

Figure 2. The easiest way to cut out the slot is with a set of dado blades. This must be done in three passes, removing ⅓ of the material with each pass. This is the third pass.

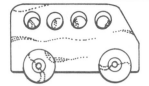
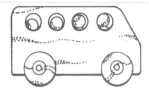
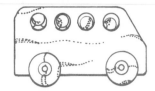
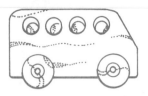

Figure 3. When you rout the top edges of the Bus, use the side of the Bus for your roller bearing support. If you lay the Bus on its side to rout this edge, the roller bearing will slip into the top holes and tear them up.

Flat sand with 80# and then 120# sandpaper. Edge sand with 80#. Rout all the edges, including all the large holes, top, and sides (*See Figure 3*). Routing the inside edges of the dado slot is not necessary. Sand the holes with a small drum sander or a dowel with sandpaper wrapped around it. Hand sand all the routed edges with 80# and then 120#.

Cut out the lifting bar (D). Flat sand the long sides with 80# sandpaper and edge sand the short ends with 80#. Hand sand all the edges and corners with 80#.

Assembly

Put the Bus on its back on the workbench and drop the lifting bar (D) into place. To cut the axles to length, measure the actual width of your sanded Bus. Add the thickness of the two wheels, 1/8" for clearance, and 1/32" for the slightly protruding axle ends to be sanded flush to the wheel hub. Position the cams in the slot, and slide the axles into place through the cams until they are

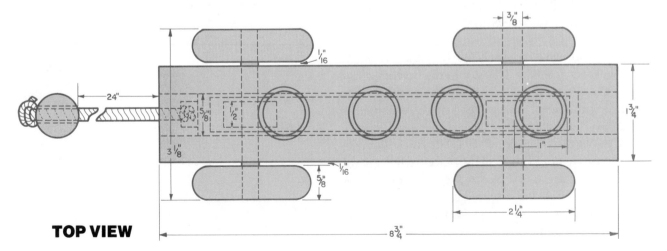

TOP VIEW

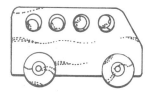
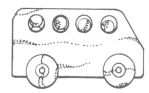
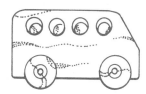
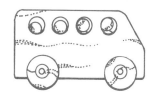

perfectly centered. With the greater part of the cams hanging below the axle (so they won't tend to move as you drill them), drill a ⅛″ hole through each cam and its corresponding axle (*See Figure 4*). Glue in the ⅛″ pre-cut dowels. Glue the wheels on and let them dry. Edge sand the axle ends flush to the wheel hubs.

Finishing

Finish the Bus and the people with either Danish oil, latex paint, or food coloring and then oil. A brightly colored Bus with painted people makes quite an attractive toy.

When the finish is dry, attach the pull cord (if you've planned for one) and it's off to the next bus stop to pick up or discharge passengers.

Figure 4. With most of the cam hanging below the axle, drill the ⅛″ peg holes.

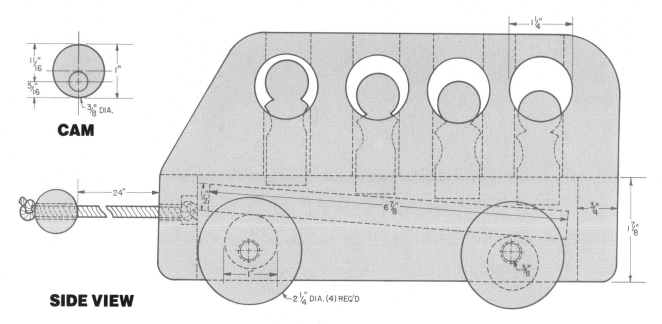

CAM

SIDE VIEW

159

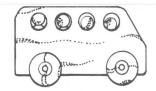

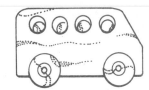

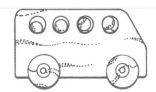

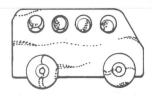

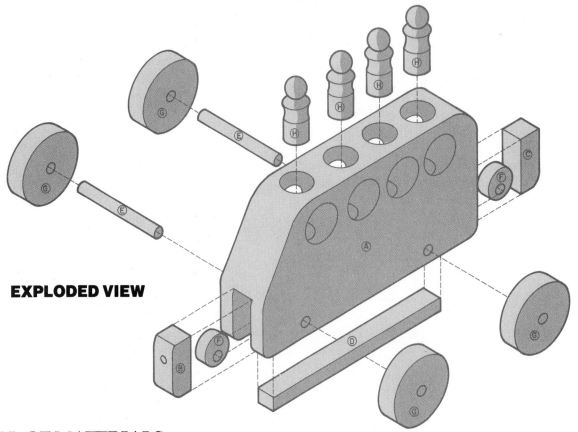

EXPLODED VIEW

BILL OF MATERIALS

PART	DESCRIPTION	QTY	THICKNESS	WIDTH OR DIAMETER	LENGTH
A	Body	1	1¾″	4″	8¾″
B	Front filler	1	¾″	¾″	1⅞″
C	Rear filler	1	¾″	¾″	1⅞″
D	Lifting bar	1	½″	⅝″	6⅞″
E	Axles	2		⅜″ dia.	3⅛″
F	Cams	2	½″	1″ dia.	
G	Wheels	4	⅝″,	2¼″ dia.	
H	People	4		⅞″ dia.	2¼″
J	Acrylic cord (optional)	1		¼″ dia.	24″
K	Bobble (optional)	1		⅞″ dia.	

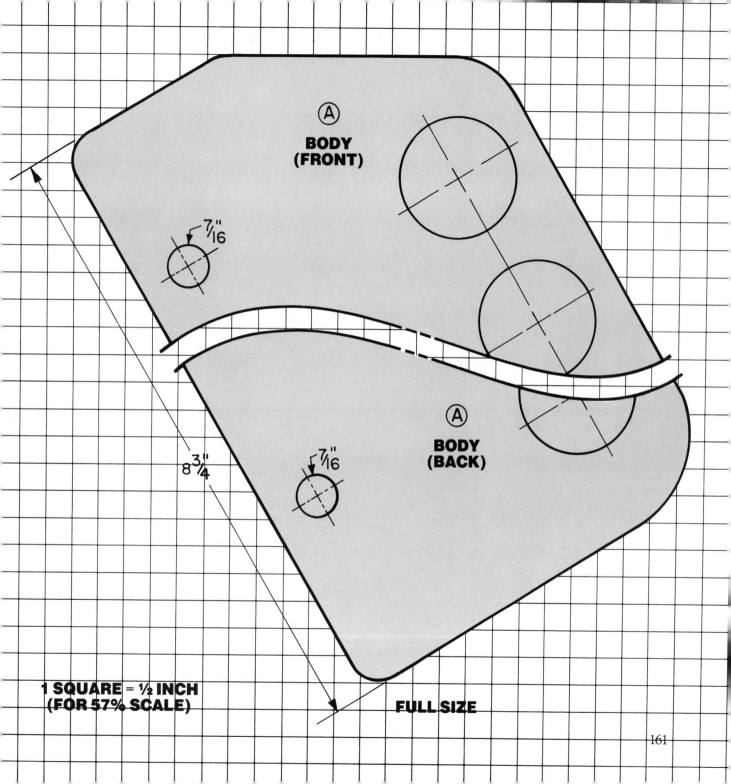

Ⓐ
**BODY
(FRONT)**

$\frac{7}{16}''$

$8\frac{3}{4}''$

Ⓐ
**BODY
(BACK)**

$\frac{7}{16}''$

**1 SQUARE = ½ INCH
(FOR 57% SCALE)**

FULL SIZE

161

The Gay Nineties HANDCAR

I think everyone, at one time or another, has looked at the Handcar with fascination. There's something almost magical about the way it flies along the tracks under manpower. The delicate burns and small parts of this Handcar, combined with its fluid reciprocating motion, put it high on the list of my favorites. The people on this toy would look great painted, too! Try food coloring, it'll let the grain of the wood show through.

The Car

Cut a 3" x 1¼" rectangle out of 1¾" stock. Make sure all the edges are perfectly square. Mark the arches and the axle holes. Drill the axle holes. Now stand the block on its rear end and locate the pull cord hole. Holding the block vertical and square on the drill press, drill the pull cord hole. Cut the arches out and save them to use when clamping the people in place later. Drill the ½" hole in the top front for the pull cord knot.

I use a 2" multispur bit to remove the drive area. If you don't have a multispur bit, drill four ½" holes all the way through the body at the corners of the drive area and cut the material out with a coping saw or a jigsaw. Clean the hole out neatly with a four-in-hand rasp. Flat sand all the sides with 80# sandpaper. Sand the arches on the roller end of the belt sander. Be careful not to dig the sharp bottom edge of the arch into the belt or it may catch and rip the belt. Rout all the edges (including the drive area hole); be careful as you pass the pull cord hole in the front. Flat sand again with 120#, and hand sand any burns or roughness with 80# and then all the routed edges with 120#. Locate and drill the ⅜" hole for securing the fulcrum piece (B).

The Rocker Arm

Transfer the rocker arm pattern (C) to a piece of ¾" stock with the grain running lengthwise. Drill the two ⁷⁄₁₆" holes and the two ⁵⁄₁₆" holes oversize so the dowels will pivot freely. Cut the part out on the bandsaw. Flat sand it with 80# and 120# sandpaper. Edge sand it with 80#. If you're good with the router, rout all the way around both sides of the piece and then edge sand again with 120#. If you have any doubts at all, edge sand it with 120# and break the edges with a four-in-hand rasp and/or sandpaper. Sand all burns or roughness with 80# and then sand all the edges with 120#.

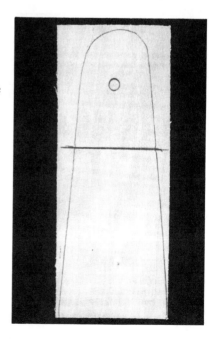

Figure 1. Lay out the fulcrum pattern on a rectangle with the bottom edge flush to an end grain edge. This will enable you to drill the ⅜" hole in the bottom and cut the notch easily.

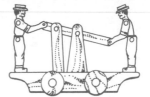

The Fulcrum

Cut a 1½" x 3⅞" rectangle out of 1¾" stock. Transfer the pattern for the fulcrum (B) to the piece, making sure the flat bottom edge is flush against a square end grain edge (*See Figure 1*). Locate, mark, and drill the ⅜" hole in the bottom as well as the ⅜" hole for the rocker arm. Now lay the block on its side and mark the bottom of the notch on both sides of the piece. Set the rip fence on the bandsaw to ⅜" and saw to this line. Flip the block over and repeat.

Remove the rip fence and cut across the bottom of the notch to remove it. A curved pass from either side will do it. Now slowly cut out the shape of the fulcrum. Flat sand it with 80# and then 120# sandpaper. Edge sand with 80#.

Here again, if you're comfortable with the router, rout around both sides of the outline (not the bottom edge) and edge sand with 120# sandpaper. If you're apprehensive, round over the edge with the four-in-hand rasp and/or sandpaper. Next, smooth roughness or burns by hand with 80# and then hand sand all the edges with 120#. Depending on your sander, you may need to do this on the back half of the belt (*See Figure 2*).

The Pitman Arm

Lay out the pitman arm pattern (D) on a 1¾" piece of stock. Drill the upper hole (⅜" for snug fit) and the lower hole (5/16" for pivot). Flat sand with 80# and

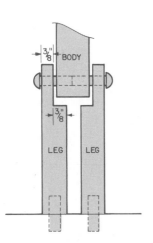

PERSON

FULCRUM

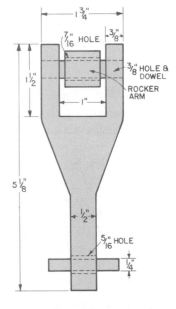

PITMAN ARM

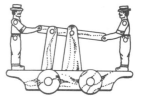

120# sandpaper. Edge sand with 80# and 120#. Once more, if you're comfortable with the router, rout the outline on both sides. If not, wait on the rounding over until you've cut it out entirely.

Cut the notch out of the top (use the same procedure as for the fulcrum). Mark a line across both sides of the piece at the point where the bottom starts getting wider. Set the rip fence to remove ⅝″ and saw up to the line. Flip it over and repeat. Now mark the rest of the curve from the tongue to the outsides of the upper part of the arm. Remove the rip fence and saw these sides off. Edge sand these sawn areas with 80# and 120# sandpaper. Round over the edges with the router and/or the four-in-hand rasp. Hand sand the edges with 80# and 120#. Hand sand the edge-sanded tapers to remove the edge sander marks.

The People

Round up enough ½″ stock to make all eight arms and legs, and enough ¾″ stock to make both bodies. Flat sand both sides with 80# and then 120# sandpaper. Transfer the images (including the hole locations). Drill the holes (⁷⁄₃₂″ in the body, ⁹⁄₃₂″ in the shoulders and hips, and ¼″ in the hands).

Now carefully burn the images on one side. The flip side of the bodies will have to be burned after they're cut out (to locate the image properly). Cut the pieces out very carefully; try to leave a consistent thickness of space around all the lines. Don't cut right up to the line; it won't look as good. Make sure you cut perfectly straight across the bottom of the feet for secure gluing.

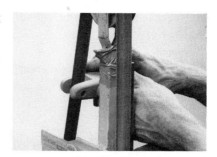

Figure 2. Depending on the type of edge sander you have, you may have to sand the sides of the notch on the back half of the belt.

Secure each leg (one at a time or together) on the drill press with the sole of the foot parallel to the drill press table. Locate, center punch, and drill the ¼″ holes in the bottom of the feet.

With the rip fence on the bandsaw, cut the notches out of the legs. Now carefully edge sand all the pieces with 120# sandpaper (using 80# is likely to take away too much material). Break the edges by hand with 120#, be careful not to sand off the burns.

To assemble the people, cut the pegs to length (*See Techniques and Production Procedures, Figure 14*). Round over the ends. Put glue in the body holes. Peg the arm and leg on one side using the clearance gauge (*See Techniques and Production Procedures, Figure 28*). Do not tap them all the way in or they won't pivot. Now rest the body on a scrap so that when you tap on the second arm and leg, you don't push the opposing pegs in (*See Figure 3*).

Assembly

Put dowel centers in the holes in the feet of one of the people. Carefully locate the person and press the feet down to locate the ¼″ holes on the car. Repeat for the

165

other person, keeping track of which person is at which end, as the hole locations will probably be slightly different. If you don't have dowel centers, position the person and, with a sharp pencil, outline the feet and measure the location of the holes on the feet to mark the location on the car. Remember you are reversing

Figure 3. Use a scrap to support the body as you tap on the second arm and leg or you will push the opposing pegs in too far as you hammer.

the feet as you flip them soles upward to measure the hole location. Repeat for the other person and drill all four ¼″ holes.

Now glue the ¼″ dowels (with the ends rounded over) into the holes in the car. Apply glue to the soles of the feet and in the holes, and place the people in their respective positions with the car in a vise. With the top of the body bent forward, place a small scrap on each person's waist. Position the arches that you cut away from the car in their respective positions and, using C-clamps, clamp the two people down. Make sure both feet are clamped flat to the car.

As the glue dries, you can assemble the fulcrum (B), rocker arm (C), and the pitman arm (D). Using the wheel jig (*See Techniques and Production Procedures,*

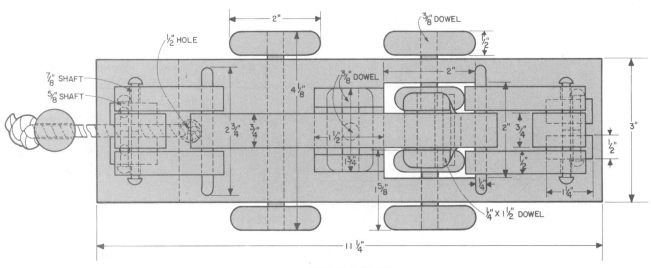

TOP VIEW

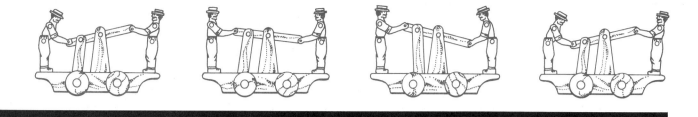

Figure 17), drill the ¼″ holes for the ¼″ dowel that joins the two 1½″ pitman arm drive wheels (S). Ream the axle hole out to ⅜″ with a twist drill (holding the wheels with pliers). Glue the ¼″ dowel in one wheel, slip the pitman arm on and glue the other wheel on. Make sure the two wheels are perfectly opposed.

Now lay the pitman arm (D) and the fulcrum (B) side by side with the rocker arm (C) in position. Tap the two ⅜″ pivot dowels (J) (cut to the exact length with the ends sanded) in until they start into the holes on the opposite side. Then put a *little* glue around the dowel

DRIVE WHEEL

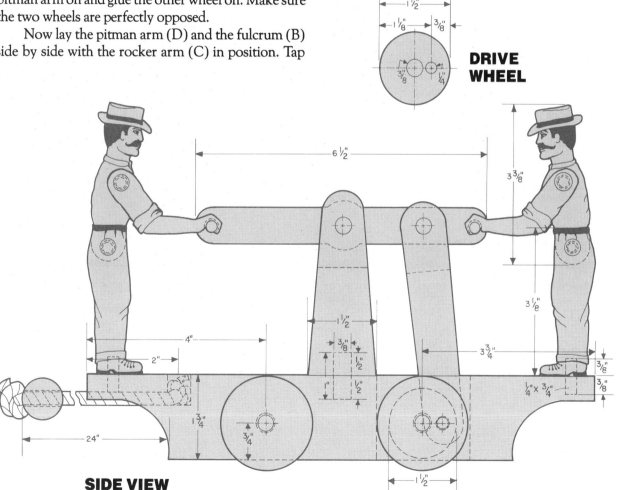

SIDE VIEW

167

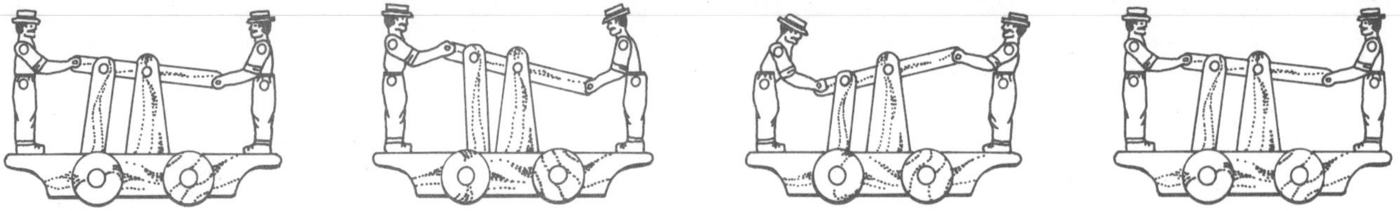

ends that still protrude and drive them home. Wipe off the excess glue and sand these areas after the glue has dried.

When the people have thoroughly dried, unclamp them and pivot the bodies back out of the way. Glue the ⅜″ fulcrum locator dowel (P) into the center of the car to attach and position the fulcrum assembly. Apply glue to the bottom of the fulcrum. (Keep glue away from the edges to avoid squeeze-out.) Clamp the assembly in place, making sure that all its edges are firmly pressed against the top of the car.

When the assembly is thoroughly dry, glue on the front wheels (T). Cut the two shorter rear axles (K) to length and round off the ends. Now apply a little glue in the ⅜″ axle holes of the pitman arm drive wheels (S). Hold the wheels firmly and start the dowel into the hole by twisting it in. Once again, supporting the 1½″ wheel (S) with your hand, glue and hammer the 2″ wheels (T) onto the protruding axles. When they are dry, edge sand all four axle hubs. Cut the two handlebars (N) to length and round off the ends on the belt sander *(See Techniques and Production Procedures, Figure 24)*. Hand sand the entire length of the handlebars until they can be twisted through the people's hands, yet still be held snugly. They shouldn't need to be glued. Make sure that you spread the hands a little so the rocker arm can move freely.

When all the glue is thoroughly dry (24 hours), oil the Handcar. Attach the pull cord and there you have it. A fine example of several of the best features of a quality wooden toy; delicate lines, concise imagery, and simple fluid movement.

BILL OF MATERIALS

PART	DESCRIPTION	QTY	THICKNESS	WIDTH OR DIAMETER	LENGTH
A	Car body	1	1¾″	3″	11¼″
B	Fulcrum	1	1¾″	1½″	3⅞″
C	Rocker arm	1	¾″	1″	6½″
D	Pitman arm	1	1¾″	1″	5⅛″
E	Abdomen	2	¾″	1⅜″	3⅜″
F	Legs	4	½″	1¼″	3⅛″
G	Arms	4	½″	1⅛″	2¾″
H	Pitman arm drive dowel	1		¼″ dia.	1½″
J	Pivot dowels	2		⅜″ dia.	1¾″
K	Pitman arm drive wheel axles	2		⅜″ dia.	1⅝″
L	Free wheel axles	2		⅜″ dia.	4⅛″

PART	DESCRIPTION	QTY	THICKNESS	WIDTH OR DIAMETER	LENGTH
M	Foot locators	4		¼″ dia.	¾″
N	Handlebars	2		¼″ dia.	2¾″
P	Fulcrum locator	1		⅜″ dia.	1″
Q	Shoulder pegs	4		7/32″ dia. shaft	15/16″ shaft
R	Leg pegs	4		7/32″ dia.	⅝″ shaft
S	Pitman arm drive wheels	2	½″	1½″ dia.	
T	Wheels	4	½″	2″ dia.	
U	Acrylic cord	1		¼″ dia.	26″
V	Pull handle	1		⅞″ dia.	

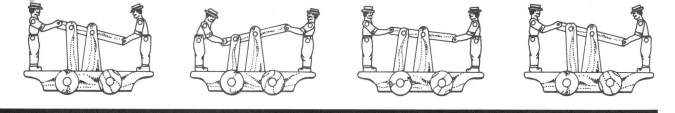

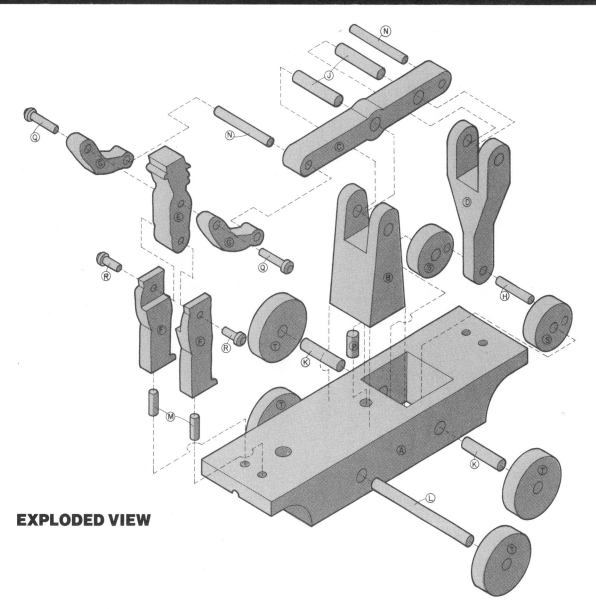

EXPLODED VIEW

169

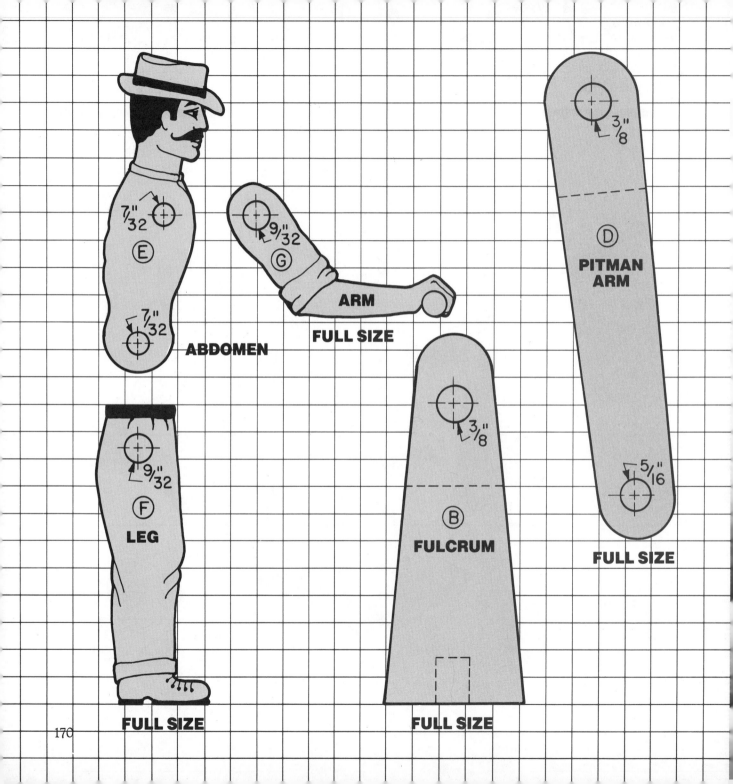

7/32"

E

7/32"

ABDOMEN

9/32"

G

ARM

FULL SIZE

3/8"

D

**PITMAN
ARM**

9/32"

F

LEG

FULL SIZE

3/8"

B

FULCRUM

5/16"

FULL SIZE

FULL SIZE

170

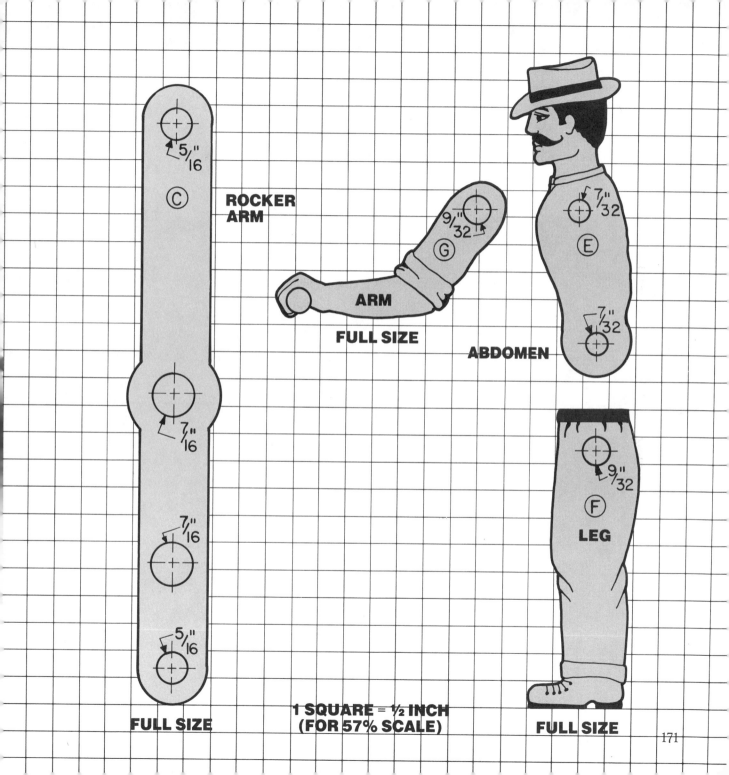

ROCKER
ARM

$\frac{5}{16}$"

C

$\frac{7}{16}$"

$\frac{7}{16}$"

$\frac{5}{16}$"

FULL SIZE

ARM

$\frac{9}{32}$"

G

FULL SIZE

$\frac{7}{32}$"

E

$\frac{7}{32}$"

ABDOMEN

LEG

$\frac{9}{32}$"

F

1 SQUARE = ½ INCH
(FOR 57% SCALE)

FULL SIZE

171

The PANEL TRUCK Collection

These toys have no action built into them, other than rolling. The burned-on logos that you choose and the cargo that the Trucks carry give them their character.

Hardwood is best for these toys, because a softer, more fibrous wood tends to "fuzz up" after it's drilled. This roughness in the 1″ hole in the back prevents the cargo from slipping easily in and out. Also, if you use hardwood, the windshield area will look much cleaner. Bear in mind that the burns don't show up very well on walnut.

Transfer the body pattern (A) onto a suitable piece of stock. Make sure you mark the center of the 1″ circle which will form the windshield and canopy. Drill this hole and the axle holes. Cut out the body shape. Try to get a smooth line where the windshield and canopy hole meets the hood line.

Clamp the body between two blocks of wood to hold it in the proper position for drilling the 1⅛″ hole in the back of the Truck. Drill this hole and leave the body in the jig for sanding. Sand the hole with a drum sander.

Next, draw and cut out the appropriate cargo for the back of the Truck. Let your imagination take over here. You can put anything in the back of these Panel Trucks as long as it will fit within a 1⅛″ circle (see end view of cargo objects).

Cut out the cargo object on the bandsaw. If you're nervous cutting out such small pieces on the bandsaw, use a coping saw (*See Figure 1*). The same applies to edge and flat sanding. Simply hand sand the cargo.

Now that all the parts are cut out, edge sand everything with 80# sandpaper. The 1″ window hole can be sanded with a small drum sander, or a dowel with sandpaper wrapped around it. Flat sand with 80# and then 120#. Next, rout both sides of the radiator top, hood, and windshield outline. Edge sand the body with 120# and hand sand any roughness or router burns with 80#. Then hand sand all the edges of the Truck body and the cargo for the back with 120#.

Figure 1. If sawing small objects on the bandsaw makes you uncomfortable, cut them out with a coping saw.

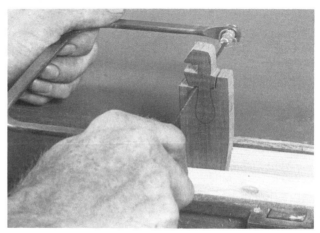

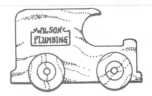 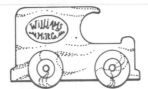 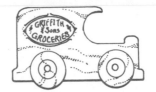 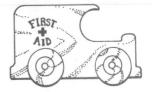

Burning

Transfer the logo onto both sides of the Truck with carbon paper and a stylus. Then use your woodburning tool to reproduce the logo on the sides of the Panel Truck.

Assembly

Once the logo is burned in, glue the wheels on the axles, and edge sand the ends of the axles when the glue is dry. Now oil your Panel Truck and the cargo, and they're ready for the "work-a-day" play world.

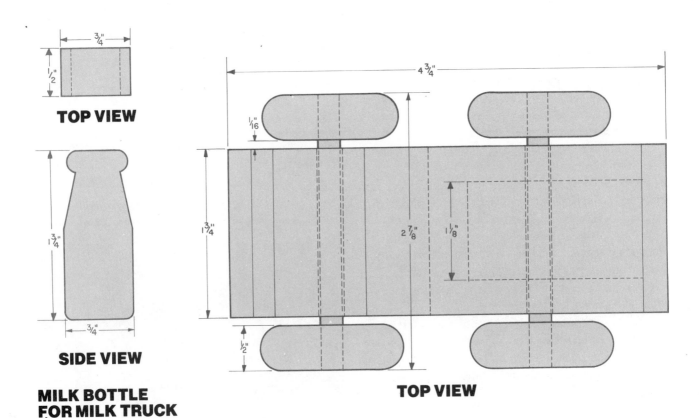

TOP VIEW

SIDE VIEW

MILK BOTTLE FOR MILK TRUCK

TOP VIEW

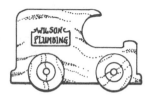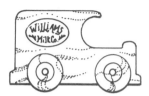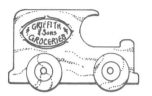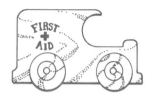

TOP VIEW

2"

1/2"

SIDE VIEW

7/8"

**MONKEY WRENCH
FOR PLUMBING TRUCK**

5/8"

3/4"

END VIEW

**BREAD
FOR GROCERY TRUCK**

1 3/4"

SIDE VIEW

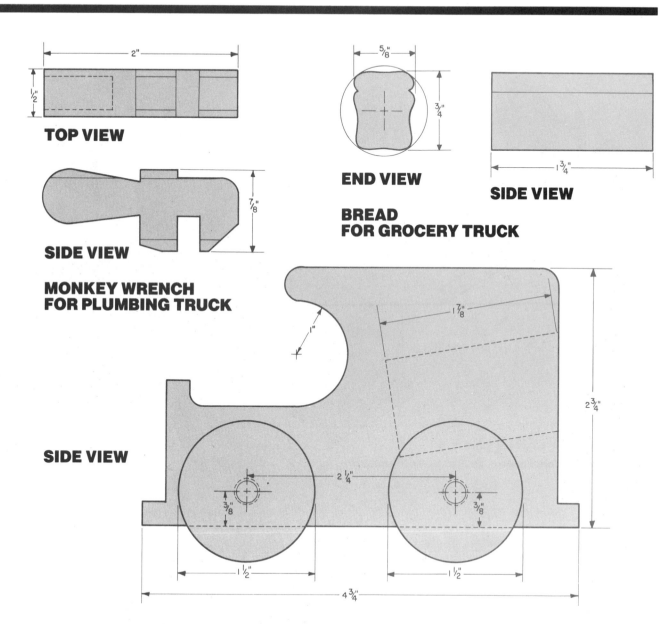

SIDE VIEW

1"

1 7/8"

2 3/4"

2 1/4"

3/8"

3/8"

1 1/2"

1 1/2"

4 3/4"

175

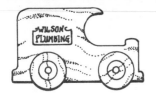
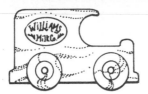

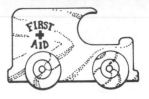

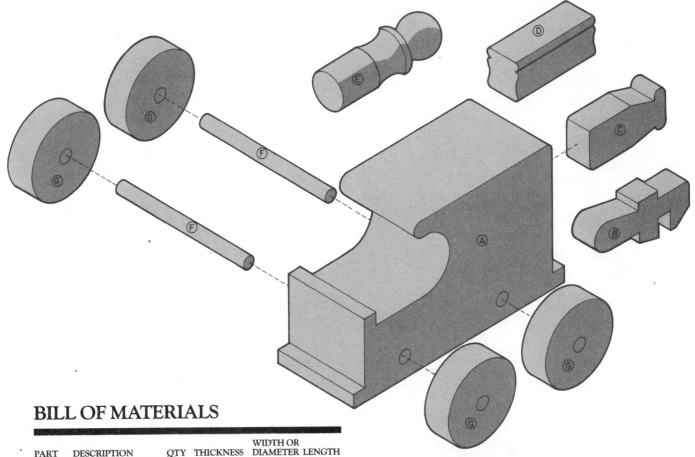

BILL OF MATERIALS

PART	DESCRIPTION	QTY	THICKNESS	WIDTH OR DIAMETER	LENGTH
A	Body	1	1¾"	2¾"	4¾"
B	Wrench	1	½"	⅞"	2"
C	Milk	1	½"	¾"	1¾"
D	Bread	1	¾"	⅝"	1¾"
E	Person	1		⅞" dia.	2¼"
F	Axles	2		¼" dia.	2⅞"
G	Wheels	4	½"	1½" dia.	

EXPLODED VIEW

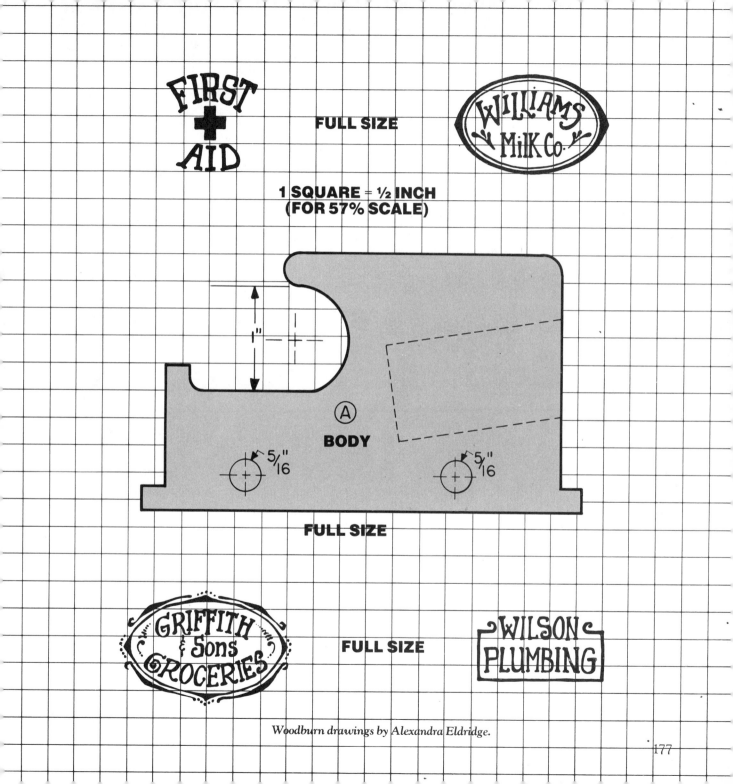

FIRST AID

FULL SIZE

Williams Milk Co.

1 SQUARE = ½ INCH
(FOR 57% SCALE)

1"

Ⓐ
BODY

5/16"

5/16"

FULL SIZE

GRIFFITH & Sons GROCERIES

FULL SIZE

WILSON PLUMBING

Woodburn drawings by Alexandra Eldridge.

The SUB on the Lookout

The periscope on the Sub raises up, scans the horizon, and then lowers again by means of a cam on the axle and a drive wheel on the periscope. This is quite a streamlined toy, but it takes a bit more work than meets the eye, with its dadoed wheel slots and compound angles.

The Body of the Sub

Cut out a square-edged rectangle of hardwood 1½" x 1¾" x 11½". Lay out the side view on the 1½" edge. Using a square, transfer the central axle hole location to the bottom to locate the 1¹⁄₁₆" (or 1⅛") hole for the periscope drive wheel. Also, lay out the slot for the cam on the axle to hide in.

Now drill the three axle holes (⁵⁄₁₆" in the center, ¼" in the bow and stern). Next, drill the 1¹⁄₁₆" (or 1⅛") hole in the bottom. Drill a ⅜" hole at both ends of the slot for the axle cam (*See Figure 1*). Chisel out the remainder of the cam slot.

Set the wobble or dado blade for ½" on the table saw and cut out the slots for the front wheel, rear wheel, and rudder. Cut the slots in two passes, raising the blade after the first pass. Glue and clamp a ½" piece of stock in the front slot so that its back edge is end grain and squared to line up with the wheel hole.

When this is dry, cut out the silhouette of the Sub and flat sand it with 80# and 120# sandpaper. Rock it to sand the tapered ends. Then lay out the top view and cut it out. Flat sand with 80# and 120#, rocking it again to sand the tapered ends. Rout what you can and round over the rest of the edges with a four-in-hand rasp. Sand any rough or burned edges with 80# and then hand sand all the rounded edges with 120#. Glue and clamp the rudder piece (C) in place in the stern slot with the rear edge flush with the stern tip of the body. When it's dry, cut the rudder at the same taper as the stern of the Sub and edge sand the tapered area. Flat sand the top and bottom with 80# and 120#.

Figure 1. Use a ⅜" drill to remove most of the slot for cam.

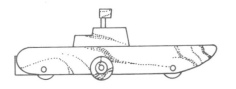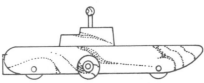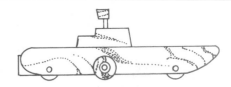

The Cabin

Lay out the side view and cut it out, leaving a ⅛″ gap where the two edges meet (*See Figure 2*). Then lay out the outline of the bottom of the cabin on the bottom of the piece. Set the bandsaw at 5° and cut out the cabin outline with the bottom up. Next, use a dovetail saw to cut the rest of the way through the side view to remove the scrap. With the table square on the edge sander, carefully edge sand the two edges where you just removed the scrap. Then set the sander/grinder table at 5° above square and edge sand around the cabin with 80# and 120# sandpaper. Break the edges by hand with 120#.

The Wheels and the Periscope

Whether you make or buy the front and back wheels, you'll have to ream the axle hole out to ⁵⁄₁₆″ so they'll spin freely on the stationary axles. Both the periscope drive wheel and the cam on the axle need to be constructed so the face on the drive wheel and the edge on the cam are flat for maximum friction. Plug the axle hole in the cam wheel and drill the offset axle hole.

The only thing about the periscope that I would mention is that you'll find it easier to drill the ¼″ hole before you cut off the short section of ½″ dowel. Then cut it off square on the bandsaw, edge sand the ends, and hand sand the edges.

Assembly

Carefully position the cabin as you glue and clamp it. When the glue has set up, put the Sub on the drill press, bottom up. If the top of the cabin is not flat, you may want to clamp the Sub so that it is perfectly parallel to the table. Then, using the hole that the center tip of the 1¹⁄₁₆″ or 1⅛″ bit made, center the twist drill and drill the ⁵⁄₁₆″ hole all the way through the cabin. Don't forget the scrap under your work to prevent tear out.

Next, put the front and rear wheels on. With the wheel in place, tap the ¼″ dowel (cut slightly long) through until it just enters the axle hole on the far side.

Figure 2. As you cut out the cabin side view, leave ⅛″ where the two edges meet. This way the piece will remain supported as you cut out top view.

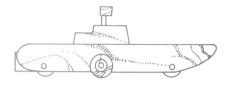
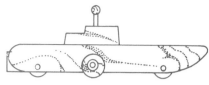
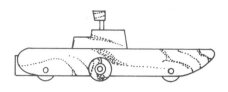

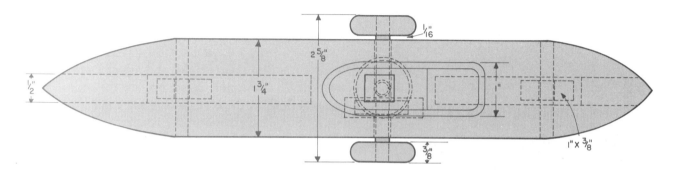

TOP VIEW

$2\frac{5}{8}$"

$\frac{1}{16}$"

$1\frac{3}{4}$"

$\frac{1}{2}$"

1"

$\frac{3}{8}$"

1" X $\frac{3}{8}$"

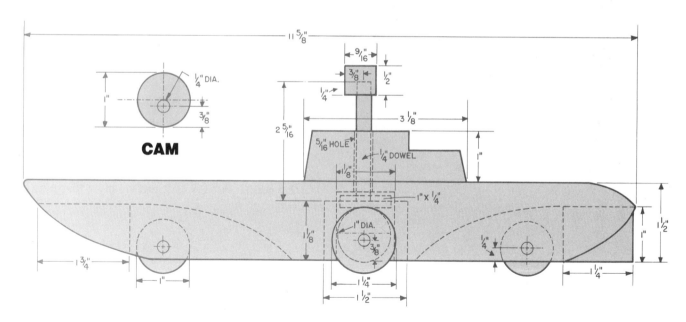

CAM

$\frac{1}{4}$" DIA.

1"

$\frac{3}{8}$"

SIDE VIEW

$11\frac{5}{8}$"

$\frac{9}{16}$"

$\frac{3}{8}$"

$\frac{1}{2}$"

$\frac{1}{4}$"

$3\frac{1}{8}$"

$2\frac{5}{16}$"

$\frac{5}{16}$" HOLE

$\frac{1}{4}$" DOWEL

1"

$\frac{1}{8}$"

1" X $\frac{1}{4}$"

1" DIA.

$\frac{3}{8}$"

$1\frac{1}{8}$"

$\frac{1}{4}$"

$1\frac{3}{4}$"

1"

$1\frac{1}{4}$"

$1\frac{1}{2}$"

$1\frac{1}{4}$"

$1\frac{1}{2}$"

1"

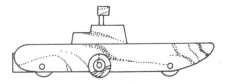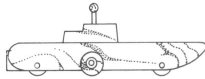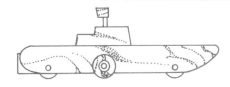

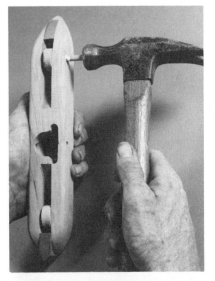

Figure 3. To glue in the stationary bow and stern wheels, drive axle through wheel until it just enters the axle hole on far side. Smear glue inside far axle hole and around protruding axle, and drive it home until it protrudes slightly on both sides.

Figure 4. To glue cam in place, drive axle through axle holes with cam in position. When it protrudes about ⅛", smear a little glue around axle next to cam, and drive dowel the rest of the way through so it protrudes equally on both sides of Sub with cam centered in its slot.

Then put glue inside the far axle hole and around the protruding axle toward you (*See Figure 3*). Now tap the axle in until a little bit of the axle peg protrudes on each side. Wipe off the excess glue and repeat for the other wheel. When the glue has set up, saw the ends of the dowels flush to the body and repeat the flat sanding with 120# sandpaper and the rocking motion at the tips.

Glue the ¼" periscope dowel to the drive wheel. Remove any excess glue and slip it into its position. Glue the viewer onto the top of the periscope.

With the Sub on its back, hold the cam in position and drive the ¼" axle (cut a little long) through both axle holes and the cam. It's easier if you drive the axle in from the side farthest from the cam so the side of the cam hole will support it as you tap the dowel through. When the axle is protruding about ⅛", spread glue on the axle on the other side of the cam (*See Figure 4*). Drive the axle the rest of the way through until it protrudes the same amount on either side of the Sub, and the cam is centered in its slot. Remove any excess glue. Now glue on both central wheels (L) and edge sand them when they're dry. Oil the Sub and it's ready to keep an eye out for any surface craft that may be approaching.

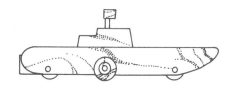
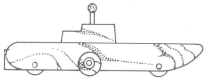
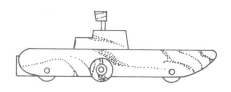

BILL OF MATERIALS

PART	DESCRIPTION	QTY	THICKNESS	WIDTH OR DIAMETER	LENGTH
A	Body	1	1½″	1¾″	11⅝″
B	Cabin	1	1″	1″	3⅛″
C	Rudder	1	½″	1″	1¼″
D	Slot filler	1	½″	1″	1¾″
E	Drive axle	1		¼″ dia.	2⅝″
F	Bow & Stern axle	2		¼″ dia.	1¾″
G	Periscope shaft	1		¼″ dia.	2⁵⁄₁₆″
H	Periscope	1		½″ dia.	⁹⁄₁₆″
J	Drive wheels	2	¼″	1″ dia.	
K	Bow & Stern wheels	2	⅜″	1″ dia.	
L	Midship wheels	2	⅜″	1¼″ dia.	

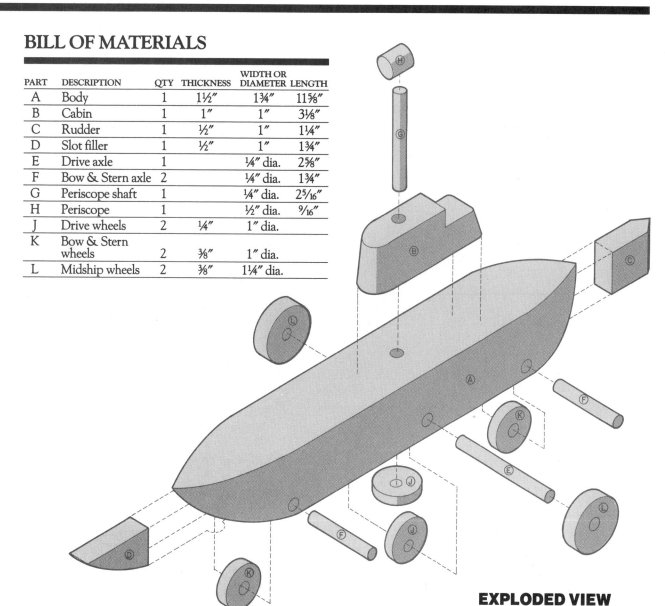

EXPLODED VIEW

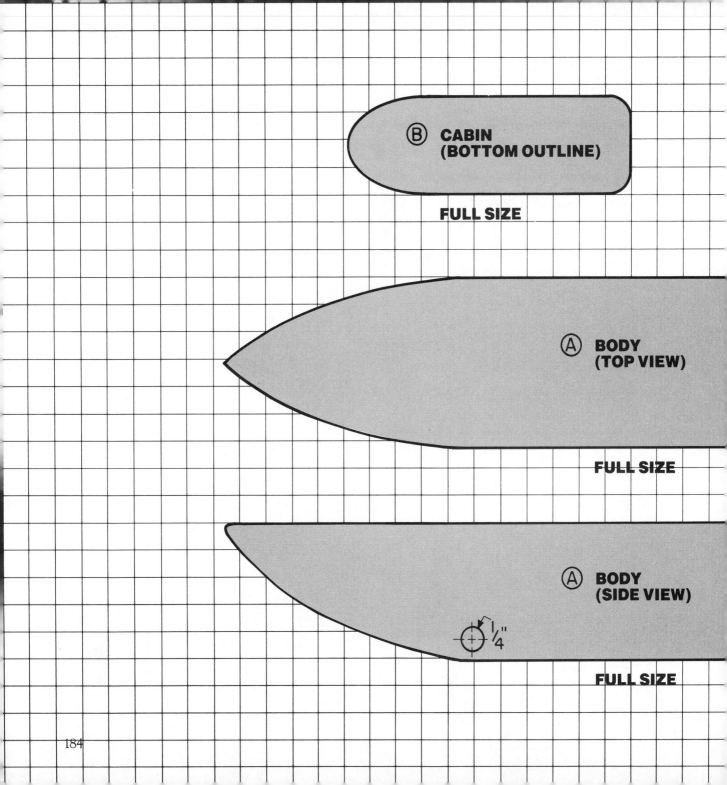

Ⓑ CABIN
(BOTTOM OUTLINE)

FULL SIZE

Ⓐ BODY
(TOP VIEW)

FULL SIZE

Ⓐ BODY
(SIDE VIEW)

$\frac{1}{4}$"

FULL SIZE

184

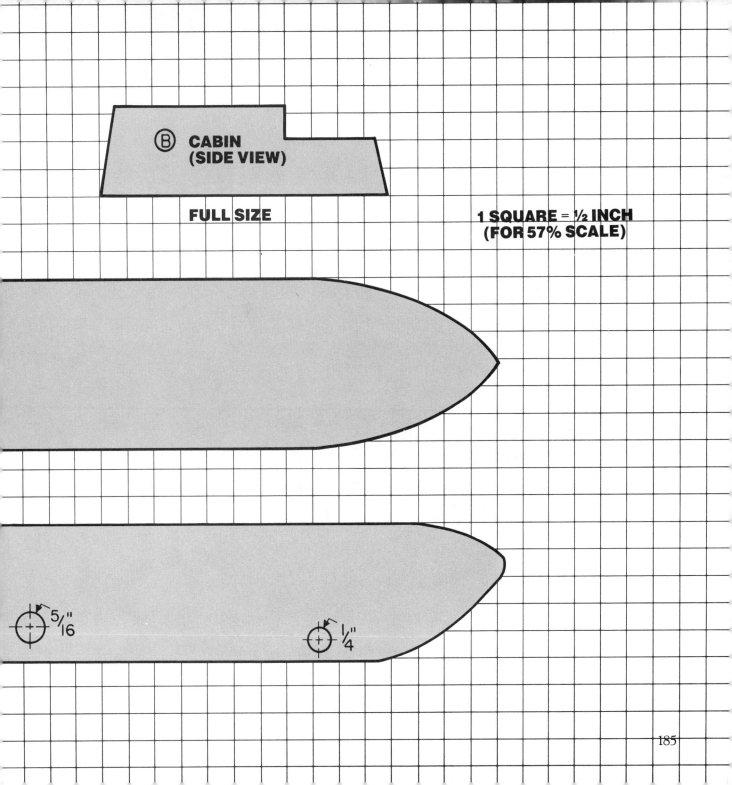

(B) CABIN
(SIDE VIEW)

FULL SIZE

1 SQUARE = ½ INCH
(FOR 57% SCALE)

5/16"

1/4"

NOAH'S ARK

ZEPHYR BOOKS

Illustrated by Pet

The Tipsy TUG and its Backwater BARGE

The diagonally opposed offset wheels give both the Tug and the Barge a simple tipping motion that turns any playroom floor into a rolling sea. You can leave the pull cord off for an older child. Why not make a whole train of barges?

The TUG's Hull

Lay out the side view of the hull (A) on a 3″ x 7″ piece of 1¾″ hardwood with the bottom flush to the edge (See Figure 1). Mark the location of the axles, pull cord, and the hole for the ⅜″ post in the rear. Draw a line through the front axle position to the lower edge, transfer this line to the bottom and mark the center of the two 1¹⁄₁₆″ holes to be drilled with a multispur bit (See Figure 2).

With the piece resting on its back edge, drill the pull cord hole. With the piece on its side, drill the two axle holes. Then with the piece on its bottom, drill the post hole in the rear. With the bottom up, use a multi-spur bit to drill the two 1¹⁄₁₆″ (or 1″) holes for the front wheel. If you don't have a multispur bit, mark the outline of the area to be removed, drill as many holes as you can fit within the outline, and chisel out the rest of the material.

Next, with the piece on its side, cut the shape out on the bandsaw. Edge sand the deck with 80# and then 120# sandpaper, trying to get a smooth curve.

Now with the piece top up, transfer the outline of the top view to the top of the boat. With the bandsaw table square to the blade, cut out the rear two-thirds of the boat (up to where it begins to curve in toward the bow). Then tilt the table 10° to the right and cut from the bow to the left side of the boat. Tilt the table 10°

to the left and cut from the bow to the right side of the boat.

Flat sand the bottom with 80# sandpaper. To sand the sides, start with the piece flat on its side and rock it to sand this area. Then tilt it and keep going to the bow. A few passes like this will smooth out the transition from the square cut to the 10° cut. Do this on both sides and repeat the entire process (including the bottom surface) with 120#. Now edge sand the stern of the boat with 80# and 120#.

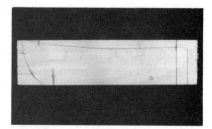

Figure 1. Lay out the side view of the Tug's hull with the bottom flush to the edge. Mark the locations of the pull cord hole, the axle holes, and the hitching post hole in the rear.

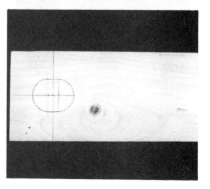

Figure 2. Using a square, transfer the front axle location to the bottom of the hull and mark the centers of the two 1¹⁄₁₆″ holes to be drilled with a multispur bit. Or draw the outline of the area to be removed if you don't have a multispur bit.

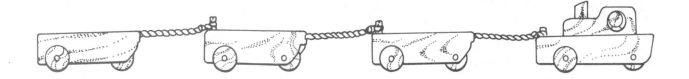

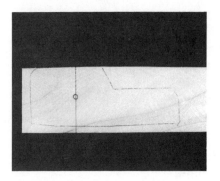

Figure 3. Lay out the side view of the cabin with the top of the cabin flush with the top edge.

If you're careful passing the rear axle holes, you can rout the bottom edge of the back two-thirds of the hull. However, there are so many multiple curves and holes that the rest of the edges should be rounded over with a four-in-hand rasp with the piece clamped in a vise. Hand sand all the edges with 80# and 120# sandpaper. Hand sand around the stern of the boat to remove the edge sander marks.

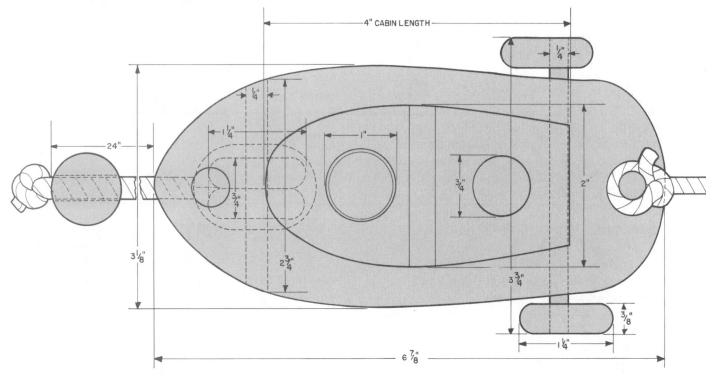

TUG/TOP VIEW

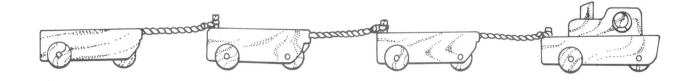

The TUG's Cabin

Cut a square-edged rectangle (1¾" x 2¼" x 4¼"). Lay out the side view of the cabin (B) on the edge with the top of the cabin flush with the top edge (*See Figure 3*). Mark the window hole location. Use a square to transfer the center of that hole to the center of the top surface for the 1" hole for the driver. First, drill the 1" driver's hole with a spade bit or multispur bit. Then clamp the cabin down securely and drill the window hole (1" or 1¹⁄₁₆") with a multispur or Forstner bit. A spade bit will catch in the driver's hole and yank the piece out of your hand. Even with a multispur bit, you'll have to hold the piece firmly and drill slowly as you pass through the other driver's hole. If you don't have a multispur bit, just drill the window hole as it will add character to the Tug even without a driver.

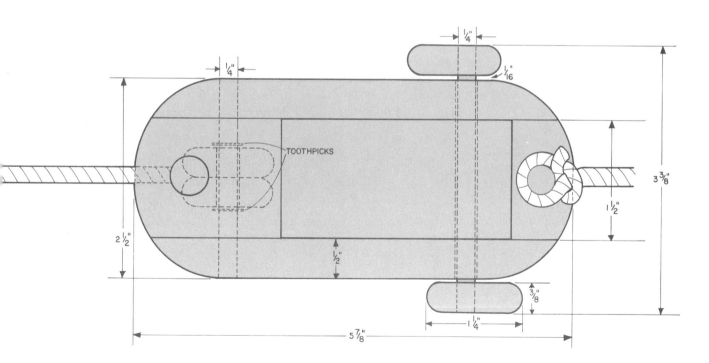

BARGE/TOP VIEW

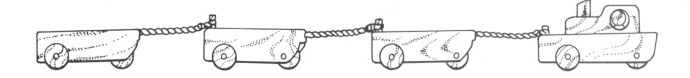

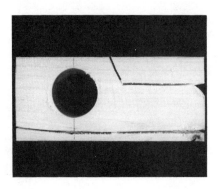

Figure 4. Cut out the outline of the cabin, leaving a ⅛″ unsawn section top and bottom to hold it together as you cut out the top view.

This piece is cut out the same way you would cut out a cabriole leg. With the piece on its side, cut out the outline leaving a ⅛″ unsawn section in the middle of both the top and the bottom line (*See Figure 4*). Now, with the piece resting on its bottom surface, transfer the top view outline of the cabin to the top of the piece. Cut this outline on the bandsaw. Edge sand the outline with 80# and 120# sandpaper. Now use a dovetail saw to cut the rest of the way through the initial cuts and remove the top and bottom scraps.

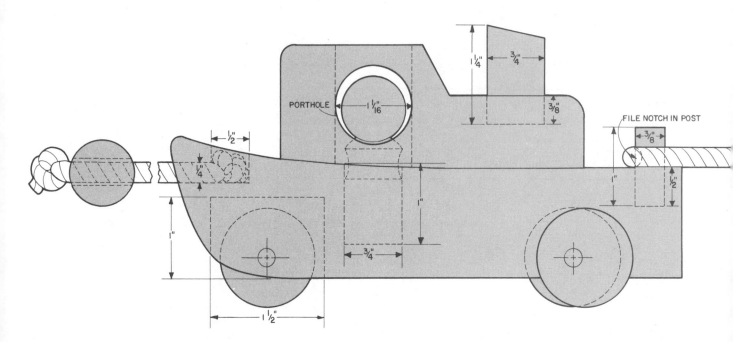

TUG/SIDE VIEW

Flat sand the bottom of the cabin, rocking it fore and aft, and checking its fit on the deck of the hull until you've matched the curve as well as possible.

Edge sand the top surfaces of the cabin with 80# and 120# sandpaper, holding the piece as flat to the belt as possible in spite of the curved sides. Now, with the piece in a vise, round over all the top edges with a four-in-hand rasp and sandpaper. Hand sand all the edges with 120#. The smokestack hole will be drilled after assembly.

The TUG's Wheels

Drill the offset axle holes in the rear wheels, using the wheel jig (*See Techniques and Production Procedures, Figure 17*). Plug the original axle holes. Glue the two front wheels together back to back. When the glue is dry, ream the axle hole out to 5/16".

Assembly of the TUG

Glue and clamp the cabin (B) to the deck of the hull (A). Glue and tap the 3/8" post (D) into the stern of the

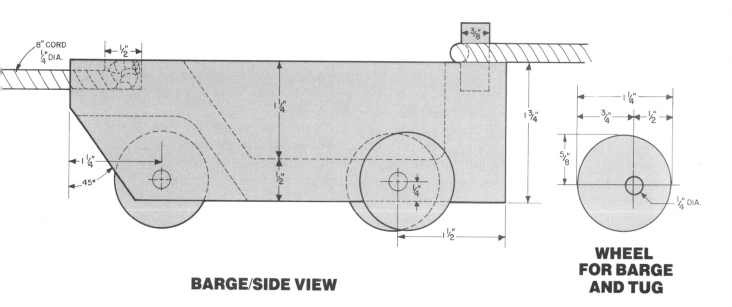

BARGE/SIDE VIEW

WHEEL FOR BARGE AND TUG

deck. When the glue has dried, use a ¾″ spade bit to drill the hole for the pilot (H). Locate and drill the smokestack hole and glue the smokestack (C) in place. Glue the back wheels to their axle with the flat side of the wheel facing out. Make sure the wheels are diagonally opposed. When the wheels are dry, edge sand them.

Position the front wheels and slip the front axle (cut a little long) through the hull and the wheels until it just enters the hole on the far side. Now spread glue inside the far hole and onto the protruding axle. Drive the axle in until it protrudes slightly on both sides. Wipe off the excess glue. When the glue is dry, saw off the axles flush to the hull and sand them smooth. Oil or paint her. With or without the pull cord, she's fit for service in any harbor the world over.

The BARGE

Lay out the side view of the center of the Barge (J) on a 1½″ x 6″ piece of 1¾″ stock. Locate and drill the ⅜″ hole in the stern for the hitching post (L) and the ½″ hole in the front for the "rope."

Next, stand the piece up on its end and locate and drill the hole for the pull rope until it enters the ½″ hole. Now, with the piece on its side, drill a ½″ hole at both ends of the bottom of the cargo area (this area will be removed). This will help you get a smooth curve. Cut out the outline on the bandsaw. Flat sand both sides of the piece; be careful to keep it square to the belt sander so the sides will remain square when glued on. This will be important when you drill the axle holes. Edge sand the inside of the cargo area and the underside in front (where the wheels will be) with 80# and 120# sandpaper.

Lay out the sides (K) and cut them out on the bandsaw. (Don't drill the axle holes yet.) Glue the sides (K) to the Barge center (J). When they are dry, mark the axle hole locations and drill the axle holes. Now lay out the top view on the top of the Barge and cut out the shape on the bandsaw.

Flat sand the top, bottom, and sides with 80# and 120# sandpaper. Edge sand the bow and stern with 80# and 120#. With the Barge face down on the router table, rout around the top. Rout the inside upper edges of the cargo area and rout as much as you can of the bottom edge. Now hand sand with 80# to remove any roughness, burns, or sander/grinder scratches in the stern and bow. Repeat with 120#.

Glue the rear hitching post (L) in (with its notch cut and the top rounded over). Glue the rear wheels on, making sure they are diagonally opposed. Before you glue the front axle in place, drill the two ¹⁄₁₆″ holes 1″ apart in the center of the axle. Then follow the same procedure as the front wheels on the Tug; make sure that the angle of the ¹⁄₁₆″ holes is diagonal, from upper front to lower back, so they won't stick out and be dangerous.

Lastly, glue the short pieces of toothpick in place on either side of the wheels (with ends rounded over). When all the glue has dried thoroughly, oil or paint the Barge. Attach the "hitching rope" and it's ready to turn the Tug into a freight train on water.

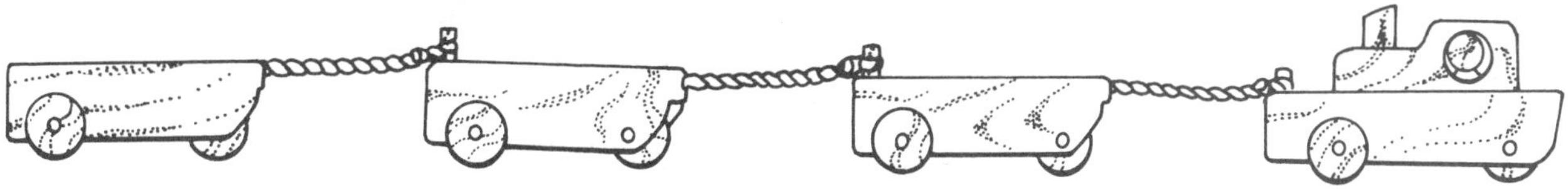

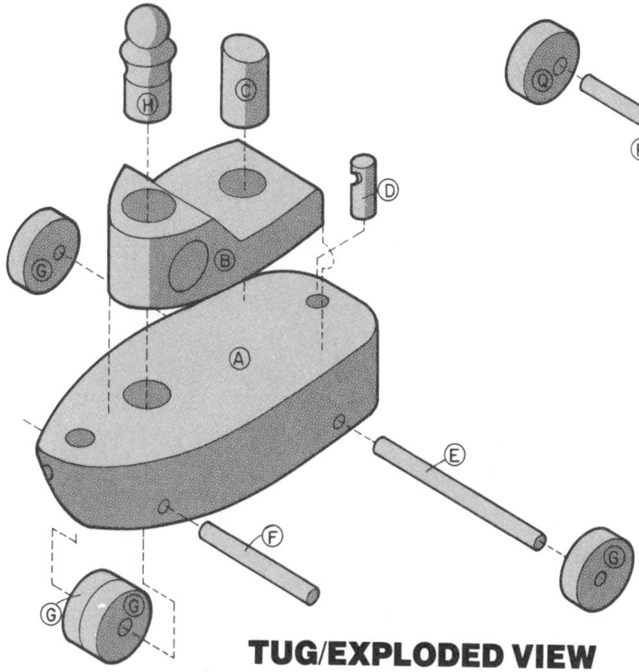

TUG/EXPLODED VIEW

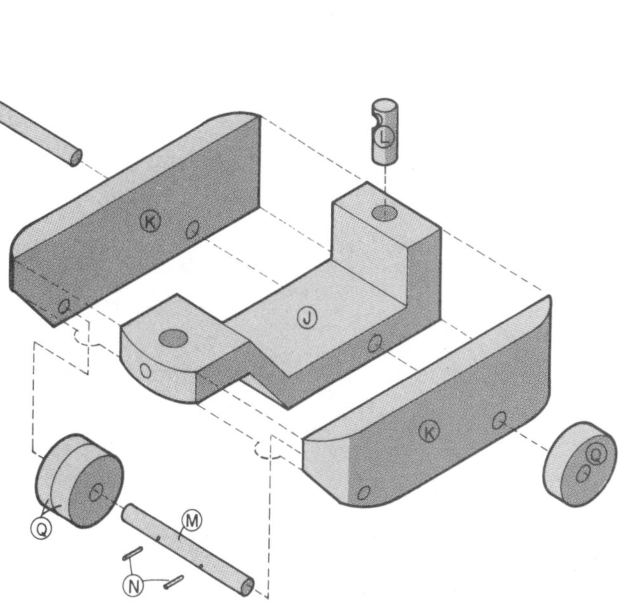

BARGE/EXPLODED VIEW

BILL OF MATERIALS

PART	DESCRIPTION	QTY	THICKNESS	WIDTH OR DIAMETER	LENGTH
A	Tug hull	1	1¾″	3⅛″	6⅞″
B	Cabin	1	1¾″	2″	4″
C	Smokestack	1		¾″ dia.	1¼″
D	Hitching post	1		⅜″ dia.	1″
E	Stern axle	1		¼″ dia.	3¾″
F	Bow axle	1		¼″ dia.	2¾″
G	Wheels	4	⅜″	1¼″ dia.	
H	Pilot	1		¾″ dia. shaft	2¼″
J	Barge center	1	1¾″	1½″	5⅞″

PART	DESCRIPTION	QTY	THICKNESS	WIDTH OR DIAMETER	LENGTH
K	Barge sides	2	½″	1¾″	5⅞″
L	Hitching post	1		⅜″ dia.	1″
M	Bow axle	1		¼″ dia.	2½″
N	Wheel locators	2		¹⁄₁₆″ dia.	½″
P	Stern axle	1		¼″ dia.	3⅜″
Q	Wheels	4	⅜″	1¼″ dia.	
R	Acrylic cord	1		¼″ dia.	24″
S	Acrylic cord	1		¼″ dia.	8″
T	Bobble	1		⅞″ dia.	

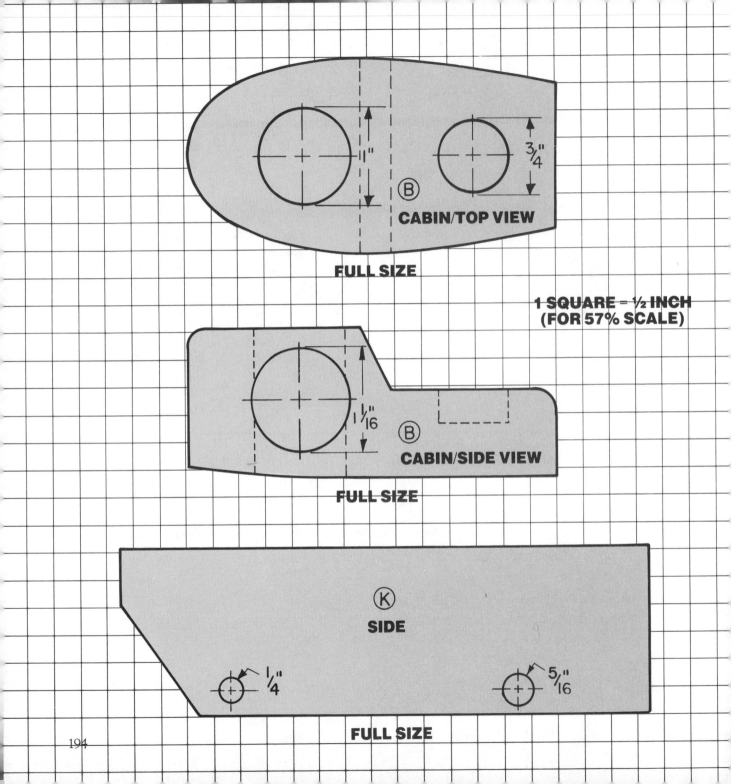

(B) **CABIN/TOP VIEW**

FULL SIZE

1 SQUARE = ½ INCH
(FOR 57% SCALE)

(B) **CABIN/SIDE VIEW**

FULL SIZE

(K) **SIDE**

FULL SIZE

194

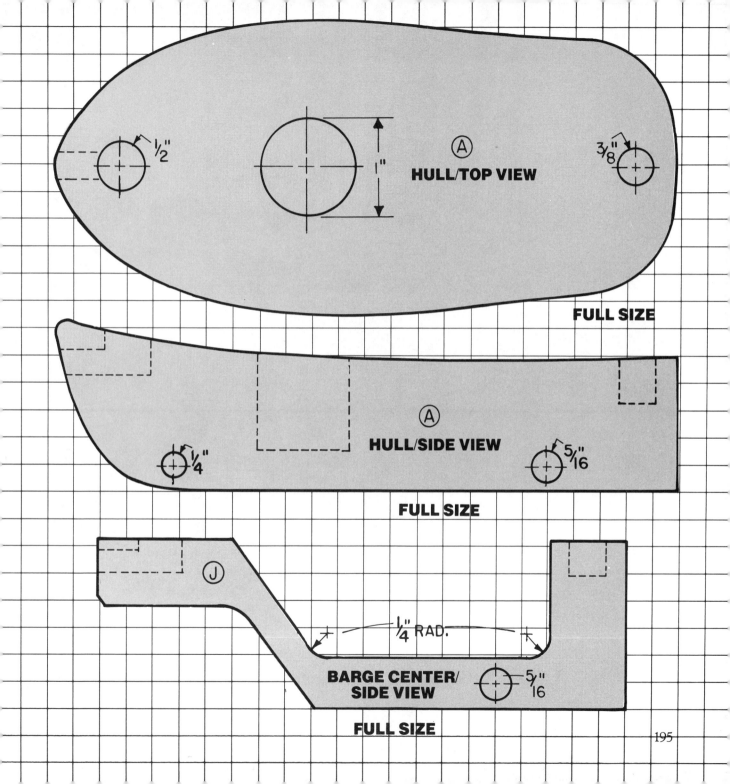

½"

1"

Ⓐ
HULL/TOP VIEW

3/8"

FULL SIZE

Ⓐ
HULL/SIDE VIEW

¼"

5/16"

FULL SIZE

Ⓙ

¼" RAD.

**BARGE CENTER/
SIDE VIEW**

5/16"

FULL SIZE

195

The Quintessential
RIVER QUEEN

This side-wheeler has a drive wheel on the axle which spins the paddles by means of a rubber band. This boat is quite authentic looking, with its vaulted upper deck, pilot's cabin, smokestacks, and concealed wheels. The many holes which must be drilled accurately, and the many small, delicate pieces which are doweled together to make the paddles, make this toy rather difficult to build. However, approached with patience, it will be a very satisfying toy, both for you to make and for children to play with.

The Hull

Cut a rectangle (4″ x 12½″) out of 1″ stock. Lay out the axle holes on the side and drill them carefully; be sure the piece is perfectly perpendicular to the drill press table. Either hold a square against the edge as you drill, or clamp a thick square-edged board to the drill press and use this to square the piece (See Figure 1).

With the piece bottom up, lay out the two holes for the hidden 1″ wheels and the hole for the drive wheels. To drill the holes for the 1″ wheels, drill a ⅝″ hole at either end of the hole and chisel out the remainder.

To remove the material for the drive wheels, drill a hole in each corner of the hole and saw out the piece with a coping saw, a jig saw, or a scroll saw.

Now carefully lay out the hole positions on the deck. Using a square to measure them will be more accurate than simply referring to the drawing or an enlarged pattern. Drill all the holes with a ¼″ bit. (There are no holes under the paddle wheel axle supports.)

Now transfer the curves (2″ circles) onto the four corners and cut them off on the bandsaw with the table square. Then draw a line around the bow and stern, ¾″ from the top. With the table at 40°, start at one axle hole and saw around to the other.

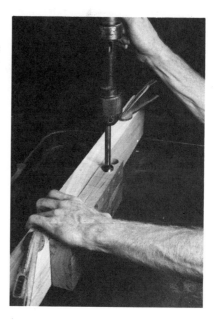

Figure 1. Clamp a square-edged board to the drill press table to hold the piece perfectly vertical as you drill the 1 1/16″ holes.

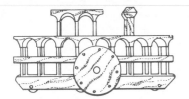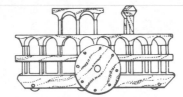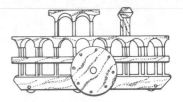

Flat sand the top, the bottom, and the long sides with 80# sandpaper. With the sander/grinder at 40°, edge sand the sawn edge of the bow and stern with 80#. With the table square, edge sand around the flat edge of the bow and stern. Now rout the entire outline, top and bottom (including the drive wheel hole). Skip the area where the roller bearing will slip into the axle holes.

Repeat all the sanding with 120#. Use a four-in-hand rasp to round over the unrouted areas, and to smooth out the junctures of the flat sides and the curved bow and stern. Then hand sand all the rough or burned edges with 80#. Hand sand all the rounded edges with 120#.

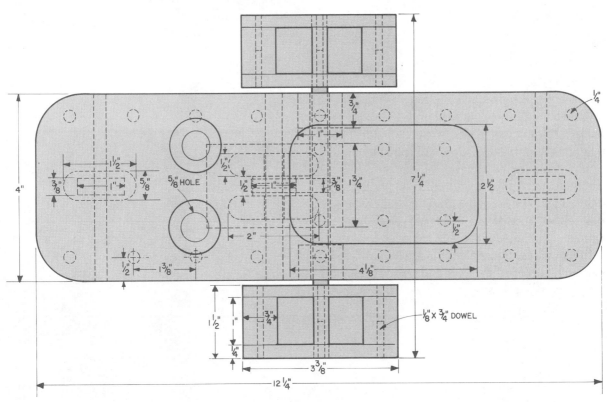

TOP VIEW

198

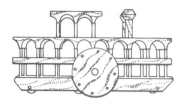 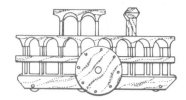 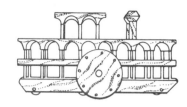

The Second Deck

Cut a 4″ x 12½″ rectangle out of ½″ stock. Locate all the holes, making sure that you lay them out identically to the holes in the deck of the hull. This time, though, drill only the four corner holes and the two holes over the paddle wheel axle supports with a ¼″ bit. Drill the rest of the holes with a 17/64″ bit; this will help greatly during assembly. Again, cut the curved edges (2″ circles). Edge sand the bow and stern with 80# and 120#

sandpaper, and flat sand the top, bottom, and long sides with 80# and 120#. Set the height of the quarter-round bit on the router to cut about two-thirds its curve and rout both sides of the deck all the way around. If you cut the full quarter round, the roller won't be properly supported on the second pass (with the piece flipped over) and the bit will dig in. Hand sand the routed edges with 80# and 120#.

AXLE SUPPORT

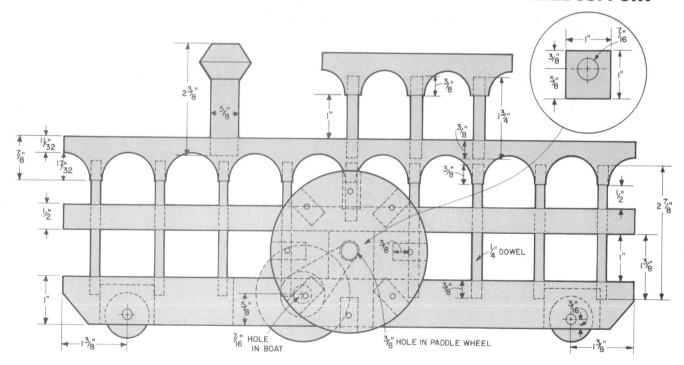

SIDE VIEW

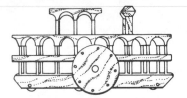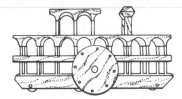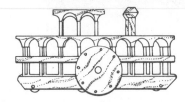

The Vaulted Roof

Square up a piece of 1¾″ stock to 4″ x 14½″. It's cut 2″ longer so you can drill the two end arches and then cut them in half later.

Carefully lay out all the holes as you did for the first two pieces. As with the second deck, drill the four corner holes with a ¼″ bit and the rest with a ¹⁷/₆₄″ bit (all the way through). Then lay out the holes for the smokestacks and the pilot's cabin (¼″) and drill them to the proper depth.

With the board on its side, measure ⅞″ down from the top edge and mark a line the whole length of the board. Using a square, transfer the locations of the ¼″ and ¹⁷/₆₄″ holes onto the side. Now carefully measure and mark the halfway point between these marks. These will be the centers of your 1¹/₁₆″ holes. A 1¹/₁₆″ multispur bit cuts a clean hole; however, a spade bit will do. Clamp a square edged board to the drill press and use that to square the piece (with or without clamps) (See Figure 1).

Using a multispur bit, you can drill all the way through into a scrap. I drill almost all the way through all of the holes, squaring the piece to the table, and then I put a scrap underneath to drill them the rest of the way.

If you're using a spade bit, drill until the tip of the bit just goes through and flip the piece over to finish the hole (using the hole that the tip made to center the bit).

Be careful that tear-out doesn't prevent the piece from sitting flat on the drill press.

Next, set the fence on the bandsaw to rip the piece in half, leaving the piece that you want ⅞″ thick. Mark out the proper length and the curved corners (2″ circles), and cut them off on the bandsaw. Edge sand the corners, and front and rear edges, with 80# sandpaper. Flat sand the top, bottom, and long edges with 80# and then 120#.

With the router bit lowered so that the roller won't slip into the arches, rout the outline of the top. Then repeat the edge sanding with 120# sandpaper.

If you used a spade bit, you'll need to do quite a bit of hand sanding on the arches (or use a 2″ long drum sander). If you used a multispur bit, they won't need sanding. In either case, hand sand any roughness or router burns with 80# sandpaper and then hand sand all the edges with 120#. Round over the edges of the arches with 120#.

The Pilot's Cabin

The pilot's cabin roof is made in the same way as the vaulted roof except all of the six dowel holes are drilled to ¼″, and they only go part of the way through the piece.

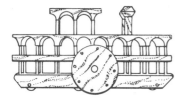 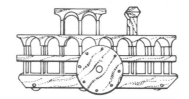 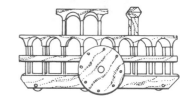

The Paddle Wheels

The paddle wheels will take a bit of time and patience, but they're not really too difficult.

With a compass, mark out the four 3½″ circles (E) in the center of a 4″ x 4″ piece of ¼″ stock sanded on both sides with 80# sandpaper. Make a deep hole with the point of the compass for later reference. Then mark out a 2¾″ concentric circle on two of the pieces. These will be used to locate the ⅛″ holes. Cut out the four circles, leaving about ⅛″ outside the line all the way around.

Next, take the two pieces with the concentric circles and divide them into eight segments. This isn't as hard as you might think if you have a ruler with inch graduations on both edges. Draw one line across the center, using the compass point hole as the center reference. To draw a perpendicular line, put the ruler across the drawn line (at the compass point hole) and shift the ruler until the graduation mark is on the drawn line both above and below the ruler (*See Figure 2*). To further divide the circle, position the ruler to divide the quarters in half. Now look at the size of the wedges below the ruler and shift it until they are equal (*See Figure 3*). Then divide the remaining two quarters. Follow this procedure for both of the concentrically marked pieces.

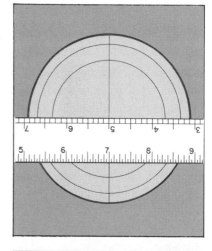

Figure 2. To draw a line perpendicular to the first one, position the ruler so that the graduations line up perfectly with the drawn line, above and below the ruler.

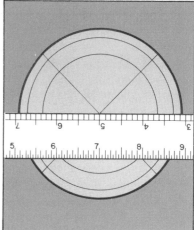

Figure 3. To bisect the quarters into eighths, position the ruler so that it bisects two of the quarters. Then shift it until the two wedges below the ruler are of equal size.

201

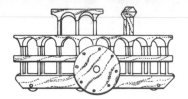 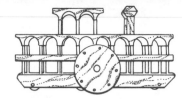 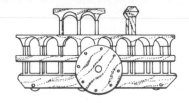

Now lay one of the divided circles on top of one of the undivided circles. Line them up carefully and drill two opposing ⅛″ holes where the inside circle intersects one of the lines that bisects the circle. Then put an ⅛″ dowel in each of the holes to keep the two circles aligned as you drill the rest of the ⅛″ holes. Draw a line on the edge of both pieces to show how they line up for assembly (*See Figure 4*).

Next come the paddle blades (F). Cut two pieces of ⅜″ stock 1″ x 12″. Flat sand all four long sides, and the edges of both pieces, with 80# and 120# sandpaper. Break the long edges with 120#. Then set the rip fence on the bandsaw to a 1″ cutoff. Clamp a scrap to the fence to measure the length of the cutoff, while allowing the piece to pass by the blade without binding (*See Techniques and Production Procedures, Figure 8*). Cut the strips into 1″ pieces. You'll have enough for a few extra pieces. You may lose a couple in the drilling process so keep these extras and continue finishing them.

Break all the sawn edges by hand with 120# sandpaper. This will ensure that they lay flat on the drill press table. Then, take two long scraps and position all the pieces between them with the edge to be drilled facing up (the end grain edges). Clamp the boards at one end. Now press all the little pieces in tightly from the other end and clamp that end. This will keep them from falling out when you move the assembly to the drill press.

Mark a line down the center of all the pieces and put another clamp in the middle. Now place the assembly on a scrap on the drill press table (*See Figure 5*). Make sure that it sits perfectly flat. I don't bother dividing the width of each piece. They're so thin that you can probably eyeball the center. You can, of course, mark the centers. The two end clamps can be tilted to be out of the way of the drill, but the center clamp will have to be tilted one way and then the other to drill the center pieces. Lay one of the sets of paddle wheel sides on the workbench with the marked pieces on top. Take the top (marked piece) off and set it aside. Cut thirty-two 1″ lengths of ⅛″ dowel (sixteen for each paddle

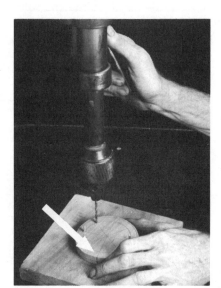

Figure 4. Drill one hole on either side of the two circles and insert ⅛″ dowels to keep them aligned as you drill the other six holes. Draw a line on the edge of both pieces to show how they should be positioned during assembly (see arrow).

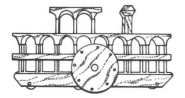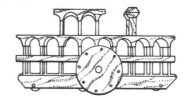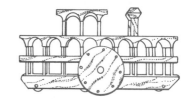

wheel). The bandsaw flings the pieces all over the shop so cut them by hand with a dovetail saw or simply cut them off with a pair of side cutters.

Put a little glue in each of the eight holes in the unmarked wheel. Slip one ⅛″ dowel in each hole. Put a little glue on the end and in the hole of each paddle and position them carefully as you slip them onto the ⅛″ dowels. Now press them down onto the wheel. If the hole is slightly off center, put the longer edge (longer from the hole to the edge) toward the outside of the wheel. That way it will be sawn off when you cut out the final circle rather than leaving a gap.

When they are all positioned, put a *little* glue on

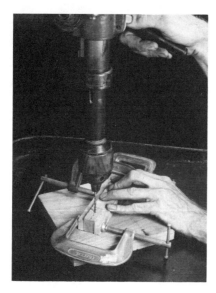

Figure 5. Clamp all the paddles together, edge grain up. Mark a line down the center and set the entire assembly on a scrap piece on the drill press; make sure they sit perfectly flat on the table.

the edge of each paddle that faces up. Put a little glue in each of the eight holes on the marked wheel with the marked surface up. Line up the pencil lines on the edges of the wheels and (without pressing the wheel onto the paddles yet) slip the ⅛″ dowels through the wheel and into their respective paddles. Make sure the paddles are still perfectly aligned and then press the marked wheel down onto the assembly. Now lift the assembly up and push in the ⅛″ dowels that you just inserted until they protrude the same amount on both sides of the assembly. If any of them are stubborn, rest the edge of the assembly on the workbench and gently tap the dowels through with a hammer until they extend equally on both sides. Now, clamp the assembly using as many small C-clamps as you can fit.

When both assemblies have totally dried, sand off the protruding ⅛″ dowels on the unmarked side on the 6″ sander with 80# sandpaper (with the grain). Lay the assemblies, one at a time on the drill press, marked side up and, with a Forstner or brad point bit, carefully drill the ⅜″ hole for the axle. (Don't forget the scrap under your work.) Now cut the final shape out on the bandsaw, leaving the pencil line.

Edge sand with 80# sandpaper to the pencil line, and then edge sand with 120#. Be careful that the belt doesn't dig in between the paddles where there is less material to resist pressure. Flat sand with 80# to remove the remaining protruding dowels (with the

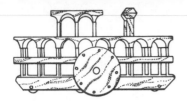
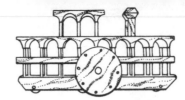
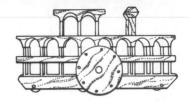

grain) and then flat sand both faces of each wheel with 120#. Break all the edges with 120# by hand.

The Drive Wheel and Balance Wheels

You can use manufactured wheels for the two outside parts of the drive wheel (R) but the center wheel (Q) should be flat-edged to give traction to the rubber band. Glue the three wheels together making sure that all the axle holes line up. Clamp the assembly in a vise. When it's dry, drill the center out to 3/8″.

The small 1″ wheels (P) under the bow and stern help to balance the boat fore and aft. The axle holes should be reamed out to 5/16″ so that they will spin freely on the 1/4″ axles.

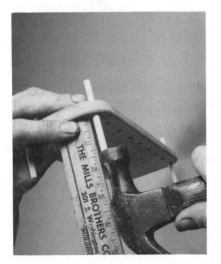

Figure 6. Drive the four corner dowels up from the bottom until the glued grooves sit in their respective holes. The dowels should all extend exactly 1⅜″ below the deck.

The Paddle Wheel Axle Support Assembly

Cut a strip 1″ x 1/2″ x 8″. Flat sand all the long edges with 80# and 120# sandpaper. Break the edges by hand with 120#. Cut off seven 1″ sections on the bandsaw in the same fashion that you cut the paddles. Four of these will serve as spacers when you glue the second deck to the hull, and the seventh is an extra in case you lose one drilling the 7/16″ holes. Mark the location of the 7/16″ hole on three of the pieces and drill the holes, holding the pieces with pliers on the drill press. Break all the outside edges by hand with 120#.

Cut all the dowels (a little long) that join the hull, the second deck, and the roof together. Round over one end of each dowel; this will help guide them into the holes in the top of the hull. Take four of the dowels, for the corners, crimp them with a pair of pliers between 1⅜″ and 1⅞″ from the rounded end. This will let more glue stay in the joint where the dowel passes through the second deck. Now, tap the four dowels into the four corner holes (from the bottom), with the rounded end down. Stop when the crimped area is just below the deck. Apply a little glue on the grooved area and spread it evenly into the grooves. Then tap the four dowels the rest of the way up until the grooves are inside the holes, and all four dowels are identically positioned (*See Figure* 6).

When the glue has dried, put glue on the bottom and top edge of the two axle support pieces (G) and position them carefully on the top of the hull. (Make

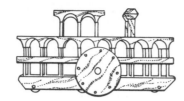

sure the hole is toward the top of each piece.) Slip a ⅜″ dowel through them to make sure they are perfectly positioned. Put glue in the four corner holes. Position the second deck and tap the dowels in from the top. When they're well started, position four ½″ x 1″ x 1″ spacers (one by each dowel) (*See Figure 7*). Tap the dowels in until the second deck rests firmly on the paddle wheel axle supports and the four spacers. Clamp the assembly over each axle support and take out the four spacers.

To attach the roof (C), put glue in each of the four corner holes. Position the roof over the four corner dowels and tap it on until the dowels protrude slightly through the roof. Make sure all three levels are parallel.

Put a little glue in one of the holes in the second deck (B) using a bent paper matchstick, or a wooden matchstick broken over at a right angle. Tap one of the ¼″ dowels through the hole in the roof, and the corresponding hole in the second deck, until it starts to enter the corresponding hole in the hull. If it's slightly off, the rounded end will help it start into the hole. Don't worry if the dowel bends.

Now apply glue to the outside of the dowel that still protrudes from the roof, and drive it home. It should extend slightly. Repeat this for all the support columns (K) including the short ones over the paddle wheel axle supports.

When the glue is thoroughly dry, take the whole assembly and flat sand all the dowels flush to the roof with 80# sandpaper (holding the assembly upside

down on the flat sander). Don't press too hard or you'll burn the ends of the dowels. Then repeat with 120# and hand sand the edges again with 120#.

Next comes the drive wheel. Hold the drive wheel in position (with the boat upside down) and tap the ⅜″ dowel into place. Use another ⅜″ dowel to tap the axle into a centered position. Drill a ⅛″ hole through the drive wheel and glue the ⅛″ x ⅞″ dowel in place.

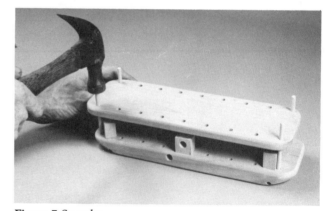

Figure 7. Start the four dowels into their respective holes. Position a 1″ spacer at each corner and drive the four dowels in until the deck rests on the four spacers, and the two axle support brackets.

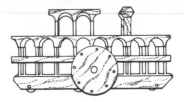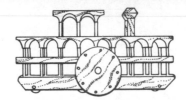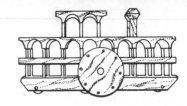

With the boat resting on scraps (to keep it up off the drive wheel), put glue in the smokestack holes and tap the smokestacks (S) into place.

Put glue into the holes in the cabin roof and tap the six ¼″ dowels all the way in (with both ends rounded over). Spread glue in the six ¼″ holes in the roof and tap the cabin roof into place using a scrap on the roof to avoid marring it with the hammer.

Holding the balance wheel in place in its slot, drive the ¼″ dowel (cut long) into its hole until it passes through the wheel and enters the other side. Then spread glue in the hole on the far side and drive the axle all the way through until it protrudes on the far side. Now carefully wipe off the excess glue, saw off the protruding ends with a dovetail saw, and hand sand with 80# and 120# sandpaper. Repeat for the stern balance wheel.

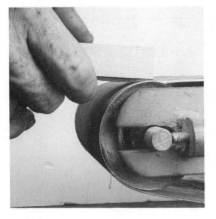

Figure 8. To taper the ends of the rubber band, use a scrap of wood to hold the strip onto the belt sander at an angle over the roller.

Cut the paddle wheel axle (M) to length (slightly long). Tap it into one of the paddle wheel assemblies until it just enters the second wheel (the outside wheel of the assembly). Then put glue on the inside of the hole it just entered and on the outside of the axle which is about to enter the inside paddle wheel. Now, with the paddle wheel flat on waxed paper, tap the axle all the way home. Wipe off the excess glue. Slip the axle through the paddle wheel axle supports (G). Rest the boat on its side (sitting on the wheel) on a piece of carpet or smooth scrap. Tap the other wheel on (using a scrap) until the axle just enters the second wheel. Repeat the gluing process and, using a scrap, drive the wheel the rest of the way onto the axle. Wipe off the excess glue. Let the glue dry.

Now comes an interesting operation. Take the entire boat and flat sand the outside of the paddle wheels (with the grain) with 80# and then 120# sandpaper to remove the glue and sand the axle ends flush to the paddle. Hold the paddle firmly as you set it onto the sander and make sure the paddle sits flat on the sander. If you are appalled at the idea of such a risk so close to the completion of a difficult toy, you can, of course, hand sand the axle ends flush.

Now oil the River Queen. Cut a ⅜″ wide rubber band to length so that there will be a good ¾″ of overlap. Taper the ends (*See Figure 8*) and glue them together with contact cement, stretching the band as you bring the tapered ends together.

Well, there you are... All ashore that's going ashore! Cast off.

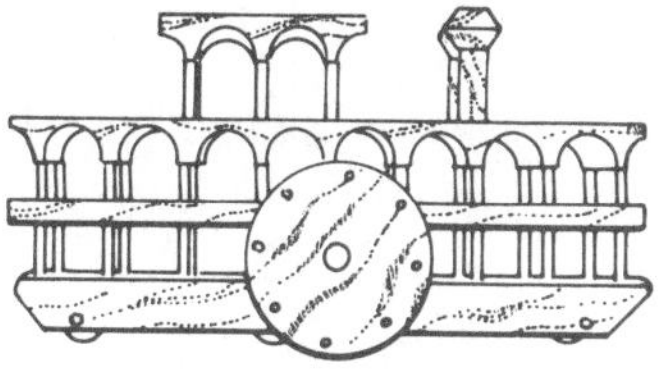

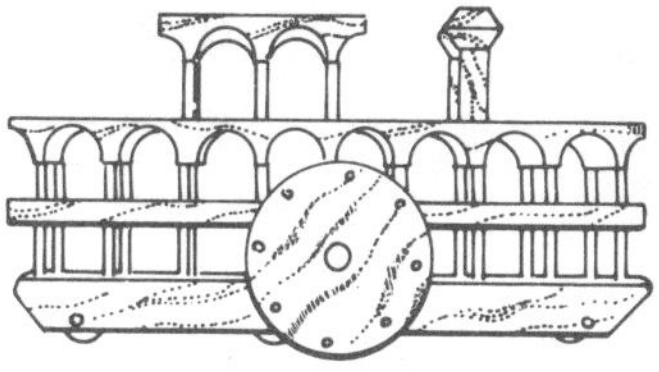

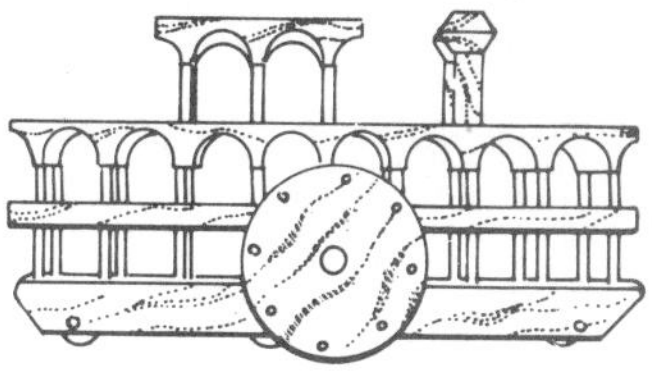

BILL OF MATERIALS

PART	DESCRIPTION	QTY	THICKNESS	WIDTH OR DIAMETER	LENGTH
A	Hull	1	1″	4″	12¼″
B	Second deck	1	½″	4″	12¼″
C	Vaulted roof	1	⅞″	4″	12¼″
D	Pilot's cabin	1	⅞″	2½″	4⅛″
E	Paddle sides	4	¼″	3⅜″ dia.	
F	Paddle blades	16	⅜″	¾″	1″
G	Axle supports	2	¾″	1″	1″
H	Drive wheel axle	1		⅜″ dia.	4″
J	Bow and stern axle	2		¼″ dia.	4″
K	Support columns	16		¼″ dia.	2⅞″
L	Cabin roof support columns	6		¼″ dia.	1¾″
M	Paddle wheel axle	1		⅜″ dia.	7¼″
N	Drive wheel pin	1		⅛″ dia.	1″
P	Bow and stern wheels	2	⅜″	1″ dia.	
Q	Drive wheel center	1	½″	1″ dia.	
R	Drive wheel sides	2	½″	2″ dia.	
S	Smokestacks	2		⅝″ dia.	2⅜″
T	Rubber band	1	⅜″		7″ approx.
U	Paddle pin	32		⅛″	¾″

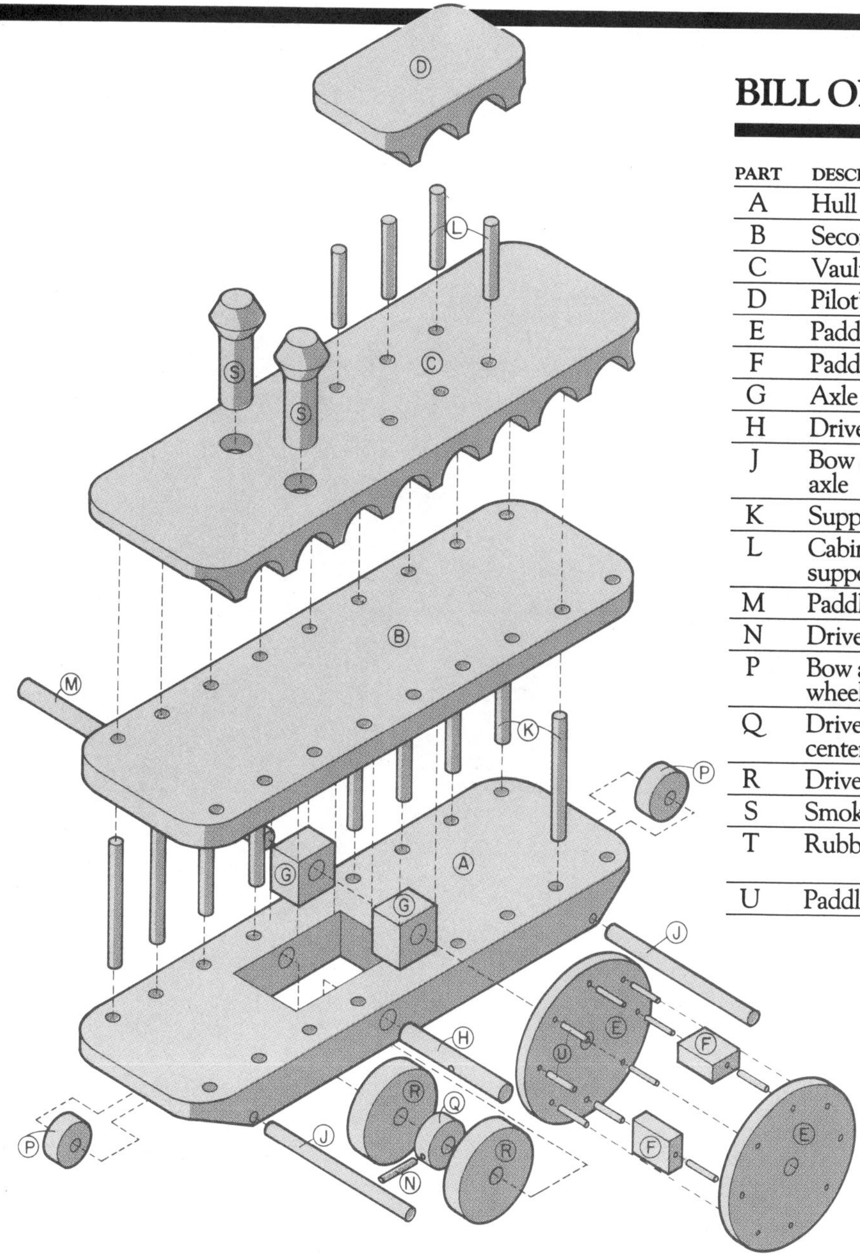

EXPLODED VIEW

The Classic MONOPLANE

I don't think there are many toymakers who haven't tried their hand at designing a wooden airplane. This is the first one I've seen, though, that has a propeller that actually spins as the plane is pushed. The rubber band around the large drive wheel on the front axle, and the smaller dowel on the propeller shaft makes the blade spin twice for every revolution of the wheels. It really whirs around quite nicely.

When the child isn't pushing it along on the ground, spinning the propeller, he or she will be flying it through the air, so I recommend making it out of a light wood like poplar. This is a good toy to paint if you are so inclined.

The Body

Lay out the body pattern (A). Draw a line straight through the center of the propeller shaft. Using this line and a square, draw a line perpendicular to it behind the back of the plane (*See Figure 1*). On the bandsaw, cut out the front of the plane where the propeller will be and then cut along the line you drew behind the plane. Now stand the plane up on its end on the drill press table (on the sawed line) and drill the 1⅛″ hole for the 1″ propeller pulley wheel to sit in (*See Figure 2*). With the plane in the same position, drill the 5/16″ hole for the propeller shaft.

Now drill the hole for the rear wheel and the two ¼″ holes to attach the rear wings. Cut out the shape on the bandsaw, except the slot for the front wings. This will be cut later.

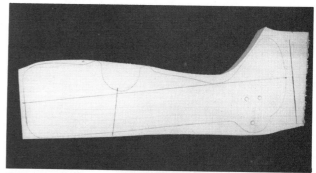

Figure 1. To drill the holes for the propeller works in the nose of the plane, draw a line through the center of the propeller shaft position and, using a square, draw a line perpendicular to this line right behind the tail of the plane.

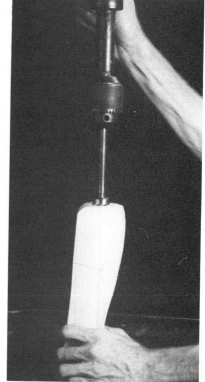
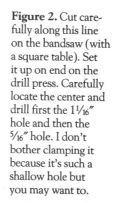

Figure 2. Cut carefully along this line on the bandsaw (with a square table). Set it up on end on the drill press. Carefully locate the center and drill first the 1 1/16″ hole and then the 5/16″ hole. I don't bother clamping it because it's such a shallow hole but you may want to.

209

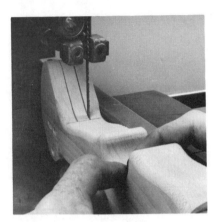

Figure 3. Set the rip fence to one side of the stabilizer and then the other, and saw to your mark.

Supporting the body at the proper angle on the drill press table, drill the hole for the pilot. Edge sand the entire outline with 80# sandpaper. Use a drum sander or a dowel wrapped with sandpaper to sand the cockpit. Flat sand the sides with 80# and then 120#.

To cut out the rear portion of the body, mark the thickness of the stabilizer on the rear of the plane. On top of the plane, mark the point at which the body of the plane starts to get thicker. Set the rip fence on the bandsaw, and using the marks on the rear of the stabilizer, saw both sides of the stabilizer until you reach your mark (*See Figure 3*). Then transfer the pattern to mark the curves from that point till it reaches full thickness, just behind the front wings. Remove the rip fence and saw along those lines. Now, edge sand this area with

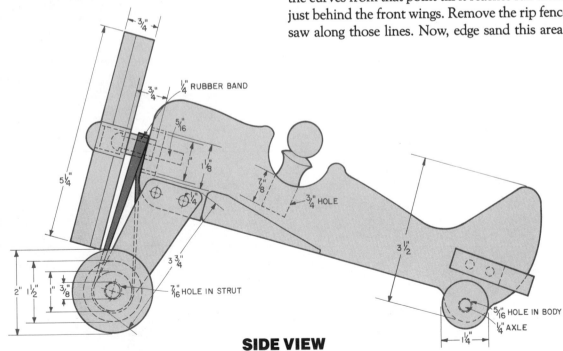

SIDE VIEW

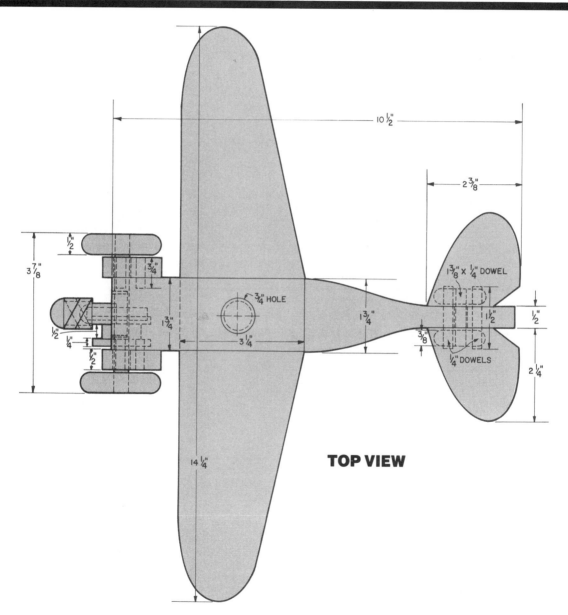

10 ½"

2 ³⁄₈"

3 ⁷⁄₈"

1⁄₂"

3⁄₄"

1 ³⁄₈" x ¼" DOWEL

¾" HOLE

1 ³⁄₄"

1 ³⁄₄"

3 ¼"

1 ½"

1⁄₂"

1⁄₂"

1⁄₄"

3⁄₈"

¼" DOWELS

1⁄₂"

2 ¼"

14 ¼"

TOP VIEW

211

80# and then 120# sandpaper. With the plane in a vise, round over all the edges of the rear of the plane with a four-in-hand rasp. Sand all these edges with 80# and then 120#, and then hand sand the tapered sides *with* the grain to remove the scratches from the sander/grinder.

Rout the front half of the plane, holding it on its nose to rout the extreme front, to avoid the roller bearing slipping into the 1 1/16″ hole as it passes by. Hand sand all the edges.

The Wings

Cut out a piece of ¾″ stock 3¼″ x 15″ with both edges jointed. Square one end and draw the side view of the wing on the end grain. Tilt the table on the bandsaw to duplicate this angle and position the rip fence to the left of the blade to guide it directly into the drawn line. Rip the wedge off the wing. Flat sand the sawn surface (and the others as well) with 80# and then 120# sandpaper. Rout the two forward edges of the wing. Round over the rear edge with the file on the four-in-hand rasp. Hand sand with 80# at one end to get a clean line for transferring the outline onto the body.

At this point, lay the body of the plane on its side and position the end of the wing board on the body where it will be slotted to fit the wing. With a sharp pencil, mark the outline *(See Figure 4)*. This way you'll get a snug fit on the wings. With the table perfectly square on the bandsaw, cut the area out, leaving the pencil line. Try the wing in the slot. It it doesn't fit, sand away a little at a time until it fits as perfectly as possible. Hand sand the edges of this cut to remove any fuzz or roughness.

Now, lay out the pattern for the wings on top of the piece you've started preparing. Cut it out on the bandsaw. Gently, flat sand the rear sawn edge of the wings with 120# sandpaper to get a nice straight edge. Then edge sand the wing tips with 80# and 120#. Rout the wing tips until the roller bearing is about to lose its support on the thin back edges. Now, round over the back edges with a file and then hand sand all the edges with 80# where necessary and then with 120# all the way around.

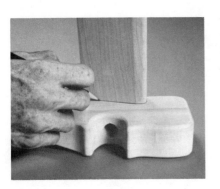

Figure 4. Rather than using the side view drawing to mark the area to be cut away for the wings, use the actual wing piece itself, and mark it with a sharp pencil. Leave the pencil line as you cut out the slot and sand or file it for a snug fit.

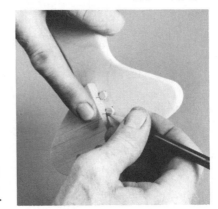

Figure 5. Holding the rear wing below where it will be glued, mark the ¼″ hole locations.

The Rear Wings

Lay out the two rear wings. Cut them out on the bandsaw. You want a very straight edge where they will meet the body. Flat sand this edge very carefully with 80# sandpaper as you flat sand the faces with 80# and 120#. Edge sand the other edges with 80# and 120#. Hand sand with 120# to break the edges. Now, hold one of the rear wings flat against the rear of the plane in the position (front to back) it will be glued in. Mark the position of the two ¼" holes onto the wing (*See Figure 5*). Clamp the two wings together so that the surfaces that are to be drilled are parallel to the drill press table. Transfer your marks onto the other piece as well. Locate the center of the holes, punch them with an awl or center punch, and carefully drill them to the proper depth.

The Propeller and Drive Shaft

Cut a ¾" piece of strong wood to ¾" x ¾" x 5¼". Set the bandsaw table to 30°. Clamp a stop to the fence 2¼" past the cutting edge of the blade. Set the fence so that the blade cuts into the wood ¼" from the left corner of the top edge. Cut to the stop (*See Figure 6*). Turn the piece over and repeat the cut (*See Figure 7*). Flip the piece end over end and repeat the last two cuts.

Remove the wedges with a dovetail saw and round the central area with a four-in-hand rasp. Edge sand all the flat surfaces with 80# and then 120# sandpaper. Round the ends of the blade with a four-in-hand rasp and then hand sand the entire blade with 120#.

When the propeller is finished, carefully mark the center and drill a ⁹⁄₁₆" hole ½" deep. Then drill the rest of the way through with a ½" bit (putting a scrap under it to prevent tearout).

Figure 6. With the table at 30° on the bandsaw and a stop at 2¼" past the cutting edge of the blade, set the fence so that the cut starts ¼" from the top left corner.

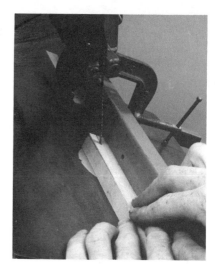

Figure 7. Turn the piece over and repeat the cut.

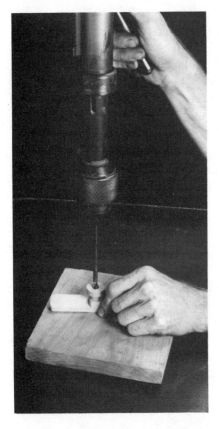

Figure 8. With the propeller assembly sitting perfectly perpendicular to the drill press table, carefully punch the ⅜″ hole location and drill it slowly with a Forstner bit.

propeller, the ½″ dowel, and the 1″ wheel together, making sure the wheel and the propeller are perfectly parallel and the ½″ dowel is perfectly perpendicular to both of them. Be sure that the dowel seats properly in both holes. Plug the ¼″ hole in the 1″ wheel. When the assembly is *thoroughly* dry, secure it in a perpendicular position on the drill press. Very carefully locate the center of the ¼″ plug in the wheel hole, center punch it and slowly drill the ⅜″ hole all the way through the assembly with a Forstner bit *(See Figure 8).*

Axle Drive Wheel

Make the three wheels for the axle drive wheel assembly. Slip a ¼″ dowel through them all to align them as you glue and clamp them together. Remove the dowel as soon as they are clamped. When the glue is thoroughly dry, ream the hole out to ¹³/₃₂″ (slightly over ⅜″) with a twist drill.

Front Wheel Struts

Lay out both pieces (D). To cut them out identically, lay them one on top of the other on the bandsaw to drill the axle holes. Flat sand them with 80# and 120# sandpaper. Edge sand them with 80# and 120#, and break the edges by hand with 120#.

Assembly

To help the propeller spin smoothly, you can rub some paraffin on the propeller peg and other working parts. Make sure you don't get any paraffin on the end which will be glued into the body. Put some glue in the peg hole in the nose of the body. Slip the peg through the propeller assembly and tap it into the nose of the plane.

For the part of the drive shaft that is set into the nose of the plane, a manufactured wheel (with the hub turned inward) will create less friction than a flat, homemade wheel, but either will work. Using the axle hole to center the bit, drill a ½″ hole ¼″ into the flat side of the wheel (outward face). Now cut the ½″ dowel to length (¾″). Round off both ends by hand. Glue the

 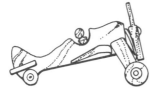  

Use a scrap of ⅜″ dowel to let you hammer the cap of the peg. Be extremely careful not to drive it in too far. It should go far enough to hold the propeller firmly with about ¹⁄₁₆″ to ⅛″ play. Cut a little less than half off the top of a wooden person's head, hand sand the rough edges and glue it over the hole in the propeller.

Hold the front wheel struts (D) in place and measure the distance across them. Add 1″ for the wheels and ⅛″ for clearance, and cut the front axle to this length. Glue one of the front wheels on. Slip the axle through the strut, through the drive wheel, and out through the other strut hole. Glue on the other wheel and sand the axle hubs when the glue is dry. Before you glue the struts in place, clamp them temporarily to the body using the side view to position them. Take a ⅛″ dowel and position it from the propeller drive shaft (¼″ out from the nose of the plane), to the forward edge of the center of the drive wheel on the front axle, and see if the propeller can turn freely without hitting the ⅛″ dowel. Adjust the strut positions if necessary to clear the propeller (*See Figure 9*). Make sure that the axle is straight and that the wheels spin freely.

Now, with a sharp pencil, lightly mark the position around the upper edge of the struts onto the body. Glue both struts and work glue back from the edges to avoid squeeze-out. Position them carefully and clamp them (using pads or scraps to prevent marring). When the glue is dry, drill the ¼″ holes and glue the ¼″ axles in place to strengthen the struts. Sand the ends flush.

With the plane on its back, position the axle drive wheel and drill the ⅛″ hole through it. Cut the ⅛″ dowel to ⅞″ and glue it in place. Wipe off any excess glue.

Figure 9. Check for clearance between the propeller and the rubber band by positioning a ⅛″ dowel in the same place that the rubber band will be. Adjust the struts if necessary and mark their position lightly with a sharp pencil to glue them accurately.

To attach the rear wings, position the two ¼″ dowels in the holes in the body. Put glue in the two holes in each small wing and put a little glue on the flat edge that will set against the body. Work the glue in from the edges to avoid squeeze-out. Press the wings on in the wood vise, pushing the plane from the nose at the same time to compensate for the tips of the wings tending to pull them back, rather than in. Leave the plane in the vise while the glue dries. Next, glue the rear wheels and axle in place.

To glue the main wings in place, apply glue to the cut-out area under the body, working it away from the edges to avoid squeeze-out. Carefully position the wing, and with a scrap over the cockpit and under the wing, clamp it in place with a large C-clamp.

When all the glue is thoroughly dry, oil or paint your plane (don't forget the pilot). When the finish is dry, it's time for the rubber band. Cut a straight strip of inner tube ¼″ wide by about 10″ long. Wrap it around both wheels with a half twist in the middle. It should come off the propeller shaft, to the front of the axle drive wheel, under the wheel, and back to the far side of the propeller shaft. Pull it fairly tight (but not stretched). Cut it to length with about a ½″ overlap. Mark the end of the overlap with a pen or magic marker and then remove it. The ends to be joined must be tapered (on opposite sides of each end). Use a scrap of wood to hold the end of the band down onto the roller on the belt sander (*See Figure 10*). Apply contact cement to the opposite tapered ends and rest the band on something that will leave both ends untouched while they dry.

When they are dry (ten minutes or so), carefully position the band on the plane (don't get the ends dirty or dusty) and pull it tight again. Press the two glued tapered ends together *firmly* and there you are. The only wooden plane of its kind with a propeller that actually spins as the plane is pushed.

BILL OF MATERIALS

PART	DESCRIPTION	QTY	THICKNESS	WIDTH OR DIAMETER	LENGTH
A	Body	1	1¾″	3½″	10½″
B	Front wings	1	¾″	3¼″	14¼″
C	Rear wings	2	½″	2⅜″	2¼″
D	Front wheel struts	2	½″	1⅜″	3¾″
E	Propeller	1	¾″	¾″	5¼″
F	Drive wheel	2	⅜″	1″ dia.	
G	Drive wheel sides	2	¼″	1½″ dia.	
H	Drive wheel	1		½″ dia.	¾″
J	Drive wheel pin	1		⅛″ dia.	1″
K	Propeller cap	1		¾″ dia.	
L	Peg	1		5/16″ dia.	1 5/16″ shaft
M	Rear axle	1		¼″ dia.	1⅜″
N	Pilot	1		¾″ dia.	2¼″
P	Rear wheels	2	⅜″	1¼″ dia.	
Q	Front wheels	2	½″	2″ dia.	
R	Wheel strut pegs	4		¼″ dia.	¾″
S	Rear wing pegs	2		¼″ dia.	1½″
T	Front axle	1		⅜″ dia.	3⅞″
U	Rubber band	1	¼″		10″

Figure 10. Taper the ends of the rubber strip by pressing them on the roller of the belt sander with a scrap of wood.

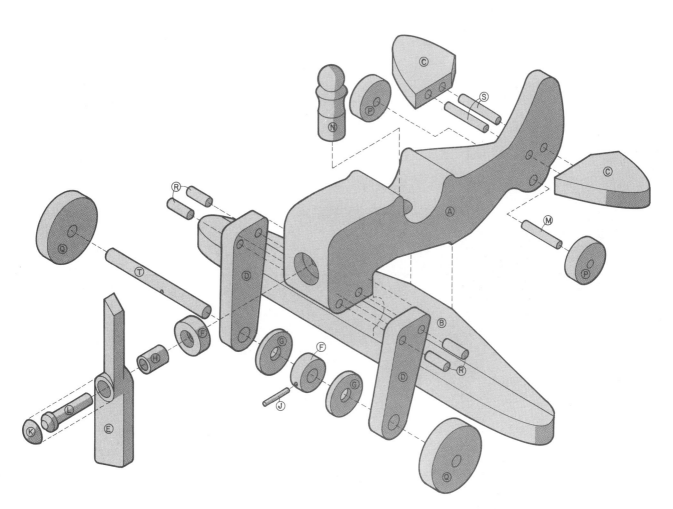

EXPLODED VIEW

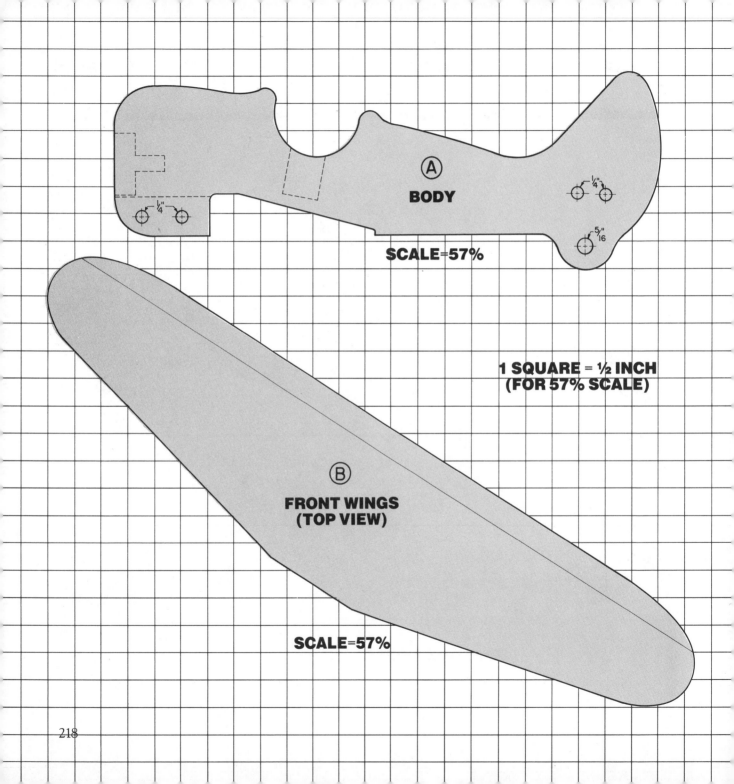

(A) **BODY**

$\frac{1}{4}$"

$\frac{1}{4}$"

$\frac{5}{16}$"

SCALE=57%

(B) **FRONT WINGS (TOP VIEW)**

SCALE=57%

1 SQUARE = ½ INCH (FOR 57% SCALE)

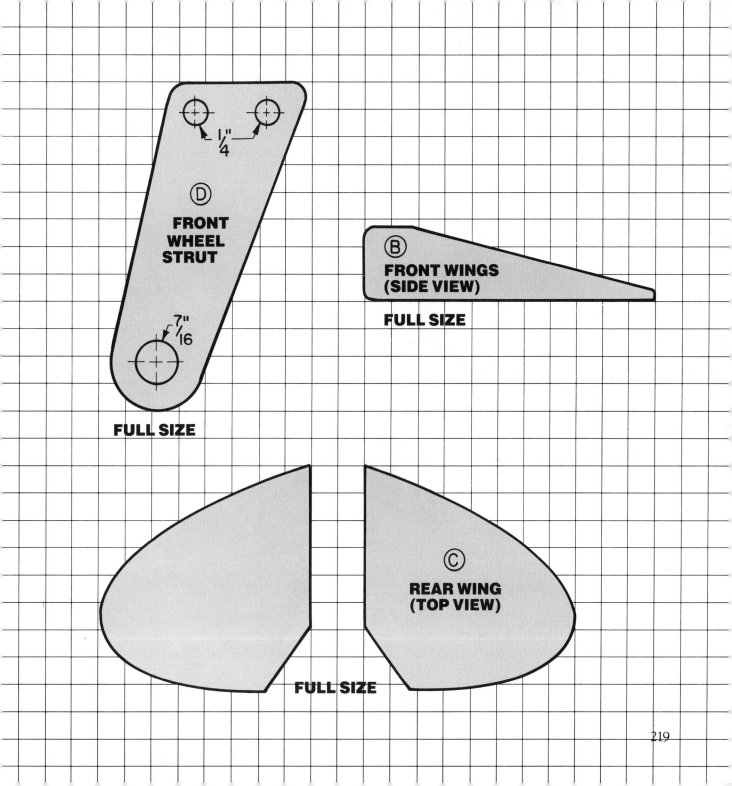

D

FRONT
WHEEL
STRUT

$\frac{1}{4}$"

$\frac{7}{16}$"

FULL SIZE

B

FRONT WINGS
(SIDE VIEW)

FULL SIZE

C

REAR WING
(TOP VIEW)

FULL SIZE

219

The Whimsical WHIRLYBIRD

Unlike most wooden helicopters, this toy helicopter actually works. A hidden wheel on the axle turns against another hidden wheel on the propeller shaft to spin the propeller. Because the mechanism that turns the shaft is hidden, the helicopter has clean lines and the movement is quite surprising. The body of the helicopter can be made out of any wood, but the blade should be made of strong, light wood.

The Body

Lay out the body pattern (A) on a board with the grain running lengthwise. The bottom edge of the pattern should be against the edge of the board; the board's other edge should be parallel to the top of the pattern. This will enable you to cut the dado slot on the table saw (*See Figure 1*). Drill the window hole, the peg hole for the rear blade, and the axle hole. If you don't have a multispur bit or Forstner bit for the 1⅛″ hole in the bottom of the helicopter, you'll have to drill that hole with a spade bit before you drill the axle hole or the spade bit will catch in the axle hole as it passes through.

Set the bandsaw table to 25° and cut a wedge out to support the helicopter at the proper angle on the drill press table; drill the hole for the handle (*See Figure 2*). Drill the handle hole on the drill press (*See Figure 3*).

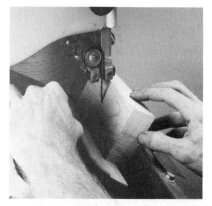

Figure 2. Set the bandsaw table to 25° and cut a wedge to support the helicopter body at the proper angle on the drill press for drilling the handle hole.

Figure 3. Using the wedge, drill the handle hole on the drill press.

Figure 1. Lay out the body (A) so that the bottom edge of the board is parallel to the top edge of the helicopter.

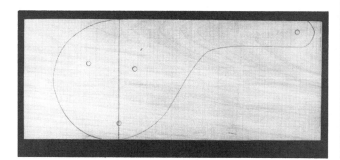

221

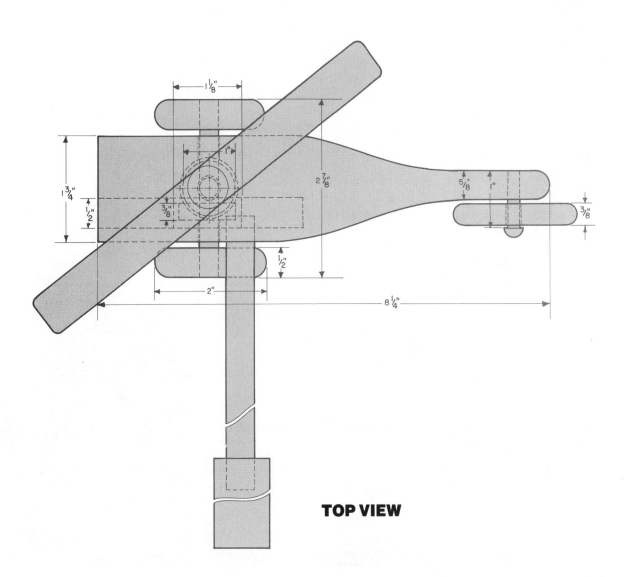

TOP VIEW

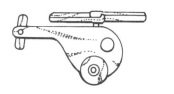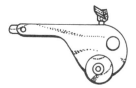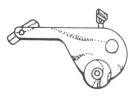

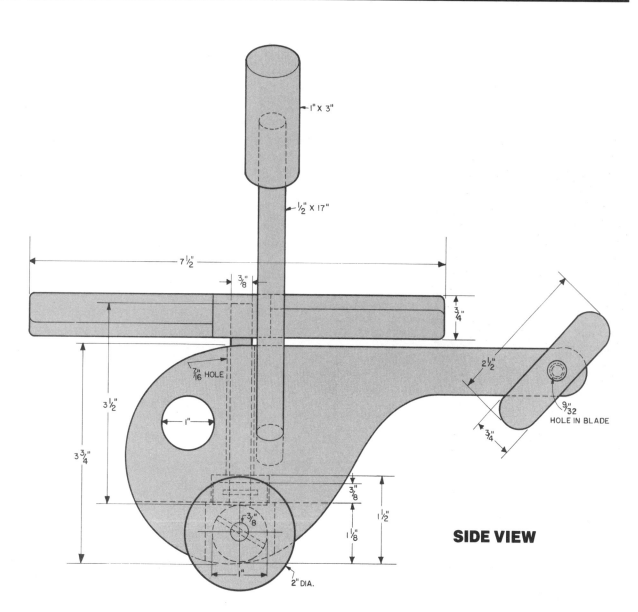

1" X 3"

1/2" X 17"

7 1/2"

3/8"

3/4"

7/16 HOLE

2 1/2"

9/32"
HOLE IN BLADE

3/4"

1"

3/8"

1 1/2"

3 1/2"

3 3/4"

1 3/8"

1 1/8"

1"

2" DIA.

SIDE VIEW

223

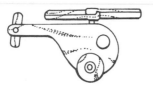  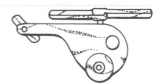 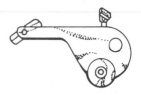

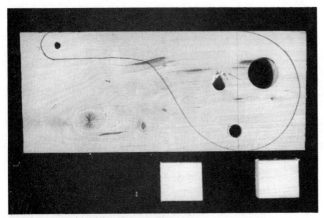

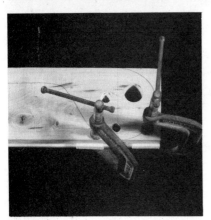

Figure 4. Cut the slot fillers so that their grain will run the same way as the body and they will have a square end grain edge to form the hole for the axle drive wheel.

Figure 5. Clamp the slot fillers in place with C-clamps using scraps or pads to protect the sides of the body.

Now, using the side and top views, locate the 1⅛″ hole on the bottom edge of the board and drill the hole where the propeller drive wheel will fit. Using the hole that the tip of the 1⅛″ bit left, center the 7/16″ bit and drill all the way through, making the hole for the propeller shaft. Remember to put a scrap under your piece to prevent tearing out as the bit breaks through.

On the table saw, cut out the slot for the axle drive wheel. Use a dado or wobble blade if you have one; if not, several passes with a regular blade will do it. Cut two slot fillers (C, D) out of ½″ stock. You'll want a square end grain edge on the insides of the hole that they are lining (*See Figure 4*). Leave the pieces large; they'll be sawn off with the outline of the helicopter later. Put glue in the dadoed slot, being careful to put it only as far into the slot as the slot fillers will go. Slip the pieces into place, positioning them carefully as in the side view. Clamp them, using pads or scraps to prevent marring the surface of the chopper (*See Figure 5*).

When all the glue is thoroughly dry, cut out the silhouette of the body on the bandsaw. Edge sand the outline with 80# and then 120# sandpaper. Flat sand the body with 80# and then 120#. Now, lay the body upside down and mark the shape of the rear of the body on the underside of the body. Cut it out on the bandsaw. With the body upside down, edge sand this area with 80# and then 120#.

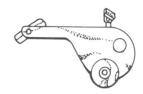

With the body on its side, rout the front half of the body and the window hole on both sides. Don't rout the bottom edge where the 1 1/16″ hole is or the router bit will slip into the hole. Round this area over with a four-in-hand rasp and sandpaper. Then, with the body on its back, rout the top edges of the back of the body. The rest of the outline will have to be rounded over with a four-in-hand rasp and 80# sandpaper. Now, sand the rough spots and burns with 80#. Hand sand all the edges and the rear section *with* the grain with 80# and then 120#, to remove all the edge sanding scratches and to smooth out all the edges.

The Blades

Cut out the small blade and drill the 9/32″ peg hole. Flat sand it with 80# and then 120# sandpaper, either on the flat sander or by hand. Edge sand with 80# and then 120#, and break the edges with 120# by hand.

To make the main blade (E), cut a piece of light, strong wood to 3/4″ x 3/4″ x 7 1/2″. Set the bandsaw table to 30°. Clamp a stop to the fence 3 3/8″ past the front edge of the blade. Set the fence so that the blade cuts into the wood 1/4″ from the left corner of the top edge (*See Figure 6*). Cut to the stop. Turn the piece over and repeat the cut (*See Figure 7*). Now, flip the piece end over end and repeat the last two cuts.

Figure 6. With the table at 30° and a stop at 3 3/8″ past the cutting edge of the blade, set the fence so that the cut starts 1/4″ from the top left center.

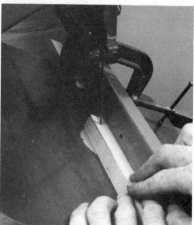

Figure 7. Turn the piece over and repeat the cut.

  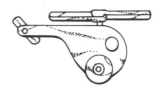 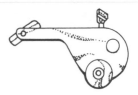

Figure 8. The propeller shaft wheel needs grooves on the face, whereas the axle drive wheel needs them on the tread surface. The more grooves, the smoother the blade will turn.

Remove the wedges with a dovetail saw and round out the central area with a four-in-hand rasp. Edge sand all the flat surfaces with 80# and then 120# sandpaper. Round the ends of the blade with the four-in-hand rasp. Drill the shaft hole and hand sand the whole blade.

Wheels and Handle

Manufactured wheels won't work for the drive mechanisms of this toy. The wheels need to have a flat face and a flat tread for friction. So, make the wheels out of strong wood with a fly cutter or hole saw. Make several extras because they are so small that they may split when you're enlarging the axle holes. Plug the ¼" hole and redrill it with a ⅜" Forstner bit to prevent splitting the small wheel. You can wrap a small piece of inner tube around the wheel and grip it with pliers to prevent it from spinning as you drill the axle hole. The wheel (N) that goes on the propeller shaft will need grooves in the face for friction, whereas the drive wheel (P) on the axle will need them on the tread (*See Figure 8*). With the wheel in a vise, make these cuts with a dovetail saw. The more slots, the more smoothly the blade will turn.

To make the handle, cut a 3" length of 1" dowel and drill a ½" hole in the end. Flat sand both ends, and round both ends on the belt sander (*See Techniques and Production Procedures, Figure 24*). Spread a *little* glue on the inside of the hole and drive the ½" dowel (with the ends rounded) into the handle.

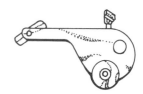

Assembly

The main blade is first. Glue the drive wheel onto the end of the propeller shaft with the grooved face downward. Use a scrap with a square edge to support the ⅜″ dowel and hold the wheel perpendicular to the shaft as you drill the ⅛″ hole through the wheel (across the grain to prevent splitting) (*See Figure 9*). Put glue in the hole and tap the ⅛″ dowel (⅞″ long) into place. After it's dry, sand off any glue or protruding dowel that might interfere with its movement in the hole in the body.

Now slip the shaft into place. With the body upright, use a 1″ dowel under the drive wheel to support it as you drive the glued propeller onto the top of the shaft. Make sure it is parallel to the top of the body.

Hold the axle drive wheel in position and slip the precut axle through the axle holes and the drive wheel. Use two blocks under the body to support it (up off the propeller) as you drill the ⅛″ hole through the wheel and the shaft, across the grain (*See Figure 10*). Cut the ⅛″ dowel slightly short so that it won't protrude and glue it into place. Wipe off any excess glue. Glue and tap the wheels on, and edge sand the axle hubs after the glue is dry.

Put glue in the peg hole in the rear and peg the rear propeller in place with a peg sawn off to 1″ shaft length. Wipe off excess glue and hand sand after the glue is dry.

Spread some glue inside the handle hole and drive the handle into place using a block to keep the body up off the wheel. Now your child is ready to fly away into the wild blue yonder!

Figure 9. With the glue still wet, support the dowel with a square-edged scrap which will hold the wheel perpendicular to the shaft as you drill the ⅛″ hole.

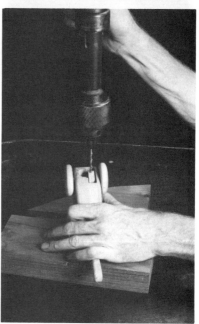

Figure 10. Use blocks under the body to keep it up off the blade as you drill the ⅛″ hole through the axle drive wheel.

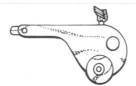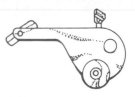

BILL OF MATERIALS

PART	DESCRIPTION	QTY	THICKNESS	WIDTH OR DIAMETER	LENGTH
A	Body	1	1¾"	3¾"	8¼"
B	Rear blade	1	⅜"	¾"	2½"
C	Rear slot filler	1	½"	1"	1½"
D	Front slot filler	1	½"	1"	1½"
E	Main blade	1	¾"	¾"	7½"
F	Front axle	1		⅜" dia.	2⅞"
G	Blade drive shaft	1		⅜" dia.	3½"
H	Blade drive wheel pin	1		⅛" dia.	1"
J	Axle drive wheel pin	1		⅛" dia.	15/16"
K	Handle arm	1		½" dia.	17"
L	Handle	1		1" dia.	3"
M	Rear blade peg	1		7/32" dia.	1" shaft
N	Blade drive wheel	1	⅜"	1" dia.	
P	Axle drive wheel	1	⅜"	1" dia.	
Q	Wheels	2	½"	2" dia.	

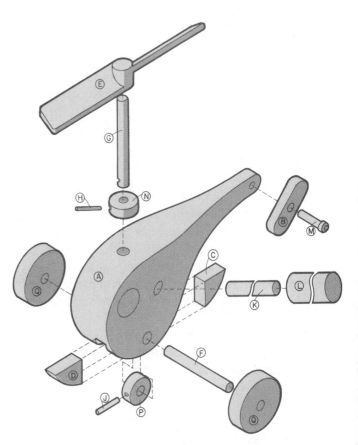

EXPLODED VIEW

228

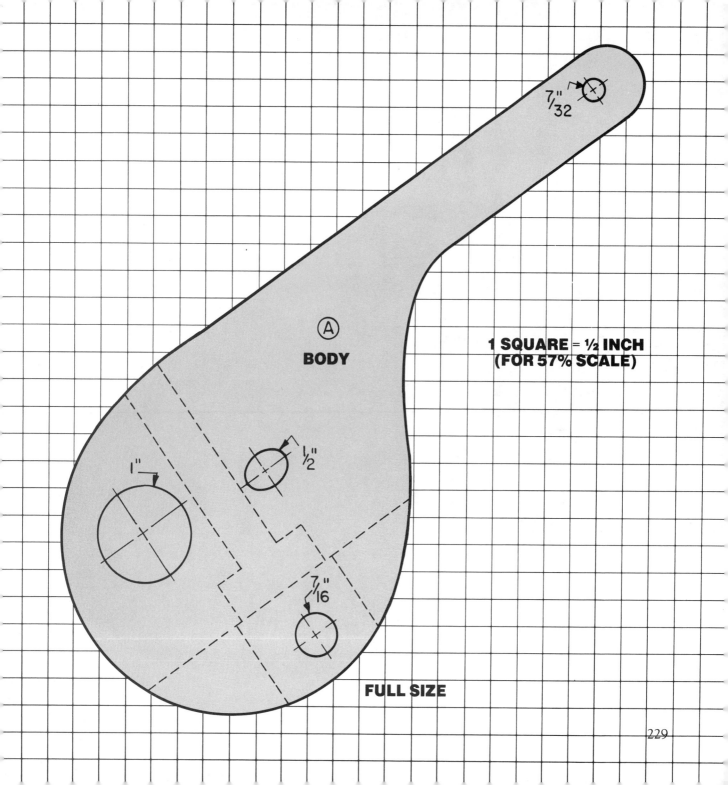

$\frac{7}{32}"$

Ⓐ
BODY

**1 SQUARE = ½ INCH
(FOR 57% SCALE)**

$\frac{1}{2}"$

1"

$\frac{7}{16}"$

FULL SIZE

229

U.F.O. on the Go

To all outward appearances this is a simple toy, but it's not as easy to build as it is to play with. The circular shape and sloped sides of the toy make some of the drilling operations a bit tricky. The hidden pivot dowel gives the U.F.O. a wobbling, hovering motion as it spins. I suggest making the saucer out of either light hardwood or softwood; this will make it easy to spin and play with. This is a great toy to experiment with. You can paint all the details you want on the U.F.O., and the pilot can be as strange or as simple as you like.

The Saucer Base

Scribe a 7″ circle on the piece of wood you've chosen. Transfer the wheel holes and axle positions onto the bottom of the piece (the same side with the circle drawn on it). Draw a straight line through the center of each axle position till the lines reach the edge of the circle. Once the circle is sawn out, these lines will be used to locate the drilling positions of the axle holes. Also, divide the circle into eighths and locate the light positions (See Figure 1).

Use a ½″ Forstner bit to drill out the wheel holes. This will enable you to overlap the holes and drill out most of the material. Set the depth on the drill press so that the tip of the bit drills to the bottom of what will be the hole. After you've drilled with the Forstner bit, use a ½″ twist drill to deepen the hole to where it should be.

This way you won't drill through the upper surface with the tip of the Forstner bit. Now if the edges of your twist drill are sharp, you can slide the saucer back and forth and clean away the rest of the material. If this doesn't work, use a sharp chisel and be careful not to cut all the way through. Now drill the ½″ hole for the pivot dowel on the bottom of the saucer.

Figure 1. Mark out wheel hole positions, axle positions (three), and light positions (eight) on the bottom of saucer base (A).

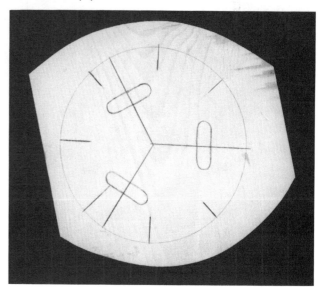

231

Figure 2. Use the axle lines you drew and a square to position the saucer base as you clamp it to a square block for drilling axle holes.

Next, cut the circle out on the bandsaw with the table perfectly perpendicular to the blade. Leave the pencil line for the final cutting. Punch the axle hole locations with an awl. Clamp a square-edged block to the saucer on the drill press and, using a square and the axle line you drew to position the saucer, drill the $^{17}/_{64}''$ axle holes *(See Figure 2)*.

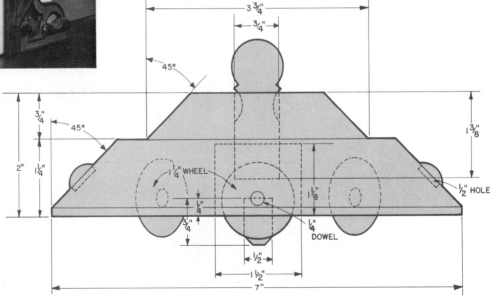

SIDE VIEW

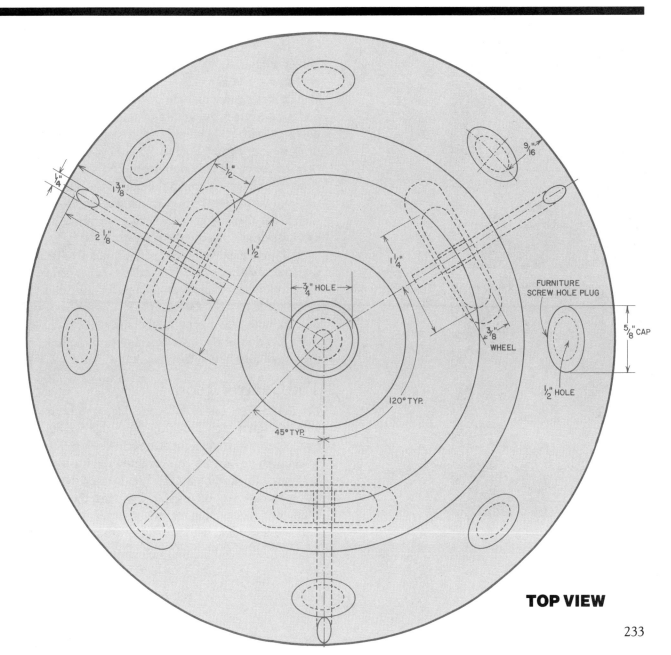

$\frac{1}{4}$"

$\frac{3}{8}$"

$\frac{1}{2}$"

$2\frac{1}{8}$"

$1\frac{1}{2}$"

$1\frac{1}{4}$"

$\frac{9}{16}$"

$\frac{3}{4}$" HOLE

$\frac{3}{8}$" WHEEL

FURNITURE SCREW HOLE PLUG

$\frac{5}{8}$" CAP

$\frac{1}{2}$" HOLE

120° TYP.

45° TYP.

TOP VIEW

233

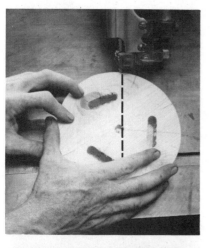

Figure 3. When cutting saucer out at 45°, be careful not to position it too far forward...

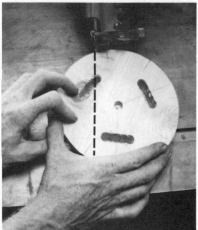

Figure 4. ...or too far back.

Now you're ready to cut out the saucer. Set the bandsaw table to 45°. Take your time and cut out as perfect a circle as possible. The piece should always remain straight to the right of the blade *(See Figures 3 and 4)*. Next, set the sander/grinder table at 45° and edge sand with 80# sandpaper, correcting any imperfections in your sawing. Using the lines you drew which divided the circle into eight segments, mark the locations for the light holes on the side of the saucer. Now flat sand the top and bottom of the saucer with 80# and then 120#. You may want to wet your fingers to grip the sloping side as you sand the bottom.

To drill the light holes, cut a 45° block to support the piece. With the drill press turned off, position the 45° block under the saucer. Clamp a board behind the block and in front of the saucer to hold it in place as you drill the holes. Now bring the Forstner bit down to the exact location of the light hole and drill the hole. Do this for all light holes *(See Figure 5)*.

The Control Room

Cut a 4″ square out of ¾″ stock. Flat sand both sides with 80# sandpaper. This piece is very hard to flat sand on the bottom after it's cut out. Scribe a 4″ circle on the wood with a compass and carefully cut it out on the bandsaw with the table set at 45°. Edge sand the circle at 45° with 80# and then 120#. Flat sand the top with 120#. Round over the top edges with a four-in-hand rasp and then hand sand the edges with 80# and 120#.

The Wheels and the Pivot Dowel

If you make the wheels, ream the axle holes out to $5/16''$. You may use manufactured wheels but they may be too thick. First ream out the axle holes of the manufactured wheels, then sand the wheels down to $3/8''$ on the flat sander. You may need to wet your fingers to hold the wheels. Watch your fingers! Don't attempt this operation if you aren't totally confident. It's easier to make your own wheels the proper thickness. To make the pivot dowel (G), sand one end of a piece of $1/2''$ dowel to a rounded point (*See Figure 6*). Cut it $3/4''$ long and hand sand the edges of the sawn end so it will slip into its hole.

The next step is to put the wheels and axles in place. Put a bit of glue inside the $17/64''$ axle hole (inward from the wheel hole). Slip the axle (cut to $3''$ long) through the wheel as you hold it in position. Put it in just far enough to keep the wheel from falling. Now put glue around the protruding axle and tap it all the way home. Glue all three wheels and axles in this manner, being careful not to get any glue in the axle hole of the wheel or it won't spin freely. Use a paper matchstick to remove any squeeze-out from the inside end of the axle. When the glue is dry, saw the ends off the dowels with a dovetail saw.

Figure 5. Use a 45° block under saucer and a board clamped behind the block to hold it in position for drilling light holes.

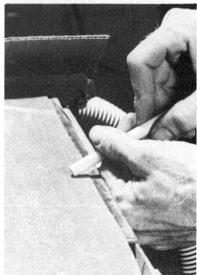

Figure 6. Make a pivot dowel by rounding the end of a piece of $1/2''$ dowel rod.

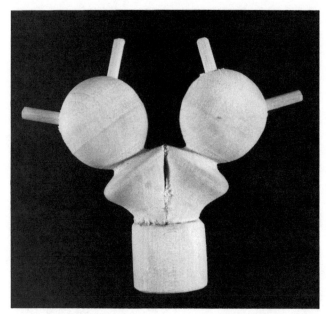

Figure 7. How alien
can you get?

Now edge sand the saucer base with 120# sand-paper. Round over the top and bottom edges with a four-in-hand rasp, and then hand sand the edges with 80# and then 120#. Glue the lights in place. You can use furniture plugs (used to cover screws) for the lights, or you can make the lights. To make the lights, take a ½″ dowel, sand the end of the dowel on the sander/grinder, round the ends on the belt sander, and cut the end off on the bandsaw.

Now put glue on the underside of the control room (B). Don't use too much glue and keep it well away from the edge to avoid squeeze-out. Clamp the control room (B) to the saucer base (A) using pads or scraps to avoid marring, and let the glue dry.

Put a block under the center of the saucer to keep it up off the wheels and drill the hole for the alien on the drill press. Glue the pivot dowel in the ½″ hole in the center of the bottom of the saucer base.

If you're going to paint the U.F.O., now's the time. Go for it! As far as the alien goes, the sky's the limit *(See Figure 7)*.

Now your children can decide if the U.F.O. is an invader or an emissary of peace and wisdom.

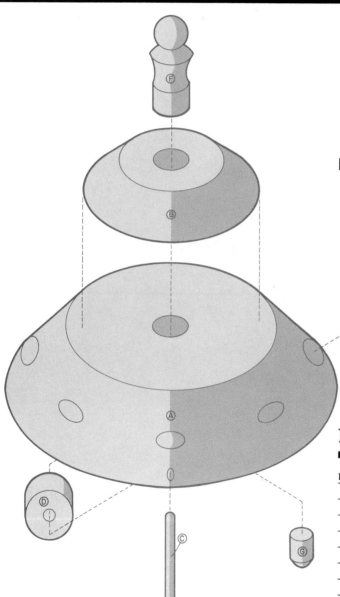

EXPLODED VIEW

BILL OF MATERIALS

PART	DESCRIPTION	QTY	THICKNESS	WIDTH OR DIAMETER	LENGTH
A	Body	1	1¼″	7″	7″
B	Control room	1	¾″	3¾″	3¾″
C	Axles	3		¼″ dia.	2¼″
D	Wheels	3	⅜″	1¼″ dia.	
E	Lights	8	½″ plug	⅝″ cap	
F	Person	1		¾″ dia.	2¼″
G	Pivot dowel	1		½″ dia.	¾″

237

Shaping the

Pressing Down
the Earth

The BULLDOZER with the Will to Work

The smooth reciprocating motion of the blade on this Bulldozer is mesmerizing for both children and adults. The blade is pinned to the back wheels in such a manner that it moves back and forth as the Bulldozer is pushed. It will actually push dirt, sand, or grain effectively. And it's just the thing for pushing that clutter of papers to one side of the executive's desk.

The blade (B) and body (A) are cut out of one piece of wood so there is no waste. If you want to make the blade and body out of two complimentary species, just cut a blade and body out of two blocks and reverse the pieces during assembly.

The 1¾″ x 4″ x 6″ block for pieces A and B must be perfectly square on all sides. When the block is squared, set the bandsaw rip fence to ½″. Using a square, draw a pencil line across the 4″ side of the block, 4⅞″ from one end on both sides of the block. Holding the block against the fence the long way, cut 4⅞″ into the block (*See Figure 1*) to the pencil line. When you back the piece out, be careful not to pull the blade off the wheels. If it starts to bind, turn off the bandsaw and back the piece out. Now flip it over and repeat.

Remove the rip fence and enter the blade into one of the cuts till it's ½″ from the pencil line. Cut a ½″ curve and then straight along the pencil line (*See Figure 2*). Remove the ½″ curve.

Figure 1. Note where the pencil line is drawn, 4⅞″ from the end of the block (on both sides). Set the rip fence on the bandsaw to ½″ and, holding the block against the fence, saw to the line. Flip the block over and repeat.

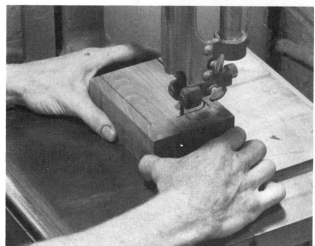

Figure 2. Cut a ½″ curve and then saw along the pencil line.

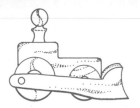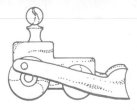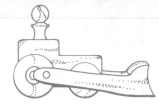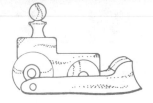

The Body

Transfer the pattern for A, including wheel holes, to the block you've just sawn out (*See Figure 3*). Cut this out and drill the axle holes. Drill the hole for the person. Flat sand the sides, top, bottom, and ends with 80# sandpaper, being careful to keep the surfaces square. If you have trouble with the top and ends on the flat sander, you can sand them on the sander/grinder with an 80# belt.

Now rout all the edges and repeat the surface sanding with 120# sandpaper. Then hand sand all the routed edges with 80# on the rough or burned areas

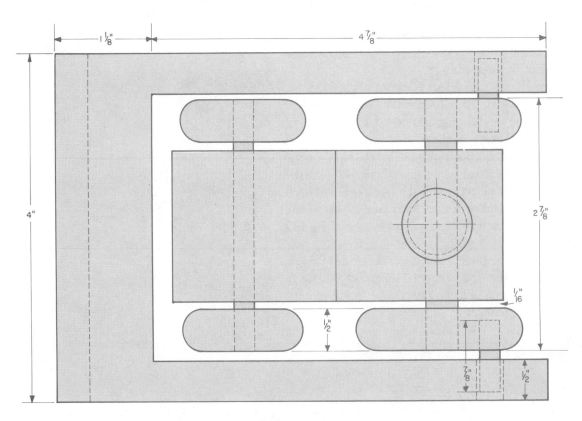

TOP VIEW

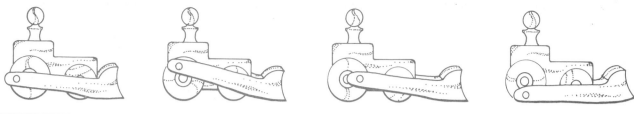

and then with 120# on all the edges. Hand sand the lip of the hole for the driver.

Figure 3. Transfer the body pattern (A) so that its back and bottom edges are flush with the square edges of the block.

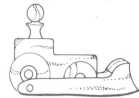

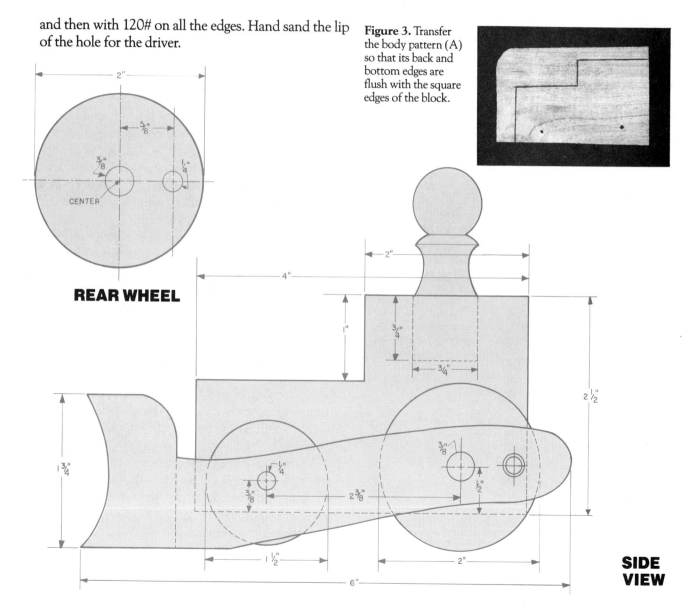

REAR WHEEL

SIDE VIEW

241

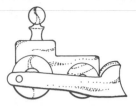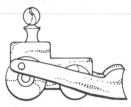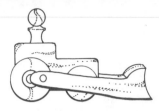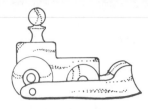

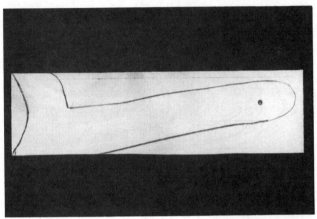

Figure 4. Lay out the silhouette of the blade pattern (B) so the bottom of the blade runs along the edge of the blank, and the back of the scoop corresponds to the cut out area.

The Blade

Mark the blade silhouette and the hole location on the side of the blade stock. Position it so that the back of the blade corresponds with the cut across the stock (*See Figure 4*). Raise the bandsaw blade guide to 4¼". Now cut out the blade slowly, holding it firmly at all times. When you're sawing the arms of the blade, go very slowly and support the upper arm with opposed pressure of your thumb and finger or it may snap off with the downward tugging of the blade (*See Figure 5*). This is not difficult, but keep track of where your fingers and thumbs are so you don't cut yourself.

Next, drill the ⁵⁄₁₆" holes in the blade arms. It would be easier to drill these holes before the block for the body is cut out, but then there would be a hole through the body. If you have a long enough bit, drill all the way through in one pass, making sure that the hole is still centered when it enters the second blade arm. If you don't have a long bit, mark the hole position on the outside of both blade arms and drill from both sides. Here again, too much downward pressure (from the drill in this case) can snap off an unsupported arm during drilling. Either put a 3" block under the arm while you drill it, or use your thumb and fingers to support it.

The scoop on the blade can be sanded on the roller on the end of the belt sander. Hold the blade firmly by both arms and press it against the roller with a 80# sandpaper belt on the sander (*See Figure 6*). Inspect the blade often as you sand to make sure you're not going

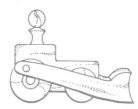
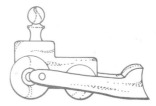
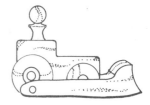

out of square. Then flat sand the sides with 80#. Edge sand the rest of the surfaces with 80#. Be careful to keep even pressure on both blade arms so that their shapes remain similar. Don't take too much material away as you sand around the holes or you will weaken them. Repeat this sanding process with 120#. Then hand sand all the edges with 120#.

Assembly

Drill the holes in the back wheels (G) (*See Techniques and Production Procedures, Figure 17*). Glue the front wheels and axle. Glue the back wheels and axle, being sure to line up the offset holes perfectly so that the blade will work smoothly. When the glue is dry, edge sand all the axle hubs. Now cut two ¼″ dowels about 2″ long, spread glue in the offset wheel holes, position the blade, and tap ¼″ pegs through the holes in the blade and into the wheel holes. Make sure they hit bottom or they will be weak. Leaving these dowels long will enable you to make sure they are perfectly perpendicular to the wheels, and parallel to each other.

Roll the Bulldozer to make sure all is working and adjust the dowels if necessary. When they are thoroughly dry, push each blade arm tightly against its respective wheel, one side at a time, and saw off the excess dowel with a dovetail saw. Now hand sand the dowel ends.

Oil the dozer and the driver and they're ready to do some serious work, from pushing sand in the sandbox to pushing bills aside on your desk.

Figure 5. As you cut the Bulldozer blade (B), support the upper arm with the opposed pressure of your thumb and forefinger, or it may break off. Watch your fingers!

Figure 6. Sand the inside of the blade's scoop on the roller of the belt sander, holding it firmly and inspecting it often for squareness.

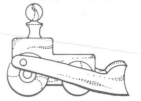

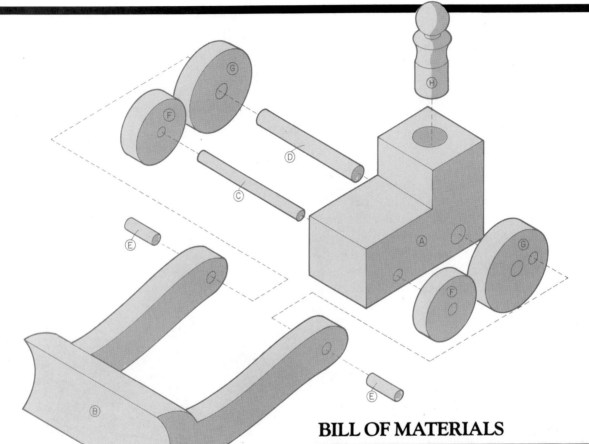

EXPLODED VIEW

BILL OF MATERIALS

PART	DESCRIPTION	QTY	THICKNESS	WIDTH OR DIAMETER	LENGTH
A	Body	1	1¾"	2½"	4"
B	Blade	1	1¾"	4"	6"
C	Front axle	1		¼" dia.	2⅞"
D	Rear axle	1		⅜" dia.	2⅞"
E	Pegs for blade	2		¼" dia.	⅞"
F	Front wheels	2	½"	1½" dia.	
G	Rear wheels	2	½"	2" dia.	
H	Person	1		¾" dia.	2¼"

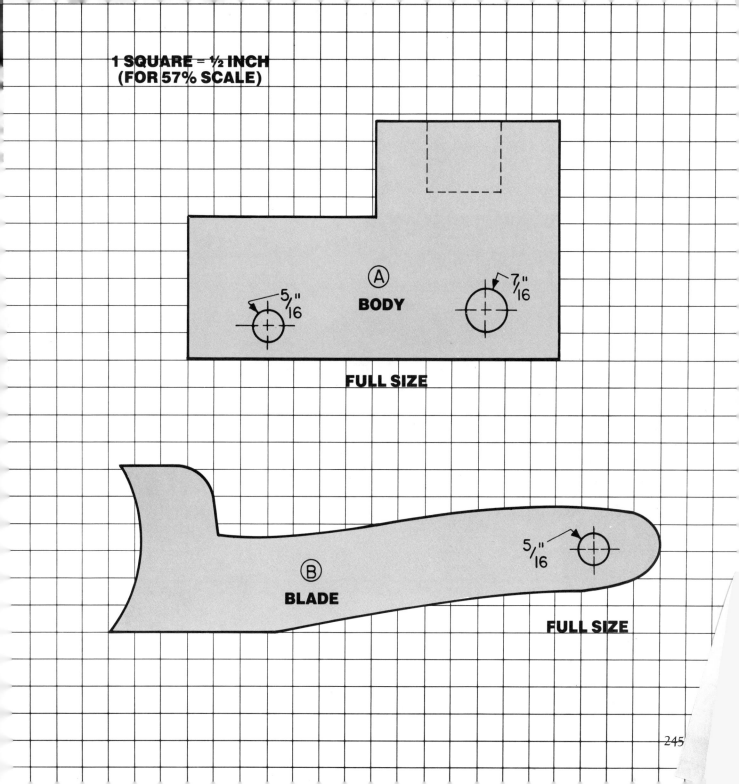

1 SQUARE = ½ INCH
(FOR 57% SCALE)

Ⓐ
BODY

5/16"

7/16"

FULL SIZE

Ⓑ
BLADE

5/16"

FULL SIZE

245

The Mixed-Up
CEMENT MIXER

This Cement Mixer has a rubber band that turns the Mixer when the axle turns. There's also a chute for pouring the concrete and a wheelbarrow to carry concrete to the areas where the chute won't reach. This toy, along with the Bulldozer and the Front End Loader, can handle any construction job.

The Cab

Lay out the cab (A) on a piece of 1¾" stock. Drill the tight inside curves around the windshield and radiator with a ⁵⁄₁₆" bit before cutting A out on the bandsaw. After you've cut out the piece, mark the hole in the back for the dowel that the Mixer pivots on, and the 1" hole on the *top* for the driver. Drill these holes on the drill press. Then, mark the position of the window hole. You'll have to drill this hole with a multispur bit or a Forstner bit. A spade bit will bind as it passes through the 1" hole and will fling the piece around. Next, flat sand the sides, top, bottom, and back with 80# sandpaper. Edge sand the remaining areas with 80#. Rout the entire cab including the window holes and the hole for the driver. Drill the holes for the headlights. Flat sand again with 120# and edge sand with 120#. Hand sand the routed edges with 80# on the rough or burned areas, and then with 120# on all the edges.

Chassis

Cut out the two chassis pieces (B) for the axles. Mark the hole locations and drill them, making sure that both pieces have the holes identically located. Flat sand all four long sides with 80# sandpaper and edge sand the ends with 80#. Make sure that all the edges remain square or the axles won't spin freely. Rout the two short end-grain edges on the top and bottom of both ends of both pieces. Then rout around the whole outline with the axle holes facing up and down so they won't interfere with the roller bearings on the router bit (*See Figures 1, 2*). Flat sand the long sides with 120#.

Figure 1. To rout the chassis pieces, rout the top and bottom end grain edges on both ends of both pieces.

Figure 2. Then you can rout the entire outline without the roller bearing on the router bit slipping into the axle holes.

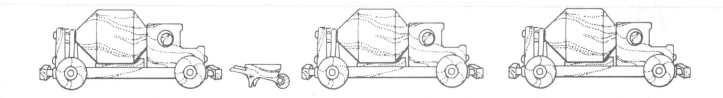

Clamp the pieces, one at a time, to a square block on the drill press. Use a square to make sure they are straight up and down in both directions and drill the ⅜″ holes to attach the bumpers later (*See Figure 3*). Glue the ⅜″ bumper dowels in (with the ends rounded over), making sure that they seat properly to the bottom of the holes. On the bandsaw, cut out the notches on the inside of each piece to allow clearance for the rubber band. Hand sand this area.

The Mixer Support Bracket

Lay out the pattern (C) with the grain running lengthwise to give strength to the little ¼″ tongue that goes

Figure 3. Use a square and a square-edged block to position the chassis pieces on the drill press as you drill the bumper dowel holes.

between the chassis pieces. Drill the ⅜″ hole. Cut the piece out on the bandsaw (leave the pencil line). Flat sand with 80# and 120# sandpaper. Edge sand with 80# and 120#, barely removing the pencil line. Drill the two holes for the tail lights. Hand sand any fuzz from drilling the light holes with 120# and break the edges with 120#. Glue the lights in place.

Bumpers

Lay out the bumpers (E) and cut them out on the bandsaw. Flat sand the tops, bottoms, and outside edges with 80# sandpaper. Edge sand the rest with 80# and 120#. If you're comfortable with the router, rout both pieces all the way around. Otherwise, round over the edges with the four-in-hand rasp. Then sand all the edges with 80# and 120#. Flat sand again with 120#. The drilling will be done later, during assembly, to make sure the holes line up properly.

The Chute

Cut the ¾″ dowel (F) to length. Make a jig to drill the center out of the dowel. Drill a ¾″ hole in the edge of a piece of 2 x 4 and clamp it to the drill press. Don't drill the hole deeper than 1″ or you'll have trouble getting it out. You may have to tap the ¾″ dowel into the hole. The dowel needs to be perfectly upright, so a snug fit in the hole is essential. Once the middle is removed, you'll find that it comes out easily enough. Mark the center of the dowel with a pencil or an awl and drill all the way through, cleaning out the hole frequently.

Mark a line ¾″ from one end. Split the dowel on the bandsaw (holding it firmly) and veer off to the edge when you reach your mark. Now, hand sand it thor-

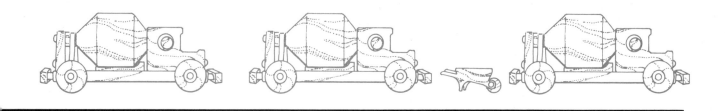

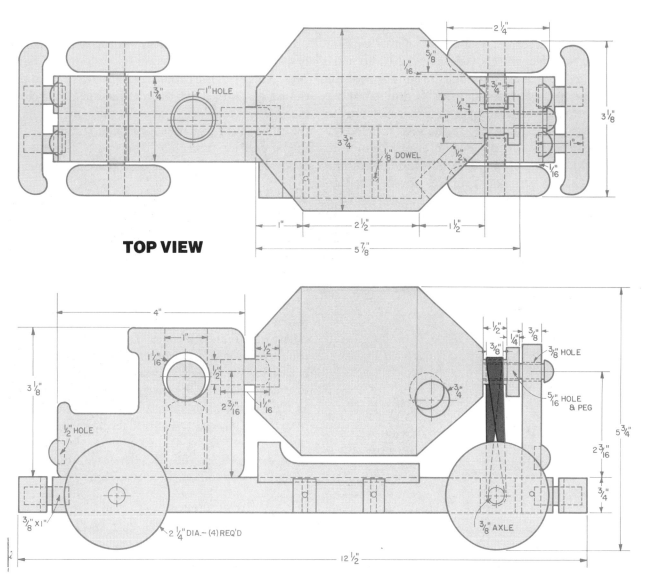

TOP VIEW

1" HOLE

1 3/4"

2 1/4"

5/8"

1/16"

3/4"

1/4"

1"

1/16"

3 1/8"

3 3/4"

3/8" DOWEL

1/2"

1"

2 1/2"

1 1/2"

5 7/8"

SIDE VIEW

4"

1"

1 1/16"

1/2"

1/2"

1 1/16"

2 3/16"

3 1/8"

1/2" HOLE

3/8" X 1"

2 1/4" DIA.– (4) REQ'D

3/4"

3/8"

1/2"

1/4"

3/8"

3/8" HOLE

5/16" HOLE & PEG

5 3/4"

2 3/16"

3/4"

3/8" AXLE

12 1/2"

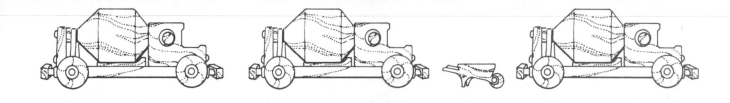

oughly with 80# sandpaper. The center of the trough will have lots of shreds, so it'll take a bit of sanding. Break all the edges with 80# and then 120#. To make the chute supports (G), lay out the pattern with the grain running lengthwise and use a ¾" drill to remove the curve in the top of the supports. Then cut them out on the bandsaw, cutting the top and sides first and the bottom last. Edge sand the sides and bottom with 120#, and hand sand the edges with 120#. Be careful not to sand the sides out of square. Now lay the supports out, as in the side view, with the chute resting on them. Put this assembly on a scrap on the drill press; drill through the chute and through the center of each support. Cut the ⅛" dowels that will hold the chute in place. Glue them into the support pieces. As the glue dries, position the chute on them to make sure they are properly aligned. When they're dry, sand the bottom of the supports flush and round over the top of the two pegs. Now, with the chute attached to keep them positioned, glue and clamp them to the side of the chassis piece. When the glue has set up, remove the chute, drill the ⅛" holes through the supports into the chassis. Cut the ⅛" pegs long and glue them in place. Saw the ends off the ⅛" dowels and sand them flush.

The Mixer

I'm not going to go into the process of turning on the lathe. That would take a whole book in itself. I'll just assume that either you know how to use a lathe or you can find someone to make this part for you. If you don't have a piece of wood big enough to turn the Mixer, glue up some boards. Use light wood so it will rotate easily. Make sure the boards are flat, and use plenty of glue and plenty of clamps. For an interesting touch, you could glue up alternate pieces of two different woods running up and down rather than the long way (*See Figure 4*). Or, turn the Mixer out of one wood and paint it with a spiral. Once you've turned the Mixer, carefully center and drill the holes in either end. Support the cylinder at the proper angle on the drill press and very carefully drill the hole for the chute, using a Forstner bit or a brad point bit.

The Wheelbarrow

Cut a piece of ¾" stock to 2" x 4½". Mark the end grain with a line running diagonally, ¼" from the upper left to ¼" from the lower right (*See Figure 5*). Position the piece behind the bandsaw blade and tilt the table until

MIXER SUPPORT

CHUTE SUPPORT

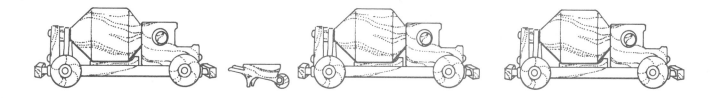

Figure 4. You can glue different types of woods together, on edge, to make the cylinder striped. Make sure the boards are flat and use plenty of glue and plenty of clamps. Any gaps will look unsightly after you've turned the piece.

Figure 5. Mark the end grain of the board to set the angle of the bandsaw table (about 9°) and the rip fence. Rip the halves of the wheelbarrow using a push stick to finish the cut.

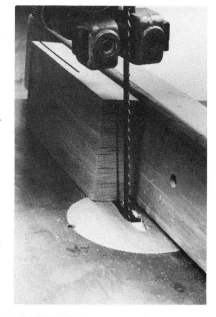

the blade corresponds to the line you drew (approximately 9°). Now, position the rip fence to guide the piece in this position and rip the board in half (*See Figure 6*). Flat sand the sawn edge with 80# sandpaper, as this is the side you'll mark the patterns on. Transfer the patterns with the top of the wheelbarrow flush to the top edge of the piece so they'll end up identical. Carefully drill the ¼" holes for the wheels and cut out the two pieces. Lay out the pattern for the center of the wheelbarrow on a 3" x 3" piece of ¾" stock which has been flat sanded on both sides with 80#. As with the sides, put the top of the pattern flush to the top of this piece. Cut it out on the bandsaw, cutting the scoop out first, then the sides, and finally the bottom. This way you'll have plenty to hold onto as you cut. Now edge sand (or file and hand sand) the inside. Use a sanded ¼" dowel through the wheel holes to line them up as you glue the assembly together. If you have soft wood face plates on your vise, they'll grab it in the middle and apply enough pressure to clamp it. If not, cut two more

Figure 6. Place the piece on the bandsaw table and use the line to resaw the halves for the wheelbarrow sides.

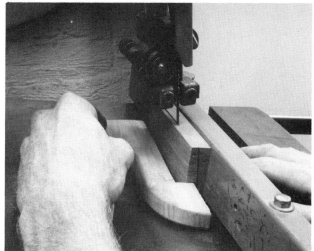

251

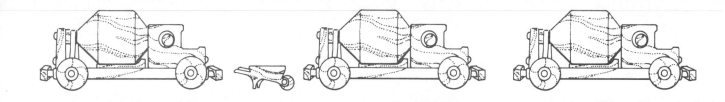

wedges with the bandsaw at 9° and use them to give you parallel surfaces for clamping. When the glue is dry, flat sand the sides of the wheelbarrow with 120#. Carefully edge sand what you can with 80# and then 120#. Hand sand all the rough edges with 120# to break corners off.

A homemade wheel will look better in this situation, as both sides of the wheel are exposed. Make a 1" wheel with a "flycutter" or a hole saw, and enlarge the axle hole to ⁵⁄₁₆". Put glue in one of the axle holes, hold the wheel in position and slip a ¼" dowel (cut long) through the wheel, but not into the glued hole yet. Apply glue around the protruding axle and tap the dowel through until it protrudes slightly on the other side. Let the glue dry, saw the ends off the axle, and give it a touch on the belt sander with 120#.

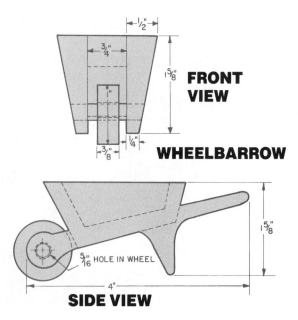

FRONT VIEW

WHEELBARROW

⁵⁄₁₆" HOLE IN WHEEL

SIDE VIEW

Assembly

Apply glue to the undersides of the shoulders on the rear mixer support. Put glue on both sides of the ¼" tongue. Line the chassis pieces up perfectly with a ¼" scrap or dowel at the front to keep them properly spaced. Carefully position the support, and clamp it from the top and bottom as well as from the sides (*See Figure 7*). When it's dry, drill the ⅛" hole through the chassis pieces and the support and glue the dowel in place. Saw the ends off and sand them flush.

Glue the lights onto the front of the cab. Cut the dowel mixer support (J) to length. Round off both ends (*See Techniques and Production Procedures, Figure 24*) and glue it into the back of the cab. Don't use too much glue or it won't seat properly.

Using a ¼" spacer between the chassis parts (B), glue the cab down onto them. When the glue has set up, hold the front bumper up to the ⅜" bumper dowels. Center it carefully and mark the hole positions on the bumper. Drill the holes. Repeat this for the rear bumpers. Now spread a little glue on the insides of all four holes and use a pole clamp to pull the bumpers on until they're square. Be sure to use pads or scraps to protect the bumpers.

Glue the front and back wheels onto their respective axles and edge sand the axle hubs after the glue has dried. Now oil everything including the driver, the wheelbarrow, the chute, the Mixer, and the peg for the back of the Mixer. When the finishing is done, slip the front of the Mixer cylinder onto the ½" dowel. Hold the back of the Mixer in position and glue the peg into the rear hole passing it through the rear support. Cut a strip of inner tube ⅜" x 8". Pass it under the rear axle

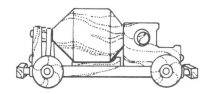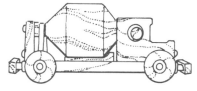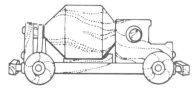

and over the back of the Mixer cylinder. Bring both ends together (there should be a half twist in the middle) over the top of the drive area of the Mixer cylinder. Pull the band fairly tight (stretch it a bit) and overlap it ¾". Cut it to length (*See Figure 8*); taper opposite sides of each end of the band (*See Figure 9*).

Apply contact cement to the opposite tapered ends. When the cement is dry, carefully position the band around the axle and the Mixer and press the glued ends firmly together (*See Figure 10*). Now...off to the work site for some serious play!

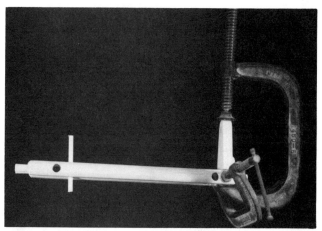

Figure 7. Clamp the rear mixer support from the sides and the top and bottom as you glue it. Note the ¼" spacer in front to keep the chassis pieces lined up properly.

Figure 8. With the rubber band stretched around the back axle, cut it to length. Leave a ¾" overlap.

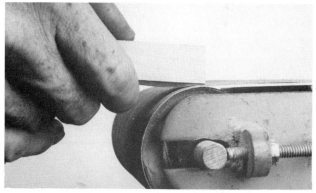

Figure 9. Taper the ends of the rubber band by pressing them onto the roller of the belt sander with a scrap of wood.

Figure 10. With contact cement on both tapered ends of the band, stretch it and press the ends together for 30 seconds.

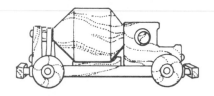

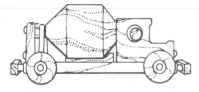

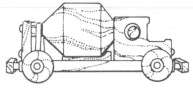

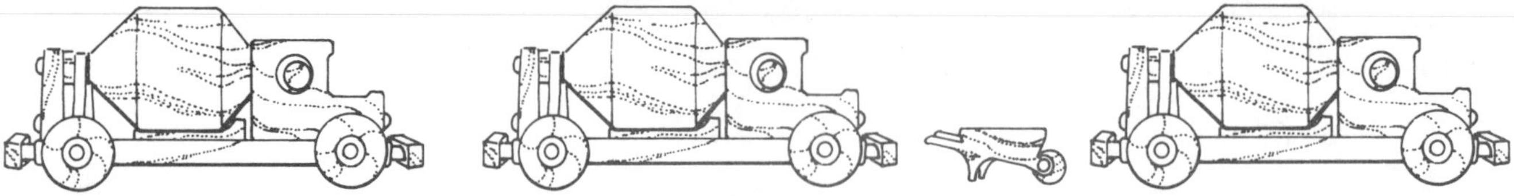

BILL OF MATERIALS

PART	DESCRIPTION	QTY	THICKNESS	WIDTH OR DIAMETER	LENGTH
A	Cab	1	1¾″	3⅛″	4″
B	Chassis	2	¾″	¾″	11″
C	Mixer support	1	⅜″	1¾″	3¼″
D	Mixer barrel	1	3¾″	3¾″	5⅞″
E	Bumpers	2	¾″	¾″	3⅛″
F	Chute	1		¾″ dia.	3½″
G	Chute supports	2	½″	¾″	¾″
H	Lights	4		½″ dia. plugs	
J	Mixer support dowel	1		½″ dia.	1¹⁄₁₆″
K	Bumper dowels	4		⅜″ dia.	1″
L	Axles	2		⅜″ dia.	3⅛″
M	Chute support dowels	2		⅛″ dia.	1½″
N	Mixer support pin	1		⅛″ dia.	1¾″
P	Chute pins	2		⅛″ dia.	¾″
Q	Mixer pivot peg	1		⁵⁄₁₆″ dia.	1⁹⁄₁₆″
R	Person	1	¾″ dia. body	⅞″ dia. head	2¼″
S	Wheels	4	⅝″	2¼″ dia.	
T	Wheelbarrow sides (split)	1	¾″	1⅝″	4″
U	Wheelbarrow center	1	¾″	1⅛″	2½″
V	Wheelbarrow axle	1		¼″ dia.	1⅜″
W	Wheelbarrow wheel	1	⅜″	1″ dia.	
X	Rubber band	1	⅜″		8″

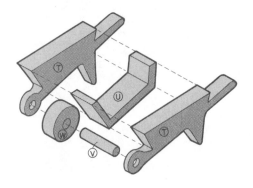

WHEELBARROW/ EXPLODED VIEW

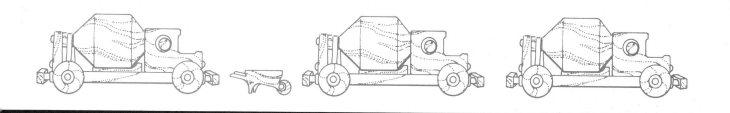

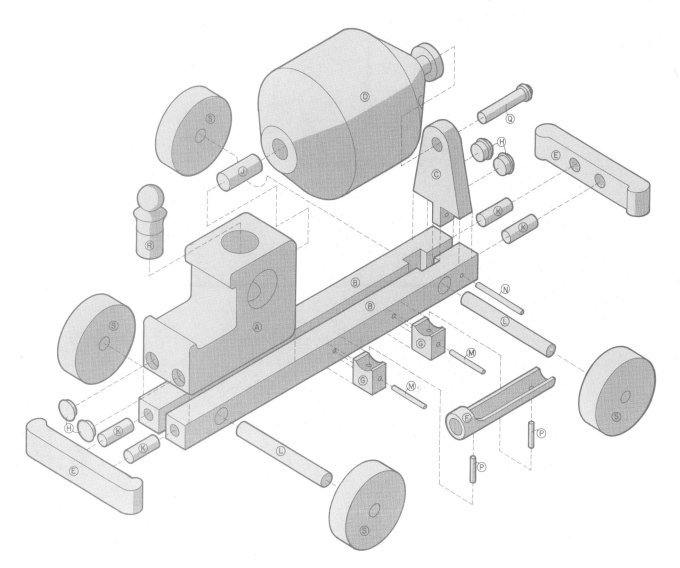

CEMENT MIXER/EXPLODED VIEW

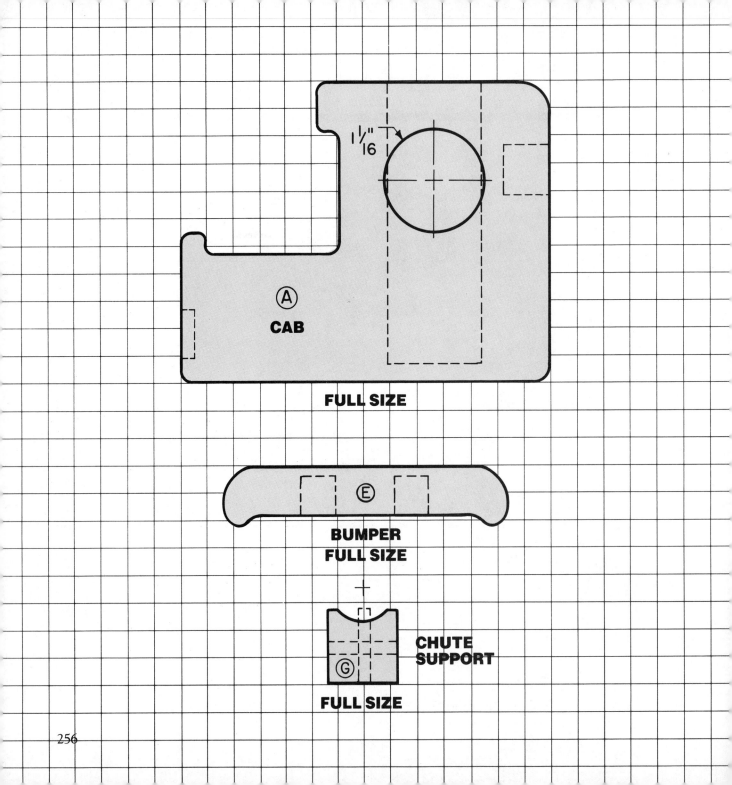

1 1/16"

Ⓐ
CAB

FULL SIZE

Ⓔ
BUMPER
FULL SIZE

CHUTE
SUPPORT
Ⓖ
FULL SIZE

256

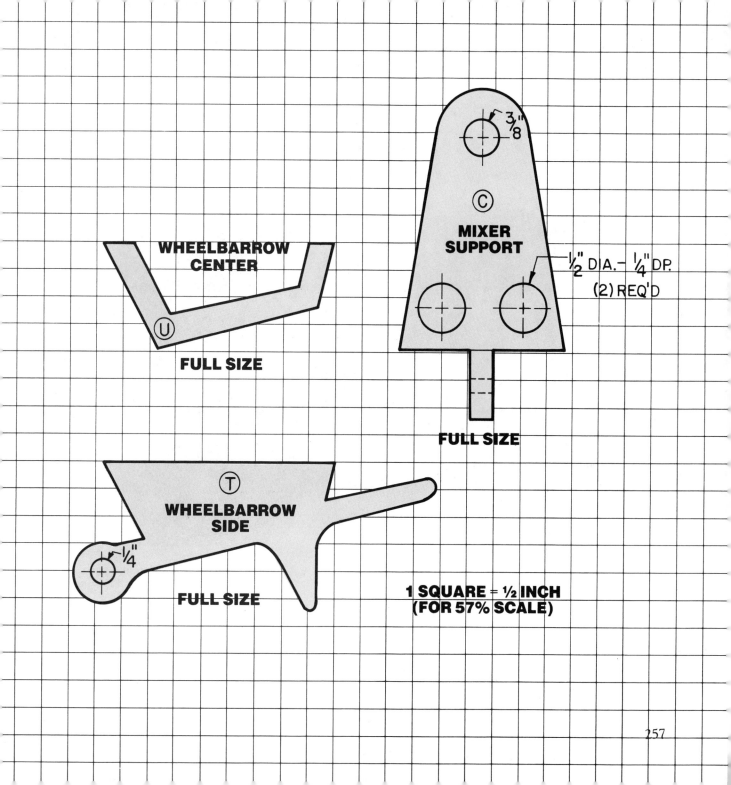

WHEELBARROW
CENTER

U

FULL SIZE

MIXER
SUPPORT

C

$\frac{3}{8}$"

$\frac{1}{2}$" DIA. – $\frac{1}{4}$" DP.

(2) REQ'D

FULL SIZE

WHEELBARROW
SIDE

T

$\frac{1}{4}$"

FULL SIZE

1 SQUARE = ½ INCH
(FOR 57% SCALE)

257

The Foremost Front End LOADER

This toy is a real workhorse when it comes to moving dirt, sand, or just about anything. Unlike most of the toys in this book, though, it needs a little explaining. It works a lot like the Bulldozer, by means of a peg on the back wheel. But if you just push it along, the shovel goes up and down senselessly. To play with this toy, a child must hold the back wheels to keep the scoop from rising. When the Loader reaches the dirt that's to be lifted, the wheels are released and the scoop digs in and lifts the material. When the scoop reaches the top of its lift, once again the back wheels are held as the child maneuvers the Loader to the dumping place. Then when the wheels turn again, the load is lowered. It sounds a little complicated, but it's really obvious once you see how it works.

This toy should be made entirely out of strong hardwood. The thin pieces need to be strong for obvious reasons, whereas the body has some thin areas where the scoop and the roof attach.

The Body

Transfer the body pattern (A) onto a 1¾″ thick piece of hardwood. Drill the axle holes and cut out the body on the bandsaw. Don't drill the peg holes for attaching the scoop until the roof is attached. With the rip fence on the bandsaw, cut away the areas for the front wheels. Flat sand the sides, back, and bottom with 80# and then 120# sandpaper. Edge sand all the other surfaces with 80#. Rout all the edges that you can. Rout the end grain edges first and then rout around the corners with the body on its side. Drill the hole for the driver and the four ¼″ holes for the roof posts. Pay special attention to the depth of these holes so that the roof will end up

flat later on. Edge sand again with 120#. Round over the unrouted edges with a four-in-hand rasp. Hand sand all the rough or burned edges with 80#, and then hand sand all the edges with 120#.

The Scoop

Mark out the sides of the scoop (B), locate the holes very carefully. Mark the hole locations with a punch or an awl and drill them. Cut out the pieces. Flat sand the pieces with 80# sandpaper, and edge sand the arms of the scoop with 80# and 120#. Cut the scoop claw (C) out of 1⅞″ stock on the bandsaw. Mark the teeth on the scoop claw and cut them out with a ⅛″ blade on the bandsaw, or with a stationary jigsaw or a coping saw. Hand sand the teeth, the inside, and the back of the scoop with 80#.

Figure 1. Position the ¾″ x ¾″ x 1⅞″ block (with the 7/32″ hole through it) between the two sides of the scoop. Tap the sanded pegs through the side holes and into the block. Slip a ¼″ dowel through the top holes in the sides. The two scoop sides should be perfectly lined up to glue the assembly together.

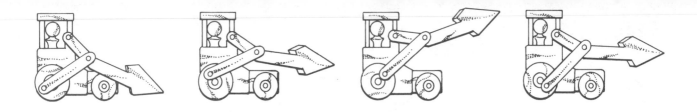

You'll need to make a simple jig to glue the scoop together. Cut a ¾" x ¾" square out of 1⅞" stock. Drill a ⁷⁄₃₂" hole through the center of it, the long way. Now take two ⁷⁄₃₂" pegs (M) and sand enough off so they will fit through the ⁷⁄₃₂" holes in each scoop arm. To glue the scoop together, apply glue to the sides of the scoop claw (C) and slip a ¼" dowel through the top hole in the scoop side (B). Position the jig between the center of the scoop sides, slip the sanded pegs through the sides and into the jig (*See Figure 1*). This will keep the sides perfectly lined up as you glue the scoop together. Now clamp the assembly together with the center of the scoop (C) lined up as well as possible. When the assembly is dry, flat sand the sides with 120# sandpaper, and edge sand the scoop claw (not the sides) with 80# and then 120#. Now break all the edges by hand with 120#.

The Roof and Drive Arms

Mark out the roof and drive arms. Drill all the holes in the roof (E), cut it out on the bandsaw, and flat sand it with 80# and then 120# sandpaper. Edge sand the roof with 80# and then 120# and break all the edges by hand with 120# (the 1" hole too). Cut out the two drive arms (D) and lay one on top of the other as you drill the holes to make sure they are identical. Flat sand the drive arm with 80# and then 120#. Edge sand them with 80# and 120#, then break all the edges with 120#.

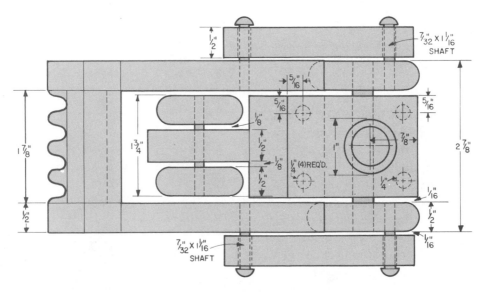

TOP VIEW

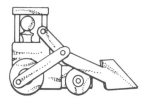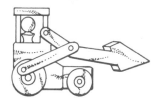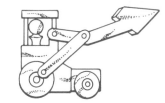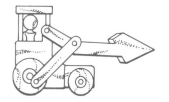

The Wheels

Using the drilling jig (*See Techniques and Production Procedures, Figure 17*), drill the peg holes in the rear wheels.

Assembly

Cut the ¼″ dowels for the roof (F & G) to the exact length. Round the ends over on the belt sander (*See Techniques and Production Procedures, Figure 24*). Apply a little glue to the insides of all eight holes. Tap the dowels into the roof piece. (Make sure which end is the front.) Locate the dowels in the body holes and (using a scrap to prevent marring the roof) hammer the roof on until the dowels seat thoroughly and the roof lays flat. Lay the body on its side on the drill press and drill the ⁷/₃₂″ peg hole. Glue the front wheels on. Glue the back wheels on, making sure the peg holes line up perfectly. When the glue is dry, edge sand the axle hubs. Glue and peg the scoop to the body using the clearance gauge (*See Techniques and Production Procedures, Figure 28*).

Using the edge of the workbench for support, glue and peg the drive arms to the rear wheels. Wipe off excess glue before it smears on the body. With the blade in the up position, glue and peg the drive arms to the scoop sides using the clearance gauge. Here again, wipe off any excess glue before it smears on the body. When the glue is thoroughly dry, oil the finished Front End Loader (don't forget the driver) and it's ready for some serious work. If you're giving it as a gift, write a little note with the instructions from the beginning of the chapter. With that little bit of help, any child will really use this toy in his or her fantasy work.

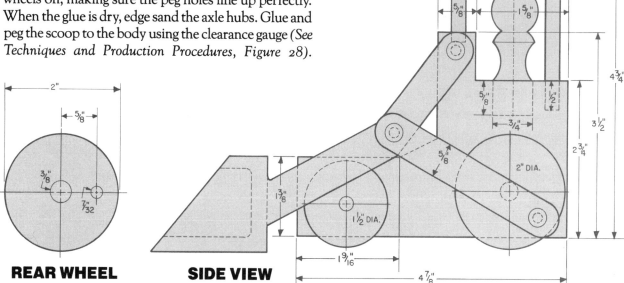

REAR WHEEL　　**SIDE VIEW**

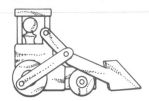

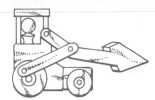

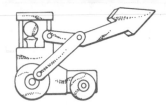

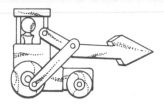

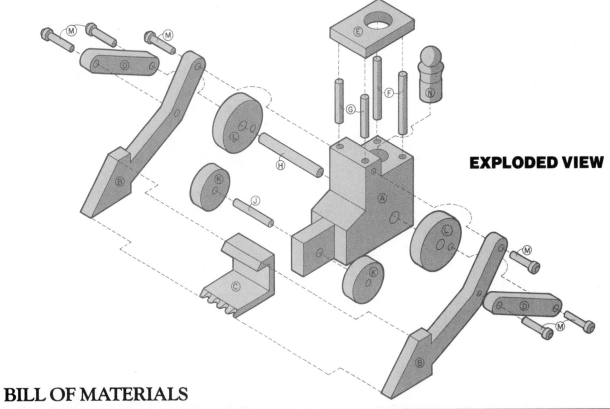

EXPLODED VIEW

BILL OF MATERIALS

PART	DESCRIPTION	QTY	THICKNESS	WIDTH OR DIAMETER	LENGTH
A	Body	1	1¾″	3½″	4⅞″
B	Scoop sides	2	½″	2⅛″	6¾″
C	Scoop claw	1	1⅞″	1¾″	2″
D	Drive arms	2	½″	⅝″	3¾″
E	Cab roof	1	⅜″	1¾″	2⅜″
F	Rear roof supports	2		¼″ dia.	2⅜″
G	Front roof supports	2		¼″ dia.	1¼″

PART	DESCRIPTION	QTY	THICKNESS	WIDTH OR DIAMETER	LENGTH
H	Rear axle	1		⅜″ dia.	2⅞″
J	Front axle	1		¼″ dia.	1¾″
K	Front wheels	2	½″	1½″ dia.	
L	Rear wheels	2	½″	2″ dia.	
M	Pegs	6		7/32″ dia.	1 1/16″ shaft
N	Person	1		¾″ dia.	2¼″

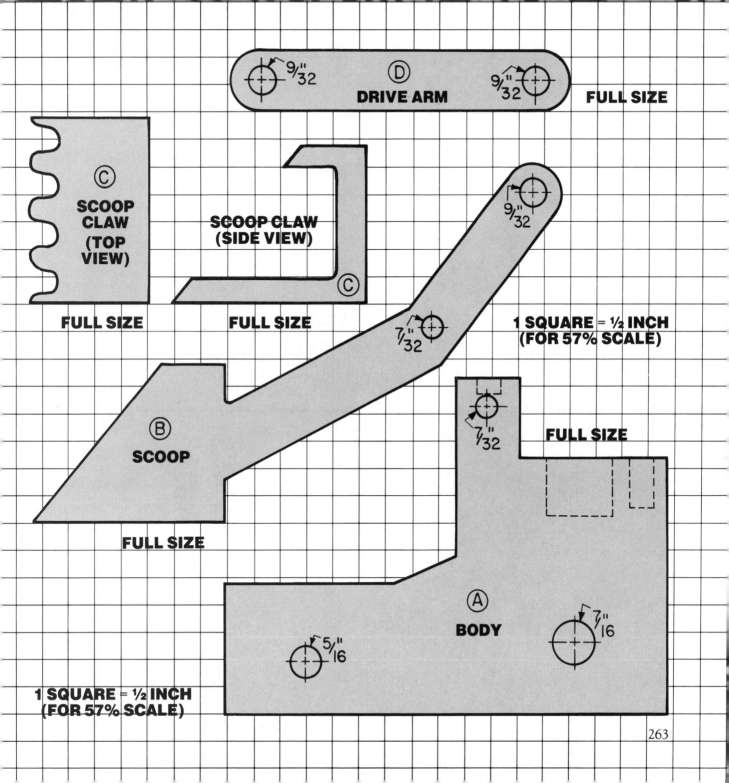

Prehistoric MONSTERS

- The Tyrannical Tyrannosaurus
- The Brawny Brontosaurus
- The Cantankerous Triceratops

The Tyrannical
TYRANNOSAURUS

The diagonally opposed, offset wheels give this monstrous dinosaur an ominous swaying gait as the cam and dowel open and close his deadly jaws. The upper arms are pinned tightly so they can be set in different positions, whereas the compound cuts on his tail give it a convincingly serpentine appearance. You can be sure this creature didn't become extinct from lack of predatory savagery.

The Body

Lay out the body (A) so the cam slot is parallel to the edge of the board (*See Figure 1*). Drill the axle and peg holes. Using a few passes with dado blades or a wobble blade, cut out the slot for the cam. If your wobble blade won't cut the slot deep enough, use a handsaw and a chisel to cut it to the proper depth.

Cut out the outline of the body, except for the teeth. Leave a flat line along the top of the teeth; this will enable you to locate and drill the ½″ hole. Draw a line on the body corresponding to the center of the dowel. Use this line to set the body at the proper angle on the drill press to drill the ½″ hole. Clamp the body securely in this position. The hole is so deep that you'll have to use a very long ½″ bit, or an extension for your spade bit. This hole will take some time. You will have to back the bit all the way out to clean the hole and the bit as you go. Also, the hole is deeper than the throw of most drill presses.

When you've drilled the hole, cut the outline of the teeth and edge sand the entire outline with 80# sandpaper. Flat sand both sides with 80# and 120#, and rout the outline on both sides (except the teeth). Now transfer the top view of the tail onto the top of the tail

and cut it out on the bandsaw. Now edge sand this newly sawn area with 80# and 120#, and edge sand the rest of the body with 120#.

With the body in a vise, round over the edges of the tail with a four-in-hand rasp and 80# sandpaper. Then hand sand all the routed and filed edges with 120#.

The Head

Cut out the head spacer (⅛″ thicker than the body) and the two ⅜″ head sides. Edge sand the lower back of the head spacer where the dowel will push it; this will keep the dowel from catching. Flat sand both sides of the two ⅜″ head side pieces with 80# sandpaper. Carefully line up the pieces as you glue and clamp them.

When they are set up, locate and drill the eye peg hole. Edge sand the assembly with 80# and 120# sandpaper. Mark the taper on the top front of the jaw piece and cut off the two wedges. Then flat sand this sawn area with 80#, rocking it onto the flat side to make a smooth transition. Repeat with 120#. Rout the outline on both sides (except the teeth). Hand sand the routed edges, and round over the teeth a bit with 80# and then 120#.

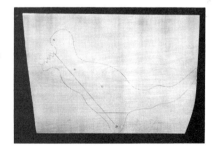

Figure 1. Lay out the body so the dado slot is parallel to and against a jointed edge.

The Arms and Legs

Lay out all six arm and leg pieces. Drill the peg holes (all 9/32″ except the lower holes in the thigh pieces which are 7/32″). Cut out the pieces, flat sand with 80# and 120# sandpaper. Break the edges with 120#.

The Wheels and Cam

Using the wheel jig (*See Techniques and Production Procedures, Figure 17*), drill the 7/32″ peg holes. Plug the axle hole and when the glue is dry, redrill the axle holes (⅜″) slightly off center. Make a cam wheel (½″ x 1¼″), plug the center hole and drill the off-center hole.

Assembly

Assemble the legs in opposite sets. Glue one front wheel to the axle. With the cam in place, slip the axle through and glue the other wheel on; make sure they are diagonally opposed, one wheel offset one way and the other wheel offset the other way. When the glue is dry, sand the axle hubs. Drill the ⅛″ hole through the cam and glue the ⅛″ dowel in place. Glue and peg the thighs to the body using the clearance gauge if necessary (*See Techniques and Production Procedures, Figure 28*).

Use the workbench to support the wheels, and glue and peg the feet to the wheels. Glue and peg the arms to the body. Drive the peg all the way in so the arms will stay where they are positioned. Glue and peg the head in place, use the clearance gauge if necessary. Cut the work dowel to length and round off the ends.

When all the glue is dry, oil the beast (and the dowel), slip the dowel in place and watch out! The unbeatable Tyrannosaurus is extinct no more!

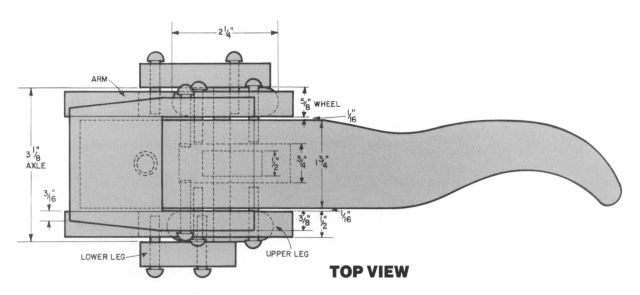

TOP VIEW

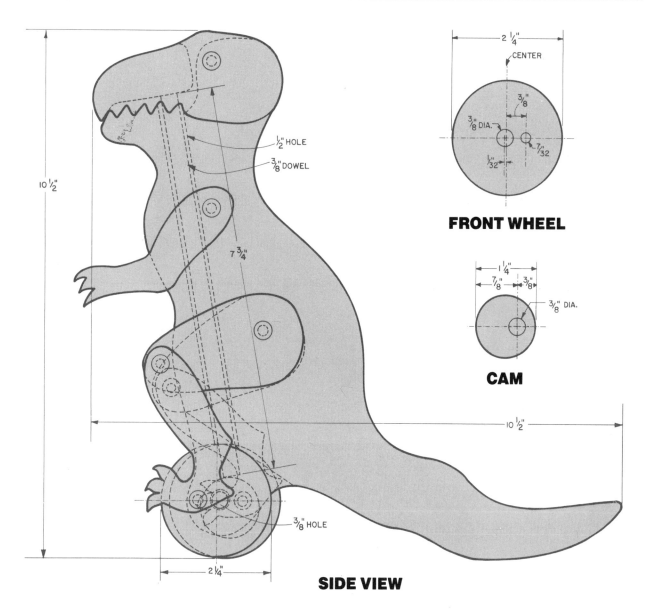

½" HOLE

³⁄₈" DOWEL

7 ³⁄₄"

10 ½"

10 ½"

³⁄₈" HOLE

2 ¼"

SIDE VIEW

2 ¼"

CENTER

³⁄₈"

³⁄₈" DIA.

7⁄₃₂"

1⁄₃₂"

FRONT WHEEL

1 ¼"

7⁄₈"

³⁄₈"

³⁄₈" DIA.

CAM

269

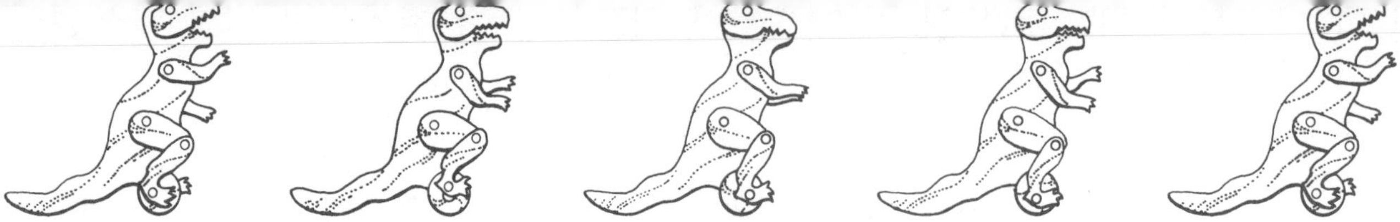

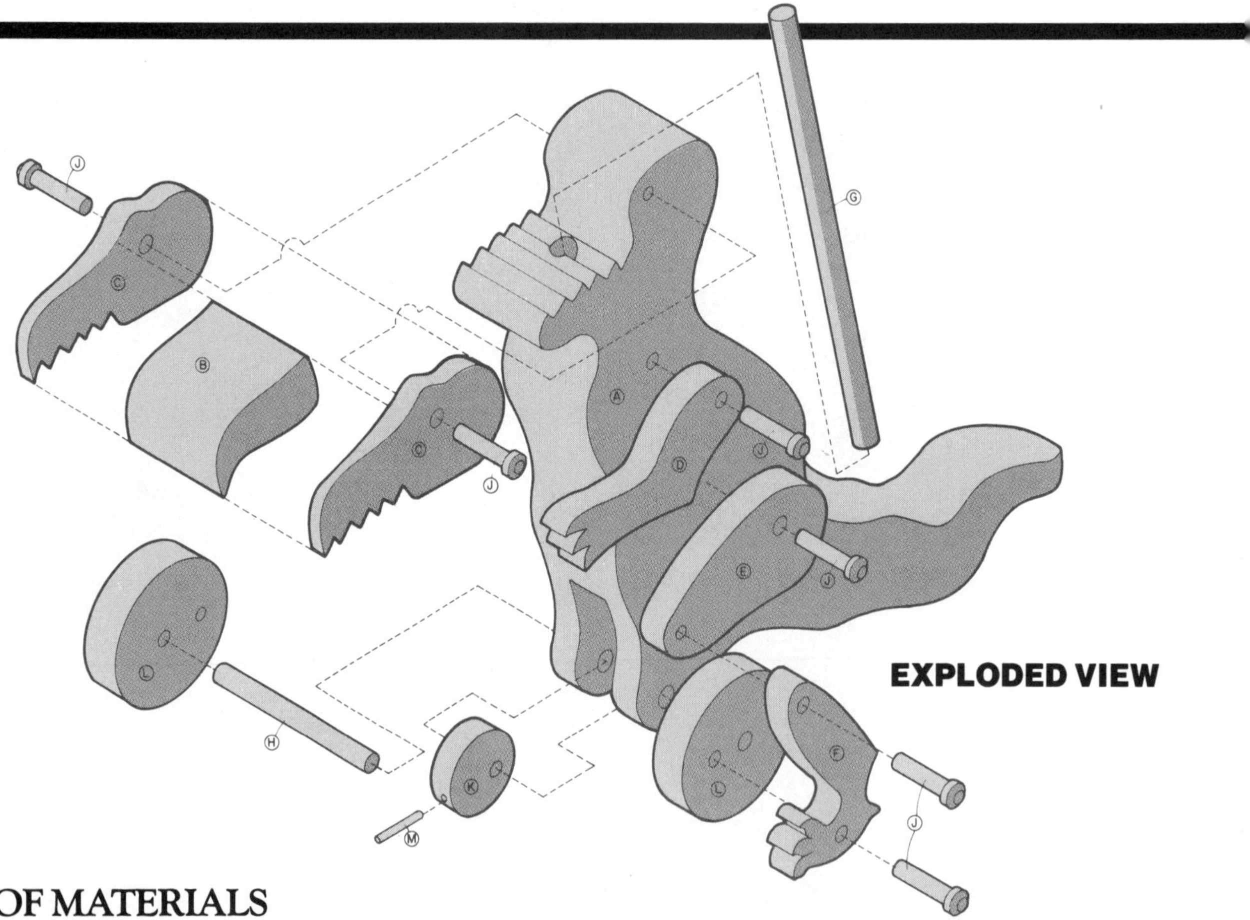
EXPLODED VIEW

BILL OF MATERIALS

PART	DESCRIPTION	QTY	THICKNESS	WIDTH OR DIAMETER	LENGTH
A	Body	1	1¾″	7¼″	12⅞″
B	Head spacer	1	1⅞″	1″	2¼″
C	Head sides	2	⅜″	1⅞″	4″
D	Arm	2	½″	1⅜″	3¾″
E	Upper legs	2	½″	1⅞″	3⅜″
F	Lower legs	2	½″	1⅞″	3⅜″
G	Work dowel	1		½″ dia.	7¾″

PART	DESCRIPTION	QTY	THICKNESS	WIDTH OR DIAMETER	LENGTH
H	Axle	1		¼″ dia.	3⅛″
J	Pegs	8		7/32″ dia.	1 1/16″ shaft
K	Cam	1	½″	1¼″ dia.	
L	Wheels	2	⅝″	2¼″ dia.	
M	Cam pin	1		⅛″ dia.	⅞″

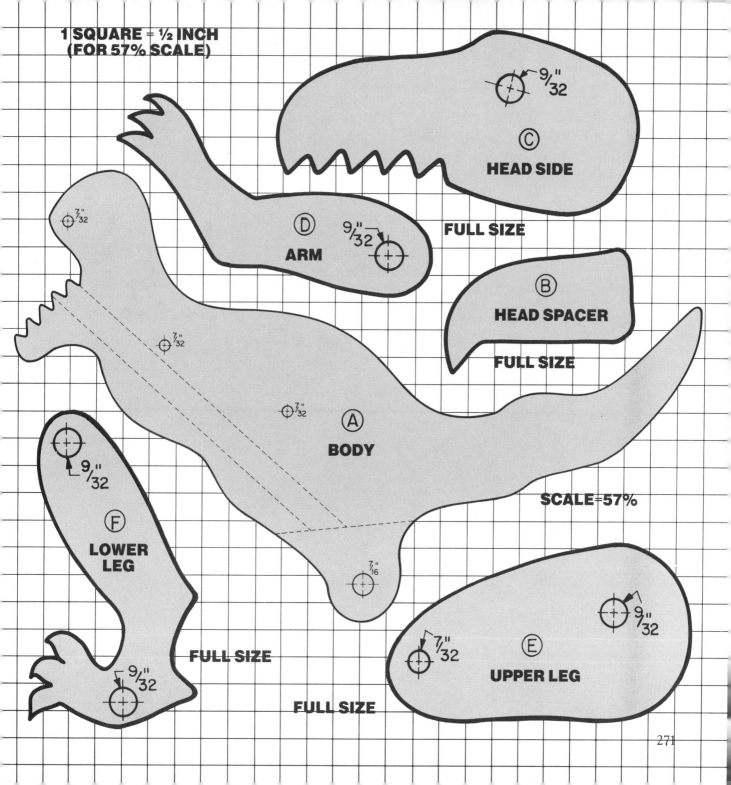

The Brawny
BRONTOSAURUS

Watch your garden; here comes the brawny Brontosaurus. This voluminous vegetarian has a brain at both ends of his body, so it's only fitting that his head and tail should gently sway up and down as he ponderously thuds along. The motion of his huge legs seems to propel him as he's pushed along.

The Head and Tail

Lay out the head and tail piece (A) on a strong, clear piece of ¾" stock. Drill the ¼" hole and the ⅜" hole and plug the eye hole with a ¼" x ¾" piece of dowel (L). Cut out the shape on the bandsaw. Cut the head out carefully. The small curves give him his character. Clamp the piece down on the workbench and flat sand both sides with 80# and 120# sandpaper. Edge sand with 80#. Rout the entire outline and then edge sand again with 120#. Hand sand any rough or burned areas with 80#; then hand sand all the routed edges with 120#. You need not worry about hand sanding the area that will be inside the body. Glue the ⅜" dowel (J) into the pivot hole; make sure that an equal amount extends on both sides.

The Legs

Lay out all eight leg pieces (E, F, G, H) on ⅝" stock. Drill all the holes, bearing in mind which holes secure the peg (elbow of upper leg) and which holes let the peg pivot (all the rest).

Cut the leg pieces out on the bandsaw and edge sand with 80# sandpaper. Flat sand with 80# and 120#. Now round the edges on all eight pieces with 120#.

Assemble the legs in opposing pairs using the clearance gauge if necessary (*See Techniques and Production Procedures, Figure 28*).

The Body

You'll probably have to glue up ½" pieces big enough to make the sides (B). Be careful to get them flat as you glue them up. Lay out both sides (B), choosing a good side of each board. Cut out both pieces on the bandsaw when the glue is dry. Now flat sand them on both sides with 80# sandpaper.

Mark the hole locations on one of the pieces and lay it on top of the other on the drill press. With a scrap under your work, drill the holes through both pieces so that they will line up perfectly. The front and the rear (where the head and tail will come out) cannot be sanded after assembly, so edge sand these areas with 80# and 120# sandpaper.

Now cut pieces C and D out of 1" stock. Lay one of the sides (B) (good side down) on a block; this will hold it up off the workbench so you can apply C-clamps. Put glue on both sides of C and D, and position them. Place the head and tail piece (A) in its proper position, with the ¼" dowel sitting in the ⁵⁄₁₆" hole (*See Figure 1*). Carefully place the other B piece in position, with the ¼" dowel sitting in its ⁵⁄₁₆" hole. Place two ⅜" dowels through the axle holes to make sure that they line up properly. Clamp the whole assembly together using three C-clamps over the C piece, and two over the D piece. Don't forget to use pads or scraps to prevent marring the sides.

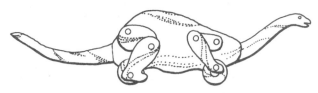

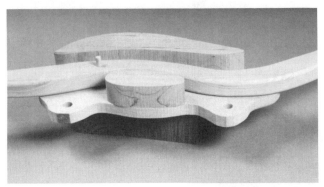

Figure 1. Glue both sides of C and D; position them with B up on a block to make clamping easier. Then position the head and tail piece (A).

When the assembly is thoroughly dry, saw off any large discrepancies in B, C, and D on the bandsaw. Now edge sand the entire outline except where the head and tail come out. Flat sand both sides with 120# sandpaper. Rout both sides of the outline (except areas already routed). Lift the head and tail as you rout under them so the top of the router bit doesn't touch these areas. Edge sand with 120#. Hand sand any roughness or burns with 80#. Then hand sand all the routed edges with 120#.

The Wheels and Cam

Using the wheel drilling jig (*See Techniques and Production Procedures, Figure 17*), drill the 7/32″ holes in all four 2¼″ dia. wheels.

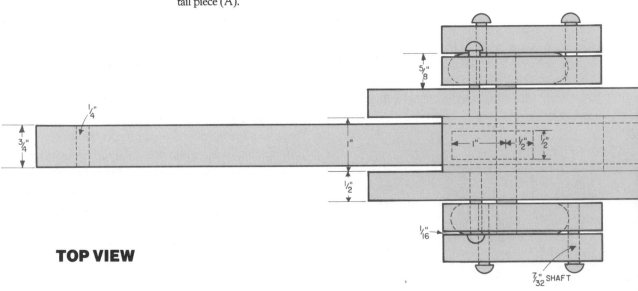

TOP VIEW

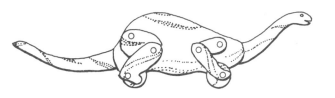
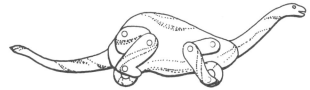

A manufactured wheel will work just as well as a handmade one for the cam. In either case, use the wheel jig mentioned above; drill the off-center ⅜" hole. A Forstner bit will be less likely to split the wheel. Then plug the original axle hole.

Final Assembly

Cut the two axles to length (a little long). Glue one of the rear wheels to its axle. Slip it through the rear axle hole. Make sure that the ⁷⁄₃₂" peg holes are diagonally opposed (one up, one down) as you hammer the second wheel on. Repeat the procedure for the front wheels with the cam held in position as you slip the dowel through the axle holes.

With the Brontosaurus on his back on the drill press, drill the ⅛" hole through the cam and the axle. The cam should be centered with most of its mass below the dowel as you drill. Glue the ⅛" x 1⅛" dowel in place and wipe off excess glue. When the glue on the axles is dry, edge sand the axle hubs.

Glue and peg the rear thigh to the body (make sure it is the correct leg in the correct position). Then glue and peg the foot to the wheel, using the edge of the workbench to support the wheel as you tap the peg in. Repeat this process for all four legs; use a clearance gauge if necessary.

When all the glue has dried, oil the Brontosaurus and look out! Children will have fun in a big way whenever this prehistoric monster is in the room.

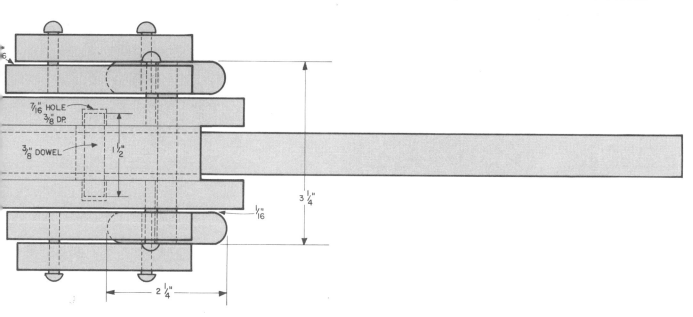

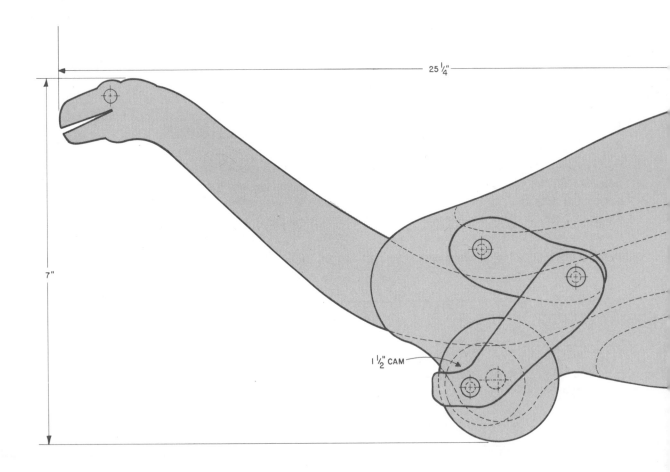

25 $\frac{1}{4}$"

7"

1 $\frac{1}{2}$" CAM

SIDE VIEW

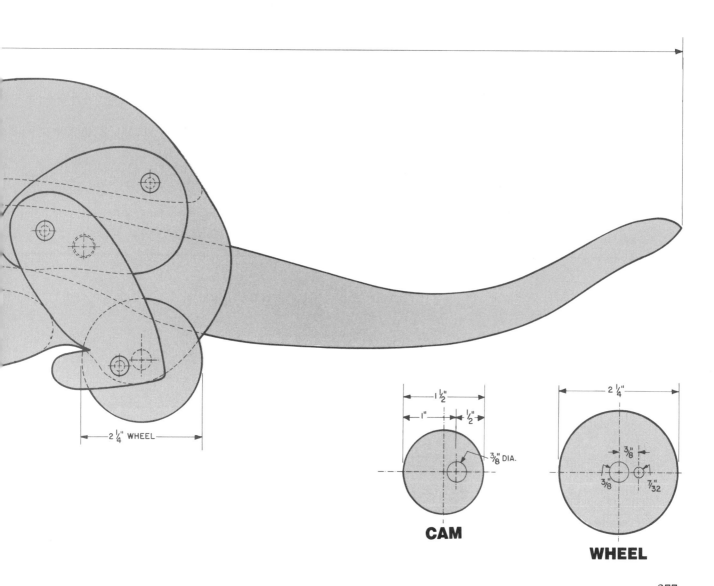

2 ¼" WHEEL

1 ½"

1"

½"

³⁄₈" DIA.

CAM

2 ¼"

³⁄₈"

³⁄₈"

⁷⁄₃₂"

WHEEL

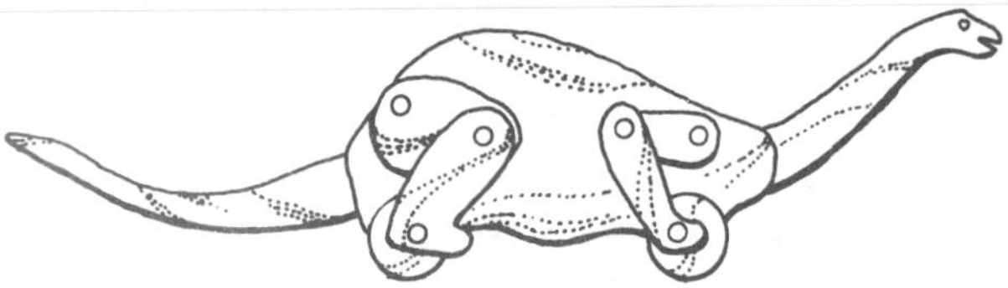

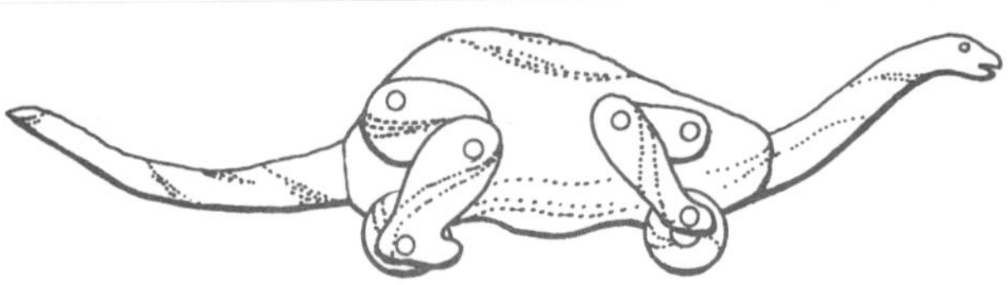

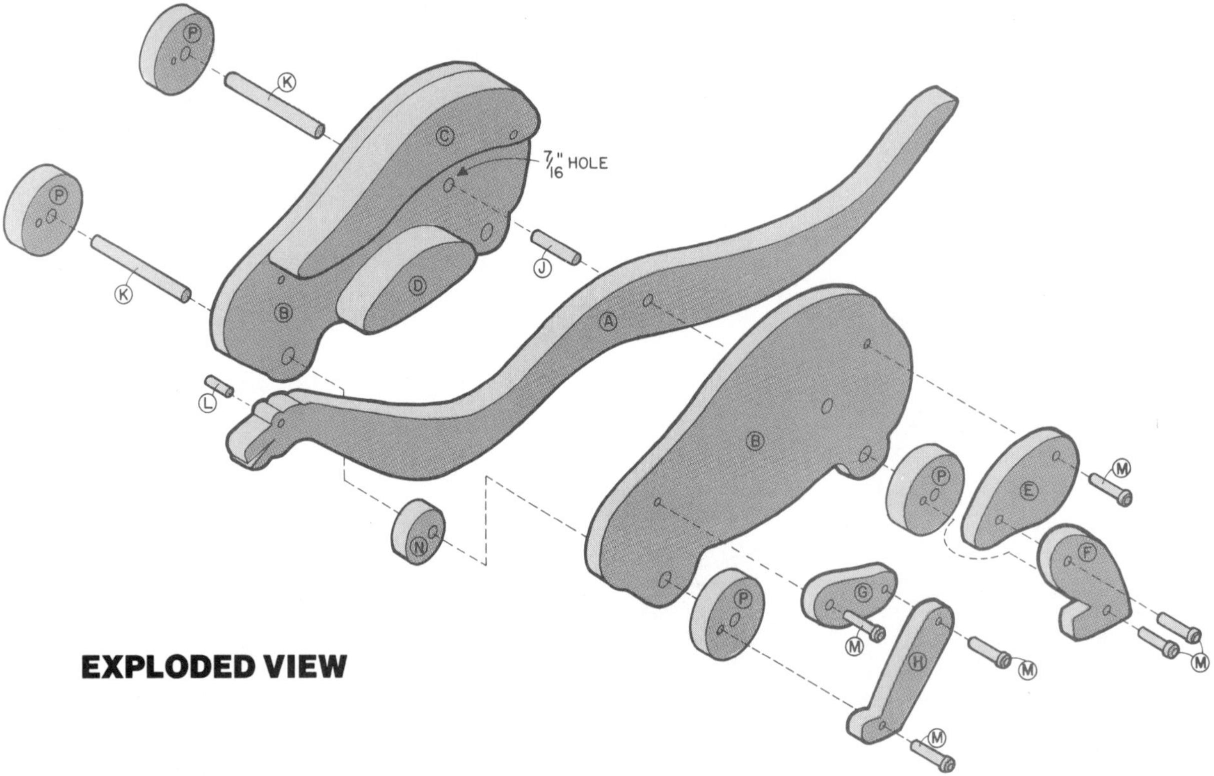

EXPLODED VIEW

BILL OF MATERIALS

PART	DESCRIPTION	QTY	THICKNESS	WIDTH OR DIAMETER	LENGTH
A	Head & Tail	1	¾″	4⅝″	25¼″
B	Body sides	2	½″	5⅝″	10⅞″
C	Top spacer	1	1″	2⅜″	8¾″
D	Bottom spacer	1	1″	1⅜″	3⅜″
E	Upper rear leg	2	½″	2¼″	3½″
F	Lower rear leg	2	½″	2⅛″	4⅛″
G	Upper front leg	2	½″	1¼″	3″
H	Lower front leg	2	½″	1¼″	3⅞″

PART	DESCRIPTION	QTY	THICKNESS	WIDTH OR DIAMETER	LENGTH
J	Pivot dowel	1		⅜″ dia.	1⅝″
K	Axles	2		⅜″ dia.	3¼″
L	Eye	1		¼″ dia.	¾″
M	Peg	12		⅜″ head 7/32″ shaft	1 1/16″
N	Cam	1	½″	1½″ dia.	
P	Wheels	4	⅝″	2¼″ dia.	

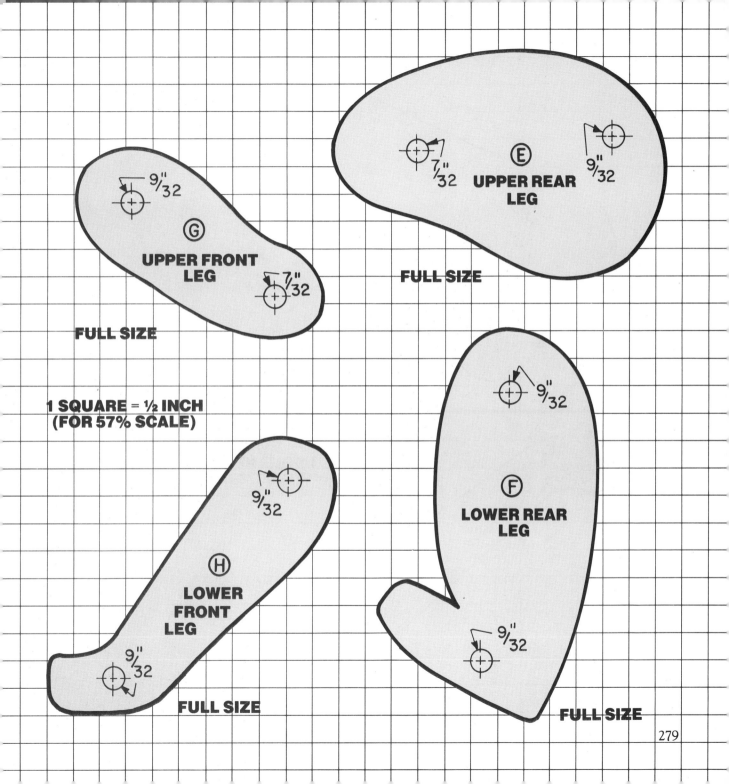

9/32"

Ⓖ
UPPER FRONT
LEG

7/32"

FULL SIZE

Ⓔ
UPPER REAR
LEG

7/32"

9/32"

FULL SIZE

1 SQUARE = ½ INCH
(FOR 57% SCALE)

9/32"

Ⓗ
LOWER
FRONT
LEG

9/32"

FULL SIZE

9/32"

Ⓕ
LOWER REAR
LEG

9/32"

FULL SIZE

279

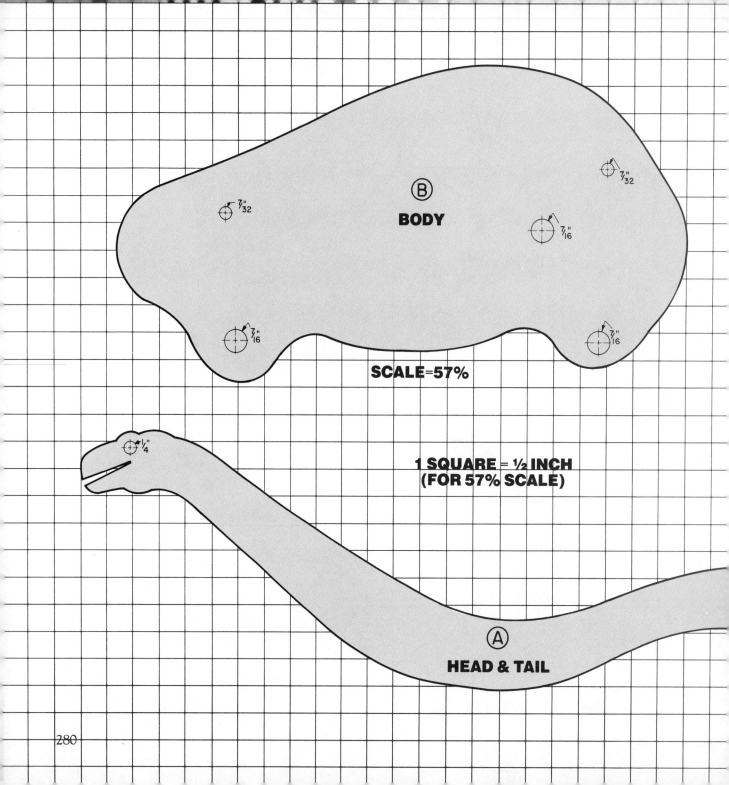

Ⓑ
BODY

$\frac{7}{32}''$

$\frac{7}{32}''$

$\frac{7}{16}''$

$\frac{7}{16}''$

$\frac{7}{16}''$

SCALE=57%

$\frac{1}{4}''$

1 SQUARE = ½ INCH
(FOR 57% SCALE)

Ⓐ
HEAD & TAIL

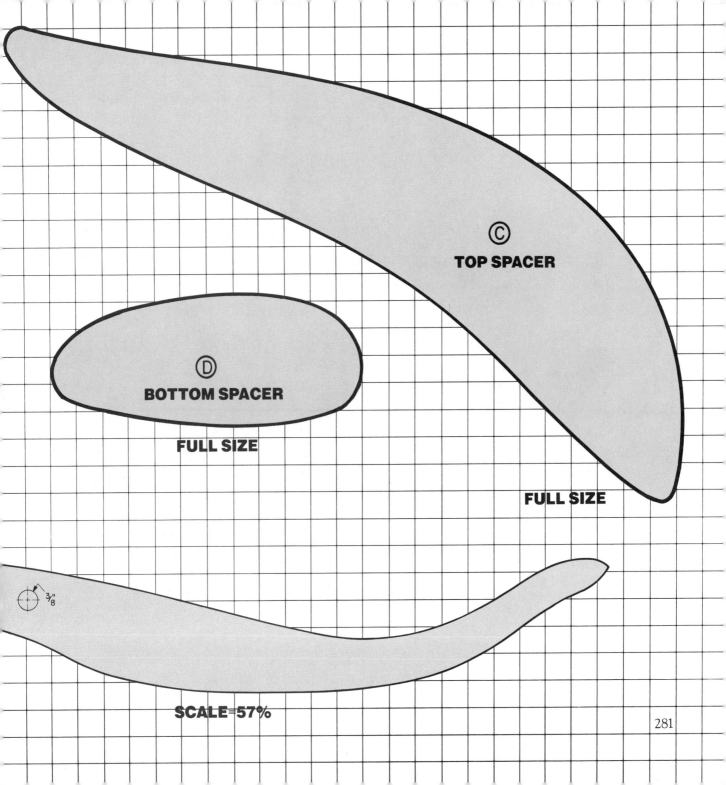

© TOP SPACER

Ⓓ BOTTOM SPACER

FULL SIZE

FULL SIZE

3/8"

SCALE=57%

281

DINOSAU

Text by Mary Packard

Illustrations by Christopher S

The Cantankerous
TRICERATOPS

This chunky monster's horned plate raises and lowers in a somewhat nasty fashion as he lumbers along, tipping to one side and then the other. He is the answer to the question: How sculptural can you get with power tools? At the risk of blowing my own horn, I have to say that I think this toy is the crowning glory of this book, and I hope you enjoy making it as much as I enjoyed designing it.

I recommend that you make him out of walnut. It is relatively strong, but still soft enough to sand the many compound angle cuts and remove the cross grain sanding marks.

The Body

Lay out the body (A) with the two slotted areas right against a jointed edge. This way you'll get the deepest cut possible with the wobble blade. Drill the front axle hole, the eye peg hole, and the peg hole for the foreleg shoulder pegs.

With two or three passes on the table saw (with a wobble or dado blade), cut the slots for the cam in the front and the wheel in the back. Be careful to stop short of the tail or you'll put a slot in it.

Cut out the outline of the body. Edge sand the outline with 80# and 120# sandpaper, and then flat sand both sides with 80# and 120#. Rout the head area. Be sure not to rout where the sides (B) will be glued on.

If necessary, deepen the dado slots with a dovetail saw and a chisel. Support the body at the proper angle and drill the ½" hole for the ⅜" dowel in the neck area.

Now lay out the two sides (B). Cut them out with the table square on the bandsaw (leave the pencil line). Flat sand both pieces with 80# sandpaper and then carefully glue them in position and clamp them. When the glue is dry, locate and drill the rear axle hole and the peg hole for the top of the rear legs. With the table square on the bandsaw, cut around the rear leg supports to cut away any overhang of the B pieces.

Now, tilt the table to 45°. Starting at the front edge of B again, saw around the top of the body following the line where A and B are joined. Repeat on the other side. To cut the belly, start the cut into the back of the left side of the belly where the leg support meets the belly. The cut will reach the juncture of A and B about ¾" forward from the top of the leg support (See Figure 1). Then continue along this joint until the edge is removed. To cut the right side of the belly, start the cut at the front of B and cut until you are across from the point where the other cut met the juncture of A and B.

Figure 1. Enter the left side of the belly at the top of the rear leg support and curve sharply forward till you meet the juncture of A and B.

Figure 2. Start at the front and cut along the juncture of A and B until you are across from where the other belly cut met A and B. Curve outward sharply and the cut should leave the piece at the top of the leg support.

Curve outward sharply at this point. The cut should leave the piece at the top of the leg support where the opposite cut entered (*See Figure 2*).

Now, with the table square on the bandsaw, raise the guides all the way up. (You may have to remove the guard to raise the guides high enough. If you do, BE EXTREMELY CAREFUL!) Mark the top view onto the top of the body and tail. Be sure to use the cutout of the extended tail to mark the top view. Part of the body will be unsupported during this cut, so you may want to clamp a piece of thin material to the table to support your work. Place a C-clamp in the middle so it won't interfere with the body as you turn it from side to side while sawing.

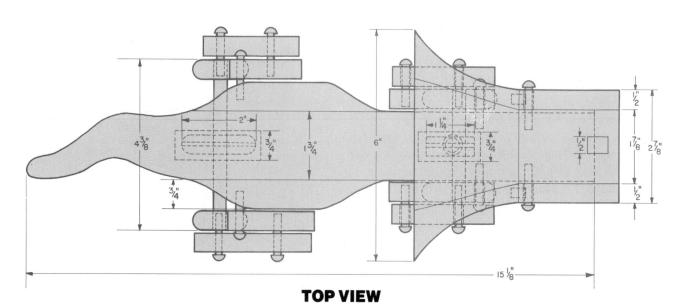

TOP VIEW

Then, starting at the front of B, where it joins the body, cut back until the cut leaves the body. Repeat on the other side. Then start at the tip of the tail and saw up either side of the tail and body (*See Figure 3*). Whew!

Now for lots of sanding. With the sander/grinder at 45°, edge sand the edges you just sawed with 80# and 120# sandpaper. Then with the sander/grinder table square, edge sand the sawn sides of the body and tail with 80# and 120#. With a little sensitivity you can do this with the piece unsupported at times. To round over the edges of the B pieces, you can either use a four-in-hand rasp and sandpaper, or you can use the sander/grinder freehand, rocking the piece by the unsupported

Figure 3. You can clamp a thin piece of material to the band-saw table to support the piece where it would otherwise go beyond the edge of the table.

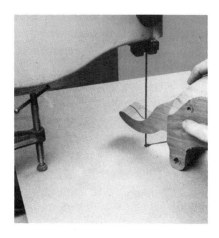

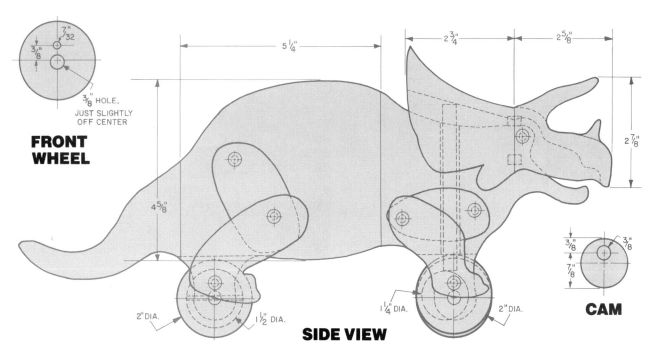

FRONT WHEEL

3/8" HOLE, JUST SLIGHTLY OFF CENTER

7/32"

3/8"

5 1/4"

2 3/4"

2 5/8"

2 7/8"

4 5/8"

CAM

3/8"

3/8"

7/8"

2" DIA.

1 1/2" DIA.

1 1/4" DIA.

2" DIA.

SIDE VIEW

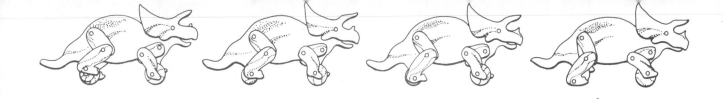

section of the belt (with 80# and then 120#) (*See Figure 4*). Using a four-in-hand rasp, round over the edges of the tail and the edges where A meets the two B pieces.

Now the arduous task of removing all the cross grain scratches left by the sander/grinder. Hand sand *with* the grain with 80# sandpaper until all of the cross grain scratches are gone; then hand sand with 120# (with the grain) to remove all the scratches left by the 80# paper. This is where you'll be thankful if you have used a somewhat soft hardwood.

The Head and Shield

Cut out the head spacer (C). Edge sand it with 80# and 120# sandpaper. With the piece in a vise, mark out the single horn location and cut away either side with a dovetail saw (*See Figure 5*). File and sand these sawn areas to conform to the curve of the head sides.

Cut out the two sides of the head (D). Flat sand them with 80# sandpaper. Edge sand whatever you can with 80# and 120#. Carefully rout the insides of the two horns, starting and stopping just short of where they will intersect the middle piece (C) (*See Figure 6*). Glue and clamp the C and D pieces, keeping their edges aligned as closely as possible.

Figure 4. You can round the edges of the top, bottom, front, and back of B by rocking it back and forth over the unsupported section of the sander/grinder.

Figure 5. Use a dovetail saw to remove the areas on either side of the single horn.

When the assembly is dry, edge sand any irregularities with 80# and 120# sandpaper. With a scrap underneath, carefully locate and drill the eye peg hole all the way through both sides. Flat sand both sides with 120#. Rout both sides, making sure not to rout the back edge.

Carefully locate the four ¼" holes on the back edge. Clamp the assembly between two blocks of wood so that the back edge is parallel to the drill press table. Center punch the holes and drill them (⁹/₃₂", slightly oversize) to the proper depth.

To make the shield that sweeps back over the Triceratops' neck, glue up a block of walnut 3¾" thick x 6" wide x 3" from front to back. I recommend you glue it up to the proper thickness, but a little wide and long so you can square it up perfectly after gluing.

When it's square on all six surfaces, lay it on the end grain edge on the workbench. Mark a line ½" up from the lower edge, across the piece. Center the head piece perfectly, resting on this line, and trace the outline of the head piece onto the shield piece (*See Figure 7*). If

Figure 6. Rout the inside of the horns. Be sure to stop just before you reach the areas that will be joined to the center piece.

Figure 7. Draw a line across the block, ½" from the edge, and carefully center the head (by measurement) on the line. Trace the outline onto the shield piece.

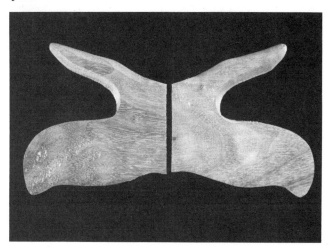

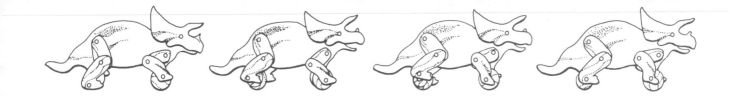

Figure 8. Cut out the side view, leaving ¼″ on the top and bottom to keep the pieces attached until later.

you have dowel centers, use them to transfer the 9/32″ holes onto the end grain of the shield piece. Otherwise, locate them by measurement. Drill them to the proper depth.

Extend the outside edges of the outline to the edges of the block (top and sides). Use these lines to help position the side and top views properly and mark them on the piece.

Now with the piece on its side, and with the bandsaw table perfectly square, cut out the side view. Leave about ¼″ on top and bottom to hold the pieces on while you cut the top view (*See Figure 8*).

Next, cut out the top view removing the two curved pieces entirely. Set the bandsaw table at 10°. Cut along the inside outline of the shield to remove the inside portion (*See Figure 9*). You'll have to leave some of the inside corners to make the two turns. This will be cleaned out later. Now, with a coping saw, remove the top and bottom pieces by sawing through the ¼″ areas that you left holding them together.

With the piece upside down in a vise, use a dovetail saw or a coping saw to square the inside corners of the underside of the shield. With the bandsaw table square again, rest the shield on its back edge and cut out the scalloped top edge.

Figure 9. With the bandsaw table set at 10°, cut out the inside of the shield piece. You'll have to cut a curve at the corners for now and clean them up later.

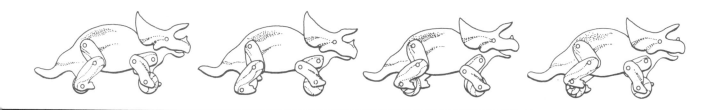

The sweeping sides of the shield can be sanded on the drum of the flat sander with 80# and 120# sandpaper. Keep the piece moving to avoid digging in. Check it frequently to make sure you don't sand it more on one side than on the other. Try to remove as little material as possible from the front edges, so they will meet up properly with the rest of the head when assembled.

Use a four-in-hand rasp to round over the junctions of the curved sides and top. Then hand sand these areas and all the remaining unsanded edges with 80# sandpaper. Break all the edges with 120# and smooth out any rough areas as well.

To assemble the head and shield, put a little glue in all eight ¼″ holes and on the surfaces to be joined. Work the glue back from the outside edges to avoid squeeze-out. Tap the four dowels (with both ends rounded over) into the head piece. Join the two pieces together and clamp them in a vise. When they're thoroughly dry, smooth out the juncture of the two parts with a four-in-hand rasp, if necessary, and then with 80# and 120# sandpaper, with the grain.

The Legs

Mark out all eight leg pieces (F, G, H, J) on ½″ stock (with the grain). Drill all the peg holes. As you do, remember that the elbow holes in the upper legs will be ⁷⁄₃₂″ to hold the tip of the pegs, whereas the remaining holes will be ⁹⁄₃₂″ to let the peg pass through and pivot.

Cut the pieces out on the bandsaw. Edge sand them with 80# and 120# sandpaper. Flat sand them with 80# and 120#. Break the edges by hand with 120#. Spread glue in the elbow holes of the upper legs and set them together in opposing sets. If there is glue forced out the back of the hole, flat sand it clean after the glue has set up.

The Wheels and the Cam

Using the wheel drilling jig (*See Techniques and Production Procedures, Figure 17*), drill the peg holes in the 2″ diameter front wheels (V) and the 1½″ diameter rear wheels (T). Plug the axle holes of the front wheels. When the glue is dry, sand the flat sides flush, set the flat side down on the drill press and use a ⅜″ Forstner bit to drill the axle hole slightly off center (directly opposite the peg hole).

To make the cam (S), cut a 1¼″ diameter wheel out of ½″ stock with the fly cutter. Plug the axle hole. Sand it flush when the glue is dry, and drill the ⅜″ hole with a Forstner bit (⅜″ from one side and ⅞″ from the other).

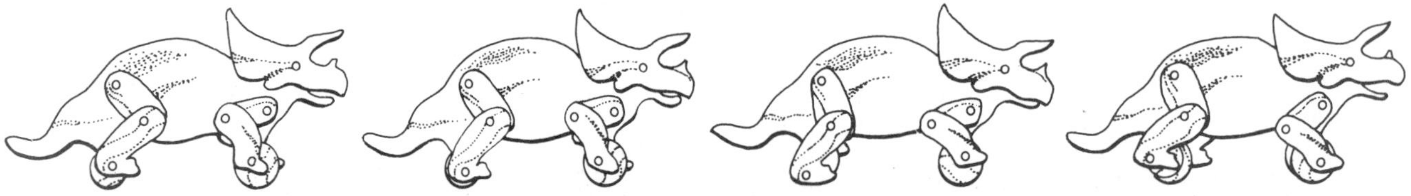

Assembly

Cut the rear axle to length (measure the body width, plus the wheels, plus ⅛″ clearance). With the 2″ wheel (U) positioned in its slot, tap the dowel through until it is centered. On the drill press, drill a ⅛″ hole through the center of the wheel until it goes through the axle. Spread glue on the inside of the hole and tap the ⅛″ dowel in place. Glue the rear wheels onto either end of the axle, making sure the peg holes are diagonally opposed.

Repeat this entire procedure for the front wheels. The only difference is that you can drill all the way through the centered cam to attach it to the axle. Now, attach the legs, one at a time, using the clearance gauge *(See Techniques and Production Procedures, Figure 28)*, if necessary. Rest the wheel on the edge of the workbench to support it as you peg the feet to the wheels.

Cut the work dowel (M) to length and round over both ends, then slip it into its hole. Put glue in the eye peg holes, position the head and tap the eye pegs into place, being careful not to insert them to the point where they keep the head from moving freely.

When all the glue is thoroughly dry, oil this fellow up and he's ready to give the Tyrannosaurus a fight for his money.

BILL OF MATERIALS

PART	DESCRIPTION	QTY	THICKNESS	WIDTH OR DIAMETER	LENGTH
A	Body	1	1¾″	4⅝″	15⅛″
B	Body sides	2	¾″	4⅝″	5¼″
C	Head spacer	1	1⅞″	1⅜″	3¼″
D	Head sides	2	½″	2⅞″	2⅝″
E	Shield	1	3¾″	6″	2¾″
F	Upper rear leg	2	½″	1¾″	3⅛″
G	Lower rear leg	2	½″	2″	3½″
H	Upper front leg	2	½″	1⅜″	2¾″
J	Lower front leg	2	½″	1½″	3⅜″
K	Balance wheel pin	1		⅛″ dia.	1″
L	Cam pin	1		⅛″ dia.	1¼″
M	Work dowel	1		⅜″ dia.	4¼″
N	Front axle	1		⅜″ dia.	2⅞″
P	Rear axle	1		⅜″ dia.	4⅜″
Q	Head assembly pins	4		¼″ dia.	⅜″
R	Pegs	14		7/32″ dia.	1 1/16″ shaft
S	Cam	1	½″	1¼″ dia.	
T	Rear wheels	2	½″	1½″ dia.	
U	Balance wheel	1	½″	2″ dia.	
V	Front wheels	2	½″	2″ dia.	

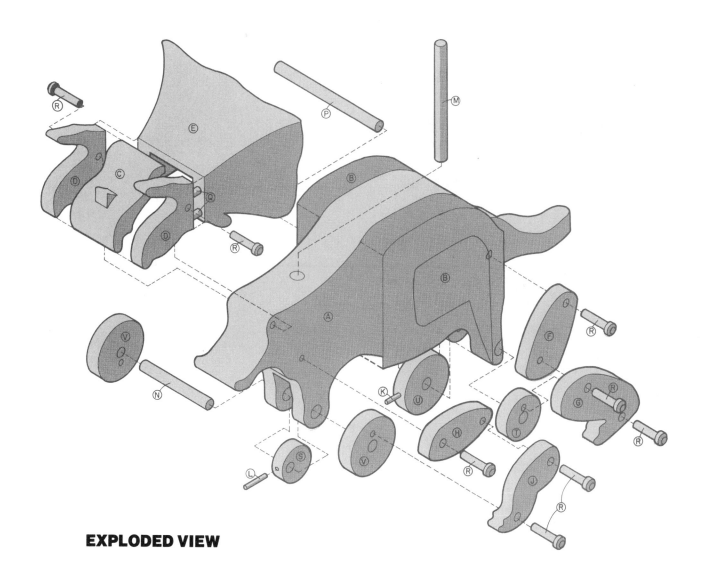

EXPLODED VIEW

291

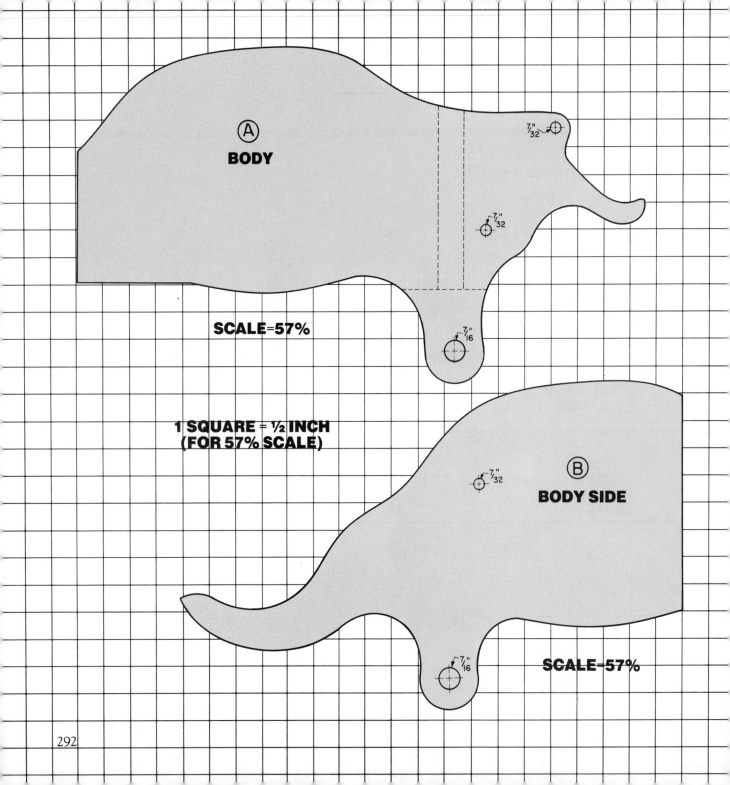

A BODY

SCALE=57%

$\frac{7}{32}$"

$\frac{7}{32}$"

$\frac{7}{16}$"

1 SQUARE = ½ INCH
(FOR 57% SCALE)

$\frac{7}{32}$"

B BODY SIDE

$\frac{7}{16}$"

SCALE=57%

292

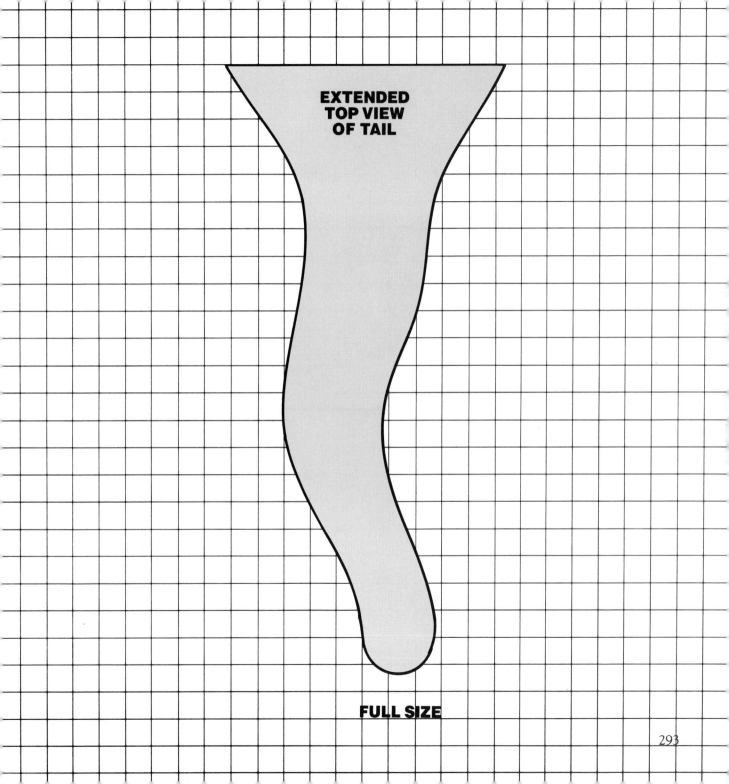

EXTENDED
TOP VIEW
OF TAIL

FULL SIZE

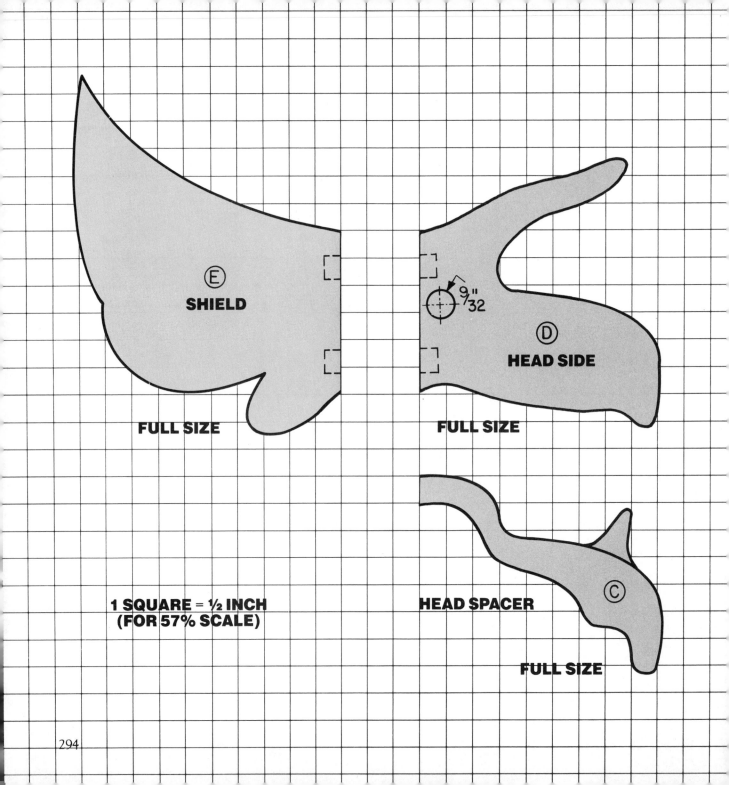

Ⓔ
SHIELD

FULL SIZE

9/32"

Ⓓ
HEAD SIDE

FULL SIZE

**1 SQUARE = ½ INCH
(FOR 57% SCALE)**

HEAD SPACER Ⓒ

FULL SIZE

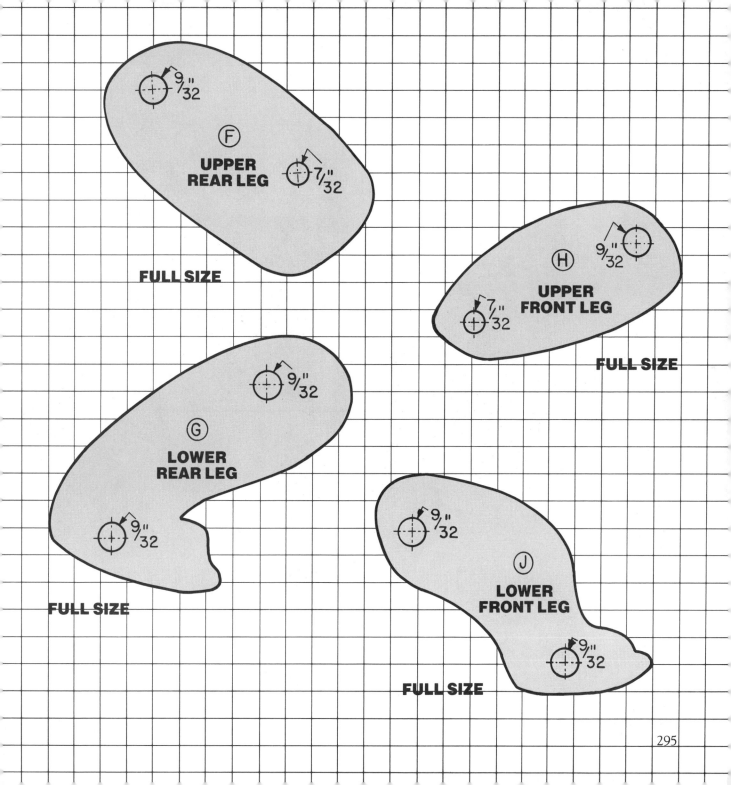

UPPER
REAR LEG

Ⓕ

9/32"

7/32"

FULL SIZE

UPPER
FRONT LEG

Ⓗ

9/32"

7/32"

FULL SIZE

LOWER
REAR LEG

Ⓖ

9/32"

9/32"

FULL SIZE

LOWER
FRONT LEG

Ⓙ

9/32"

9/32"

FULL SIZE

295

Pure MOTION

A Delightful Infant's RATTLE

The Rattle is the only toy in this book that isn't my design. However, it is such a classic that I want to include it with my toys. As far as I know, it is a very old design and, unlike my toys, is not protected by any copyright. Feel free to reproduce *this* toy for resale if you have aspirations toward becoming a professional toymaker.

Either transfer the pattern for the sides (A) onto suitable pieces of wood (any species), or simply use a compass, and scribe two 4¼" circles on the wood. Cut them out on the bandsaw keeping as close as possible to the line. The more perfect the circles, the better the toy will look, but perfection is not essential to the working of the toy.

Drill the ⅜" holes. Flat sand each piece (*with the grain*) with 80# and then 120# sandpaper. Edge sand with 80#. Rout the edges and then edge sand with 120#. Now hand sand all the routed edges with 80# and then 120#.

Cut the dowels to length. Drill the ⁷⁄₁₆" holes in the 1" dowels, making sure the holes are centered (*See Techniques and Production Procedures, Figure 17*). Sand the ends of the 1" dowels by holding them very firmly and perfectly perpendicular to the belt sander.

Sand the corners off both ends of all six dowels on the stationary belt sander (*See Techniques and Production Procedures, Figure 24*). Hand sand all of the dowels to remove any roughness or splinters, especially around the holes in the 1" dowels.

Spread glue in the ⅜" holes in one of the sides (A) and drive the ⅜" dowels (C) into the holes until they seat properly.

If you want to color the 1" dowels with food coloring, now's the time. If you decide to color the dowels, let them dry thoroughly after you apply the food coloring, and then oil them before assembly or the food coloring will rub off. Now slip one of the 1" dowels onto each of the ⅜" dowels. Be sure each ⅜" dowel has a 1" dowel on it and that the end of the 1" dowel (the end without the hole) is positioned between the other two ⅜" dowels.

Spread glue in the three holes in the second side (A). Put either carpet or a smooth scrap under the assembly so that the surface of the lower side won't be marred as you hammer the toy together. Place a scrap, which is at least as large as the side, on top of the second side as you position it on top of the assembly. This will prevent marring or even splitting the top side as you hammer it into place (*See Figure 1*). Position each of the

Figure 1. To prevent marring or splitting the Rattle during assembly, put a scrap above and below the toy as you hammer it together.

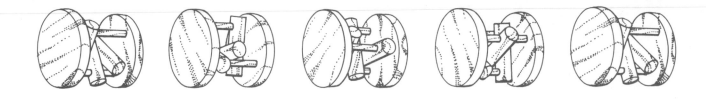

⅜″ dowel ends so that they are started into their respective holes. Now hammer on the top side, rotating around the circle, hitting the assembly directly over each ⅜″ dowel as you go around. As you're hammering, look at the assembly and make sure that the second

A piece seats all the way into the ⅜″ dowels. The sound of the hammering will change when the dowels hit bottom. The side pieces should end up parallel.

When the glue is dry, oil the Rattle and it's ready to roll!

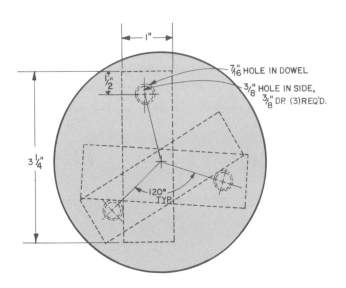

SIDE VIEW

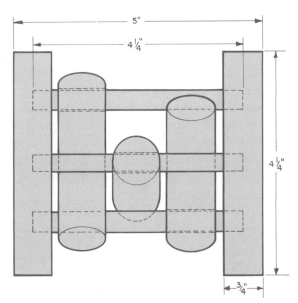

TOP VIEW

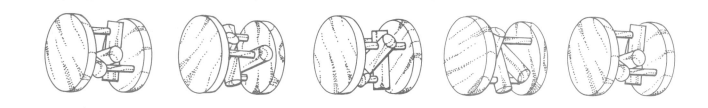

EXPLODED VIEW

BILL OF MATERIALS

PART	DESCRIPTION	QTY	THICKNESS	WIDTH OR DIAMETER	LENGTH
A	Sides	2	¾″	4¼″	
B	Rattling dowels	3		1″ dia.	3¼″
C	Connecting dowels	3		⅜″ dia.	4¼″

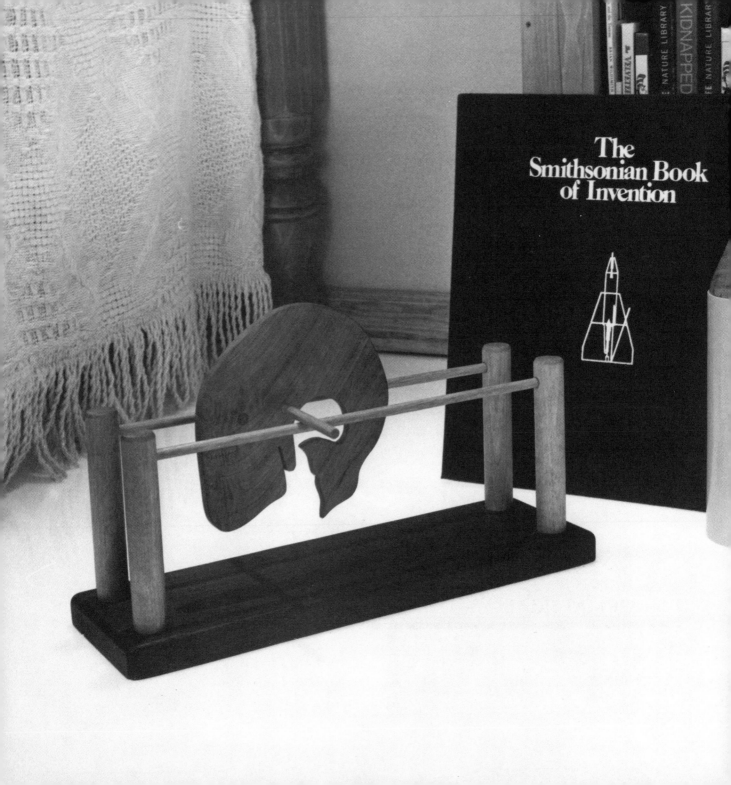

The Perpetual Motion ILLUSION

When you give the dowel just a slight twist, the animal goes head over heels along the track. The body is overbalanced to make it spin with a stop-and-go movement that makes it seem like it's bound to stop, but it keeps going right to the end of the track. The trick is to see how little you can twist the dowel and still have the animal make it across. It's quite mesmerizing when you get the hang of it.

The base of the toy can be made of any wood you have handy. The animal itself can be made of ¼" tempered hardboard, if you're making the Whale. If you plan to make the Dragon or the Toucan, you will want to use something that will show off your woodburning. One-quarter inch plywood will do, but a light colored hardwood like poplar or cherry would be more attractive.

Cut out the base and drill the four post holes. Flat sand the top and sides with 80# sandpaper. Edge sand the short end grain edges with 80#. Rout the corners (*See Figure 1*) and then all the top edges. Repeat all the sanding with 120#, and hand sand any roughness with 80# and then 120#. Cut the ¾" posts and the two ¼" track pieces to length. Round off both ends of all six dowels (*See Techniques and Production Procedures, Figure 24*). Drill the ¼" holes in the posts. Make sure the holes are centered (*See Techniques and Production Procedures, Figure 9*). Hand sand the dowels to remove any roughness around the ¼" holes and on the surface in general. Assemble posts, tracks and base without glue to make sure that these parts fit properly. Put just a little glue on the insides of the holes in the posts; too much glue will prevent the ¼" dowels from seating properly. Hammer the ¼" dowels (D) into the posts, making sure the posts

end up parallel to each other and perpendicular to the ¼" track (*See Figure 2*). Glue the post and track assemblies into the holes in the base, once again make sure they are parallel and perpendicular to the track and the base.

To make the animal, transfer the pattern onto the material. If you're making the Dragon or the Toucan, transfer the image with carbon paper and a stylus. Drill the ¼" hole and cut the shape out on the bandsaw. Hand sand the edges. Now burn the Toucan or Dragon images on the piece. Cut the ¼" dowel (E) to length and

Figure 1. Rout the corners first, then rout smoothly around the entire outline.

Figure 2. Make sure the posts are parallel to each other (in both directions), and perpendicular to the ¼" track. Either of the positions shown will present problems.

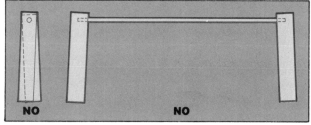

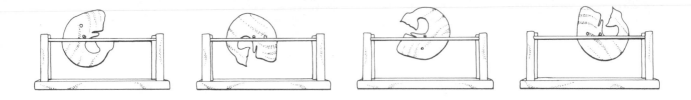

round off both ends on the belt sander. Slip the animal on the dowel until it is almost centered. Apply a ring of glue to the center of (E) and slide the animal over onto the glued area. Resting it on the track, make sure the dowel is perfectly perpendicular to the animal. Now let all the glue dry thoroughly, oil it, and twirl away. Make sure it's on a perfectly level surface and remember the trick is to twirl it as slowly as possible.

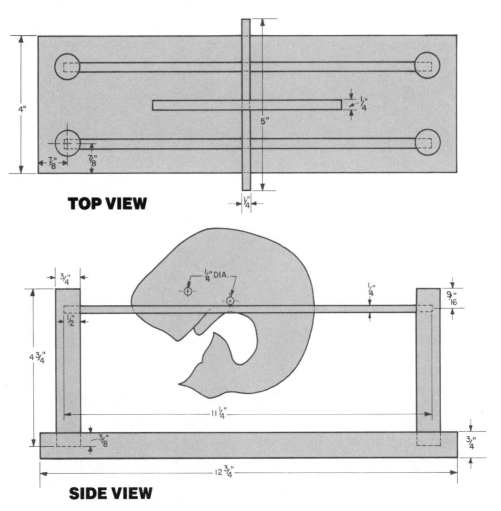

TOP VIEW

SIDE VIEW

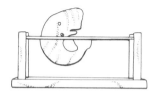 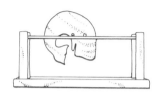 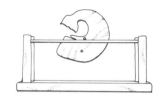 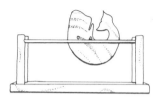

EXPLODED VIEW

BILL OF MATERIALS

PART	DESCRIPTION	QTY	THICKNESS	WIDTH OR DIAMETER	LENGTH
A	Animal	1	¼"	5¾"	5¾"
B	Base	1	¾"	4"	12¾"
C	Posts	4		¾" dia.	4¾"
D	Tracks	2		¼" dia.	11¼"
E	Dowel	1		¼" dia.	5"

305

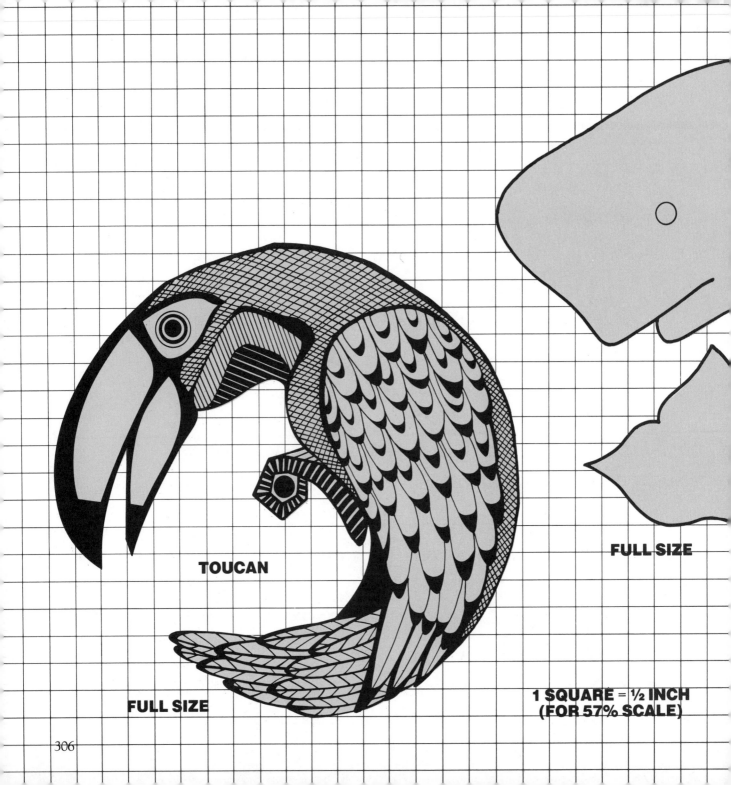

TOUCAN

FULL SIZE

FULL SIZE

1 SQUARE = ½ INCH
(FOR 57% SCALE)

306

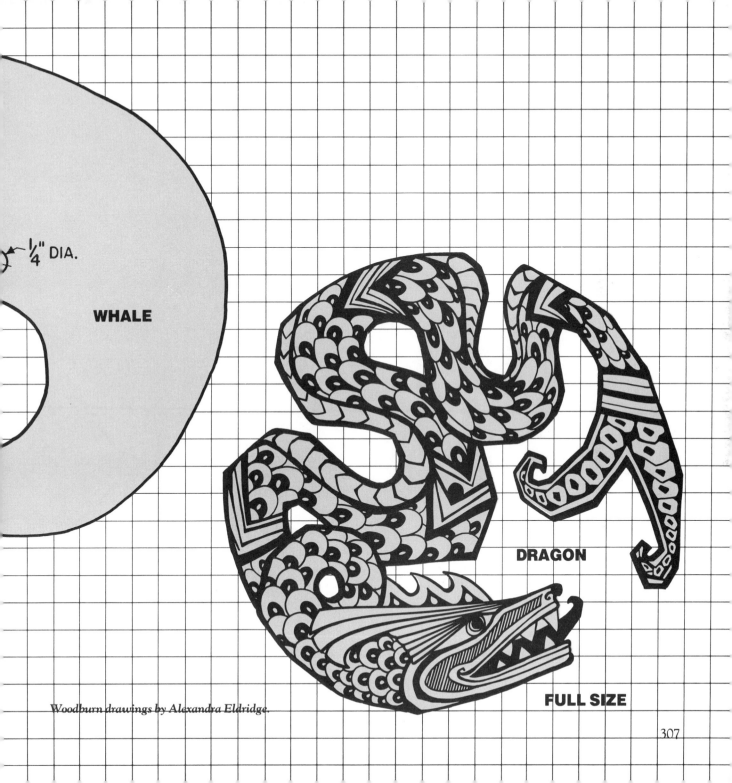

¼" DIA.

WHALE

DRAGON

Woodburn drawings by Alexandra Eldridge.

FULL SIZE

Appendix

"New-Life Abrasive Belt Cleaner"
Abrasive Service Co., Inc.
398 Broad St.
Forestville, CT 06010
203/584-2091

Dust collectors
"Ace Vacuum Systems"
Blackburn Division of
F L Industries, Inc.
Holub Operations
1701 W. Bethany Rd.
Sycamore, IL 60178

Smooth hardwood dowels
C. B. Cummings & Sons Co.
Norway, ME 04268
207/743-6326

Wax emulsion end-grain sealer, "Sealtite #60"
Chapman Chemical Co.
P.O. Box 9158
Memphis, TN 38109
800/238-2523

Sawmill directory
Department of Natural Resources (Your State)

Quicksand "165" and "671" belt sanders
Divindacon Products, Inc.
P.O. Box 17
Jackson, WI 53037-0017
414/677-3655

1/8" Bandsaw blades
Do-All Company
1547 Lockbourne Ave.
Columbus, OH 43210
614/443-6571

"Titebond Glue"
Franklin International
Corporate Center
2020 Burks St.
Columbus, OH 43207

Full-size patterns and finished toys
Howling Wolf Woodworks
Rt #1, Box 240-A
Millfield, OH 45761

"Moisture Meters"
Lignomat U.S.A., Ltd.
P.O. Box 30145
14345 N.E. Morris Ct.
Portland, OR 97230
053/257-8957

Sandpaper sheets and belts
The Midwest Buff Co.
40 Alpha Park
Highlands Heights, OH 44143
216/461-1414

Wheels and toy parts
Toymakers Supply Company
(Love-Built Toys)
105 Weiler Rd.
Arlington Heights, IL 60005

"Watco Danish Oil"
Watco Danish Corp.
Santa Monica, CA 90404
213/829-2226

Tools, supplies and toy parts
Woodcraft Supply Co.
Dept. PS105, 41 Atlantic Ave.
Box 4000
Woburn, MA 01888

To save the reader the trouble of enlarging drawings, the Author offers a complete set of full-size patterns to replace those that were published at 57% scale. To obtain these full-size patterns, send $3.00 plus $.50 postage to Howling Wolf Woodworks, Rt. 1, Box 240-A, Millfield, OH 45761.

Walk · Wend · Waddle · Wobble ·
Perambulate · Step · Stride · Stroll · S
Swing · Sway · Swerve · Shimmy · S
Lurch · Stumble · Bump · Buffet · St
Galumph · Caper · Cavort · Hop · Lea
Mince · Maneuver · Meander · Mose
Jiggle · Joggle · Jerk · Jar · Jolt · Jou
Ramble · Turn · Veer · Vault · Falter ·
Quaver · Tiptoe · Traipse · Tramp · Go
March · Hike · Walk · Wend · Waddle · W
Perambulate · Step · Stride · Stroll · S
Swing · Sway · Swerve · Shimmy · Shal
Stumble · Bump · Buffet · Strut · Stag
Caper · Cavort · Hop · Leap · Bound ·
Maneuver · Meander · Mosey · Whirl ·
Jerk · Jar · Jolt · Jounce · Dance · Rock ·
Vault · Falter · Waver · Dodder · Teeter
Tramp · Go · Gad · Agitate · Peregrina
Waddle · Wobble · Wiggle · Wander · Am
Stroll · Saunter · Sidle · Slink · Shuffle ·